'*Futureproof* provides a very practical guide for businesses with a sensible three prong approach to implementation. Importantly, Caleb and Minter astutely put collaboration and responsibility as a core mindset. Use this as a desktop reference to guide your company and career.'

Jeremiah Owyang, Founder, Crowd Companies

'This is a book that challenged me and made me think at every turn. It disrupted my mind!'

Mark W. Schaefer, consultant and speaker; author, *KNOWN*

'There are usually two responses to hearing about "disruption": panic or denial. *Futureproof* gets beyond that with helping you decide what kind of a leader you want to be in the face of constant change, with a roadmap for success.'

Scott Monty, CEO and Co-Managing Partner, Brain+Trust Partners

'In Silicon Valley, we're obsessed with disruption. What must you do to prepare for accelerating challenges and opportunities for your customers and your markets? How will you embrace change and take decisive action in a world of increasing uncertainty? Thought leaders Minter Dial and Caleb Storkey discover the deeper insights that expose the next epic shift at work in *Futureproof*.'

Mark C. Thompson, NY Times bestselling author, *Admired* and *World's #1 Executive Coach for Growth Companies*

'A refreshing, clear, concise and wonderfully actionable look at the changing business landscape and the transformative power of disruption. A superb provocative guide to the power of the new with clear steps on how leaders can drive change and unleash their potential. More than anything else this book makes the complex seem simple, refreshingly jargon free.'

Tom Goodwin, EVP, Head of Innovation, Zenith Media; #1 Top Voice in Marketing on LinkedIn

'Many people use the words "innovation" and "disruption". Few people fully understand them. Minter and Caleb are two of the people who do. *Futureproof* will help you to navigate your way through the minefield of innovation (needing to do existing things faster) and preparing for a world of further disruption (where existing business models become obsolete). Learn about the difference between Pi-shaped people and comb-shaped leaders, and educate yourself with everything you need to know about the twelve technological forces which will shape our future. You won't be disappointed.'

Jeremy Waite, Evangelist, @IBM

'The new mindset of *Futureproof* integrates the best of feminine attributes to balance the old masculine mindset. Meaning, collaboration, empathy, empowerment, transparency, sharing . . . these are the operative functions that will allow you to gracefully handle the disruptive forces of our digital future. AI, IOT, Hackers, Big Data, Genomics – they are all yours to harness for the good of man and womankind. Here is your roadmap to confidently leveraging what is about to explode your potential business opportunity. Read it and reap.'

Susan Bratton, CEO, Personal Life Media, Inc.

'Minter and Caleb's book should be required reading for marketers because it's not about marketing; rather, it's a deep dive and "how to"' on harnessing the disruptive forces impacting every job description. Their holistic analysis is a toolkit for any business leader on embracing change, but it's a particularly potent call to arms for marketers and communicators who need to narrate it.'

Jonathan Salem Baskin, author; President, Arcadia Communications Lab

'Caleb and Minter's latest book shares great insightful stories about disruption. Why it matters, why it can be hard and easy at the same time, and what you can learn from others. Definitely a must-read.'

Eric Gervet, Lead of San Francisco office, AT Kearney

'Not incremental, but disruptive and accelerating: these are the most visible characteristics of our era. But what are they made of? The book gives you 12 key driving forces of this upcoming revolution . . . Reading it not only helps to understand but lets you better focus on what is important and what is not. For everyone, students, the retired and business executive and entrepreneurs.'

Gilles Babinet, Digital Champion at France European Commission, entrepreneur, ex. Chairman at French Digital Council and Africa 4 Tech

'Practical, inspiring and rigorously researched. The authors are immersed in the world of disruptive innovation and usefully share the thinking and skills that we need to deal with in the future. My mindset was definitely shifted, and I can't wait to bring that to my work.'

Dave Duarte, CEO, Treeshake

'*Futureproof* is a handbook to the communication and technology issues impacting organisations and modern society. Minter Dial and Caleb Storkey are your guides. It's an upbeat and thought-provoking book that urges us to embrace the opportunity created by disruption. Most importantly, it's practical. The authors outline 12 forces of disruption that are an excellent foundation for benchmarking your organisation and a start point for planning for disruption.'

Stephen Waddington, Partner and Chief Engagement Officer, Ketchum; Visiting Professor, Newcastle University

'Disruption is near to my heart and in the legal sector I've seen large law firms not take innovation seriously enough.

'In *Futureproof*, Caleb and Minter not only outline the core mindsets needed to be an entrepreneurial leader but provide an outstanding practical guide to implement these technologies both into your team and into your business. I so completely recommend it. If you're working in a startup, it's a no brainer; get a copy for all your team.'

**Alexandra Isenegger, CEO of Linkilaw –
The Legal Platform for Startups**

'We are acutely aware of the disruption to business models and the challenge of long-term thinking and planning. Although this can be set as a Boardroom task and delegated down, disruption starts with a mindset. Caleb and Minter's amazing book is written to challenge business minds and help practically implement the technology, enabling organisations to realise the shift and develop the skills to succeed. Incredibly stimulating and thought-provoking. A must read for all. Someone is planning to eat your food; make sure you improve your business so you and your families don't starve.'

**Penny Power, OBE Digital Entrepreneur,
Enabler and Educator**

Futureproof

Pearson

At Pearson, we have a simple mission: to help people make more of their lives through learning.

We combine innovative learning technology with trusted content and educational expertise to provide engaging and effective learning experiences that serve people wherever and whenever they are learning.

From classroom to boardroom, our curriculum materials, digital learning tools and testing programmes help to educate millions of people worldwide – more than any other private enterprise.

Every day our work helps learning flourish, and wherever learning flourishes, so do people.

To learn more, please visit us at **www.pearson.com/uk**

Futureproof

How to get
your business ready
for the next disruption

Minter Dial and Caleb Storkey

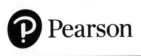 Pearson

Harlow, England • London • New York • Boston • San Francisco • Toronto • Sydney
Dubai • Singapore • Hong Kong • Tokyo • Seoul • Taipei • New Delhi
Cape Town • São Paulo • Mexico City • Madrid • Amsterdam • Munich • Paris • Milan

Pearson Education Limited
KAO Two
KAO Park
Harlow CM17 9NA
United Kingdom
Tel: +44 (0)1279 623623
Web: www.pearson.com/uk

First published 2017 (print and electronic)
© Pearson Education Limited 2017 (print and electronic)

The rights of Minter Dial and Caleb Storkey to be identified as authors of this work have been asserted by them in accordance with the Copyright, Designs and Patents Act 1988.

ISBN: 978-1-292-18639-9 (print)
      978-1-292-18693-1 (PDF)
      978-1-292-18694-8 (ePub)

British Library Cataloguing-in-Publication Data
A catalogue record for the print edition is available from the British Library

Library of Congress Cataloging-in-Publication Data
A catalog record for the print edition is available from the Library of Congress

10 9 8 7 6 5 4 3 2 1
21 20 19 18 17
Image on cover and spine by Dejan Popov

Print edition typeset in 9/13 Melior Com by iEnergizer Aptara®, Ltd.
Printed by Ashford Colour Press Ltd, Gosport

NOTE THAT ANY PAGE CROSS REFERENCES REFER TO THE PRINT EDITION

'Change is for sure. Growth is the option.'

Sam Villa, international hair stylist, performing artist

Contents

About the authors

Caleb Storkey is a seasoned entrepreneur, speaker and consultant in innovation, entrepreneurism and marketing. Founder and CEO of Gettr (an AI software consultancy) and Storkey Media (an integrated marketing agency), Caleb works internationally with a wide range of businesses from multinationals (RBS, AMEX, Canon) through to highly disruptive tech startups.

A passionate and reflective communicator, Caleb works in the intersection of business growth, human emotions and technological advancement. Hosting the 'Gett To The Future' podcast, he interviews world-class experts embracing the technologies and themes explored in this book. Caleb bridges the strategic 30,000ft view alongside creating implementable programmes that generate strategic change and transformation for leaders and their businesses.

Earlier in life, Caleb was a boy soprano with the English National Opera and Royal Opera House. Now, a lover of raucous nights of music and wholehearted conversations, Caleb is married to Kerry and daddy to Iona and Ezekiel.

Minter Dial is founder and President of The Myndset Company, a boutique agency providing specialised services on Branding and Digital Strategy. Renowned international speaker and consultant, Minter creates bespoke executive programmes designed to activate strategy and accelerate transformation. He is non-executive Board Director of the Ecole de Communication Visuelle in Paris and former

NED of Lastminute.com Group. From 2011 to 2016, he was Associate at Netexplo, a global observatory of new tech trends. Prior to The Myndset, he spent 16 years at L'Oreal, with 9 assignments in 4 countries. He was Managing Director Worldwide of Redken, Managing Director of the Canadian subsidiary and, in his last post, member of the Worldwide Executive Committee of L'Oreal Professional Products Division. He is also author of the book and award-winning WWII documentary, *The Last Ring Home*, which aired nationally in 2017 on PBS in the US and History Channel in Australia and NZ. Passionate about the Grateful Dead, padel tennis and languages, Minter is married with two children.

Authors' acknowledgements

We would like to acknowledge several important people who helped us in the writing of this book. First, we would like to thank our delightful friend, Jeremy Waite, who put us in touch with one another over a few single malts, and set us on our journey. We are also indebted to Adrian Swinscoe for introducing us to our fabulous editor, Eloise Cook, who provided us with solid, dependable guidance throughout the entire process.

We would like to thank a number of people who helped by providing inspiration, advice, feedback or actually made contributions to this book. These individuals include:

Jennifer Arcuri, Anne Bezançon, Michael Carrier, Olivier Cimelière, Antoine de Gabrielli, Yu Du, Tim Ferriss, Lutz Finger, Marco Gervasi, Eric Gervet, Giles Gibbons, Seth Godin, Jeremy Goldman, Arthur Goldstuck, Doug Hewett, Jim Hunter, Mitch Joel, Andrew Lam-po-tang, Ian Monroe, Scott Monty, Giles Morgan, Thomas Nicholls, Pippa Green, Brandon Ng, Jeremiah Owyang, Jeffrey K Rohrs, Daniel Rowles, Toby Shapshak, Duncan Stewart, Elaine Storkey, Michael Stuber, Tony Vino, Tom West, Stephen R. Williams, Bradford Worrall.

Further, no project like this gets to be put to bed without superlative friend and family support.

From Minter: Caleb, this has been an exciting journey we have embarked on and I've cherished your passion and perseverance along the way. I appreciate your thoughtful content and style, and the way you inject your personality into your words. In so doing, you pushed and cajoled me to do more and be better. A huge, hearty and meaningful thanks.

To my parents, Morsan and Papa, you have both contributed in different and wonderful ways to making me the man I am. This book has parts of both of you! Forever Grateful.

For my children, Oscar and Alexandra, I cherish and love you both. Thank you for supporting your goofy father! This book will hopefully play some part in *your* future.

Lastly, to my wife, Yendi, who is beautiful inside and out, a rock of support and always looking after my back. Merci ma déesse.

From Caleb: Minter, it's been a complete pleasure writing this book with you. I love the way your mind works, your openness and your pursuit of the new. You, my friend, are both an incredible talent and an inspiration. Thank you.

Thank you mum and dad. Not only have you inspired me with your writing, you've been the greatest source of love, challenge and support, and your integrity and the gratitude I feel for you, runs deep through me.

Thank you precious friends of mine. You know who you are. Your love, honesty and support has sustained and encouraged me to be who I was created to be. I am forever indebted and always here for you.

Kerry, Iona and Ezekiel. I love you with all of my heart. As we grow older and build for our future, with all the challenging, beautiful and exciting adventures that lie ahead, I'm so grateful and passionate to wholeheartedly live life and love life with you.

May the road rise up to meet us.
May the wind be always at our backs.
May the sun shine warm upon our faces;
the rains fall soft upon our fields
and until we meet again,
may God hold us in the palm of His hand.

Publisher's acknowledgements

We are grateful to the following for permission to reproduce copyright material:

Figures

Figure on page 89 drawing by Antonio Meza (http://antoons. net/), commissioned by The Myndset; figure on page 150 from http://blog.softwareinsider.org/2016/09/18/mondays-musings-understand-spectrum-seven-artificial-intelligence-outcomes/, reproduced with permission; figure on page 46 adapted from Jeremiah Owyang, reproduced with permission; figure on page xxx from http://irisclasson. com/2013/07/08/stupid-question-218-what-are-t-shaped-pi-shaped-and-comb-shaped-skills-and-which-one-should-i-aim-for/, reproduced with permission.

Text

Extract on pages 50–51 from Scott Monty, Collaborative economy disruption for Myndset.

Introduction: Getting ready for disruption

Disruption is uncomfortable yet exciting, painful yet liberating, destabilising yet energising. It really depends on your point of view.

I n 1992, the US ad agency TBWA successfully registered the brand name, 'Disruption'. Since then, the word has caught on rapidly. Pick up any phone and flick over to your news app. Now, disruption is seen widely as describing the effect that the internet and new tech have had on all forms of activity. It applies to business, cities, government, NGOs and life in general. Basically, we could say, disruption is an interruption, causing a change in what used to be seen as normal.

It is our position in this book that disruption does not apply only to innovation. Clay Christensen, Harvard Professor and author of *Innovator's Dilemma*[1], would define it this way. Although a great book, this is something on which we disagree. We see disruption happening in the ways people think, in the ways they communicate and act, and in how it is forcing business and operating models to change. Whether as a disruptor or a disrupted business, the new world order is in an even more impressive fight for survival. As Brian Solis has written, we live in a time of digital Darwinism.[2] It is either *disrupt* or *die*.

Christensen defines a disruptive product as one that addresses a market that could not be serviced until now. He calls this a market disruption. Alternatively, if there is a simpler, cheaper or more convenient alternative to an existing product, he calls this a low-end disruption. In Christensen's sense, Airbnb and Google AdWords would be market disruptions, whilst Uber would be a low-end disruption. Low-end or not, Uber has changed the way lots of people work and the way they experience city life. It has also upset countless taxi businesses that thought their jobs were forever secure. There is plenty of charm in a cockney London black cabbie but, if he can't pay the bills and tier one of Maslow's Hierarchy of Needs[3] isn't sustainable for his family, he may not be a happy chappie. Sorry, Guv'nor.

What is clear is that every part of our society is being impacted by new technologies. We see this from developed to developing countries, from governments to associations and from companies all the way down to startups and individual citizens. There is a need for people to adapt their *approaches* to keep up with the changes. The expression 'disrupt or be disrupted' suitably lays down the gauntlet for the world's workforce.[4]

If the rapid way in which these new technologies are sprouting up seems dizzying at times, the biggest and most problematic challenge that organisations are facing is not a technical one. It is the need for a shift in thinking and mindset. After all, are you ready for disruption?

In this book, we will be exploring a total of 15 disruptive forces. These are structured in two parts. Part 1 focuses on the thinking, where we identify the three mindsets that are needed, in combination, to be able to fully embrace disruption. Part 2 is technology-led, where we explore the 12 most technologically disruptive forces. These are formed into three groups. The first group involves those technologies that are most pervasive. Just like the three mindsets, these technological forces are virtually omnipresent. The second group looks at specific applications we can take advantage of. The final group is for stand-alone technologies. Yet, if you are to take away one message from this book, it is that no one force or mindset stands in isolation. These technologies often need to work and be used in combination with others. In all cases, having the right mindset is *the* killer app.

'The times they are a-changin' ... again and again. Bob Dylan's Nobel Prize is a testament to how a great song stays relevant through the ages. Meanwhile, some of the sites and applications we have recommended may not stand the test of time so well. However, at the risk of some 404 and 'out of business' errors, we prefer to get people into action and suggest the best versions that we can find today.

Startups and disruption

Simplistically, the name disruptors often is given to startup companies and disrupted is tagged on to big businesses. This doesn't cut it. Many intrapreneurs[5] of large companies will be disruptive in nature and vast numbers of startups do not come close to their self-acclaimed status of being disruptive.

Such is the energy behind the word in the startup community that we have seen TechCrunch run 'Disrupt' conferences since 2011.[6] The common line amongst speakers and exhibitors at this and many other conferences would be: 'Our startup X is going to bring disruption to Y.' Alternatively, with a similar meaning, they would state: 'We're the Airbnb of Y.' And with it comes the hope of a billion-dollar valuation, otherwise known as being a 'unicorn'. The vast majority of the unicorn-seeking startups are not successful.

And, even if they do truly disrupt, the fact of disrupting does not necessarily guarantee success. They may break codes and tradition, but never find a way to turn disruption into real money. The first incarnation of the file-sharing initiative, Napster, would be a prime example.[7] (Though, with co-founder Sean Parker's later successes and *Forbes*' reported $2.4 billion net worth in 2017,[8] I think he was able to put that one down to experience.)

With over 100 million new businesses started globally each year, and roughly 7 out of 10 of these disappearing in the first 3 years, startup life for most mortals is a huge struggle. For both of us growing up, the pull was to be in a rock band. It has been some time since geek became the new chic, and we have seen aspirations change some time ago. When we first started in tech, there were few startups or people we knew who were founders. Now everyone is startup crazy. The likelihood is you will know, be related to or even be the person working in a startup.

It is important to note that some entrepreneurs will struggle with the disruptive mindset more than others. Some may fail because they are so keen to succeed that they will accept any opportunity and 'pivot' too quickly, thereby losing their focus or vision. As they get stuck, they can end up in what Seth Godin would describe as a *cul de sac* in his book, *The Dip*.[9] Timing is vital. Being too early will doom a startup. Alternatively, others may be cautious, fearful and indoctrinated with a 'large business' mindset, such that they operate too slowly and forget to bring the customer true value. Some have an outlook and ecosystem that is too narrow, and can't identify a ground-breaking idea that others need. But most startups will be outpaced, outmanoeuvred and out-executed by competitors. They won't have funding, won't generate enough revenue and will burn through the cash they have. We have seen, over the decades, bands sleeping in vans, driving through the night to chase after their dream. Likewise, most startup founders have to be willing to sacrifice what feels like everything, if they are going to create the change and see the success they are dreaming of.

If reading this, you are the entrepreneur, we appreciate it often feels like you have no choice. You have to keep going. You are prepared to pay the price. We applaud and honour you for your courage. We acknowledge your determination and persistence. We hope your tenacity and efforts are fully rewarded in one way or another, with or without the dancing unicorns. Just make sure you keep friends close to you along the way. You are going to need them.

Looking back at the macro picture, it is essential for startup entrepreneurs to be aware of the transformational areas of technological change. The entrepreneurs may consider it outside the core focus of their startup. The areas of change, if given space, will bring clarity on what needs fixing. How are entrepreneurs able to address the issues and implement appropriate and value-added solutions?

Even those startups that are successful are not always disruptive. Being disruptive is not necessarily about making your products or service better, cheaper or faster. So, before we go any further, let us define what we mean by disruption.

Working in a startup, it is vital to create an environment that gives a priority to exploration. The widely used Lean Startup[10] model by Eric Ries emphasises the importance of a company-wide culture that looks to grow through *building* something new, *measuring* the results and applying the *learning* for the next stage of growth. Build, measure, learn. Build, measure, learn. It is a mantra many successful entrepreneurs have embraced.

Due to tunnel vision and single-natured goals, sometimes there is a lack of awareness and understanding of many other areas of disruption that pose a threat or provide additional value to the project. Many new businesses are moving in spaces that require multiple areas of expertise. Without a clear understanding and knowledge on how to apply these new forces, there will be significant blind spots. A startup focused on creating a sharing economy marketplace, for example, may be missing out on integrating cryptocurrencies like Bitcoin into their business model as an alternative form of payment. Or others may not be able to mine and analyse the big data that will help to craft and perfect their product in the future.

There is a lot for startups to take on board. One of the goals of this book is to help startup founders, teams, investors and consultants to develop and grow the disruptive mindset in order to leverage fully the disruptive technological forces. Up for the ride?

Bigger organisations – some challenges

For larger organisations, the challenge is a different one compared to startups. There are the legacy systems and processes. Foundational management styles and business principles that have been so important for the last 30 years are limited. They simply cannot equip leaders for both the change we are experiencing and the revolution that is coming. In order to succeed in taming and leveraging disruptive technologies, old dogs need to learn new tricks.

Being intelligent and well-read is not enough to tackle this changing landscape. Authority, analysis and advice are no replacement for trial, experimentation and action.

Most large organisations have reacted to the new world order by assigning this responsibility to an individual. We see within companies such as Starbucks, GE, Total, Burberry, McDonald's, L'Oréal and Condé Nast that the role is crystallised by the Chief Digital Officer (CDO). David Mathison, CEO of the CDO Club,[11] projected that there would be 2,500 CDOs by the end of 2016.[12] The CDO role typically involves having to evangelise and drive the digital agenda, encourage best practices, win buy-in from others to embrace the digital vision and evaluate the infrastructure. The CDO often is given the charge of leading the digital transformation. The role is, perhaps, a necessary evil to get things started but, surely, over time, we would argue that the CDO must disappear so that digital becomes everyone's responsibility. Much in the same way, the Chief Environmental Officer will not need to exist when people have learnt to switch the lights off upon leaving a room. It should be everyone's responsibility.

Transformation more than digital

This brings up an important point that we need to address from the outset. In our focus for this book, disruption is not necessarily digital. We will be covering disruption from all angles. The disruptive mindset is, therefore, not simply the digital mindset.

It is possible that, for consumer-facing companies, digital may work as a blanket term to encompass the relevant new technologies affecting their business. But, for some industries, digital would be far too narrow and simplistic. For example, the advancements in genomics and next generation sequencing are mostly separate from digital. Yet, digital technologies, platforms and applications have helped accelerate the advancements and expanded the accessibility. If companies prefer to talk about digital transformation, we prefer to consider the bigger topic and implementation of the disruptive mindset.

Depending on the sector, for some companies, the remit for the transformation falls under the person in charge of marketing or innovation. In worst-case scenarios, it will be given to a person not on the executive committee, the Chief

Technology Officer or HR. The problem with such an approach is that digital is being given a label, much like any other function, and the responsibility is delegated *away* from other people. A digital revolution cannot be delegated to a single individual. The leader must be digitally focused and the digital revolution must be lived at the top. If the CEO is not a digital agent of change and leading the change him- or herself, transformation will be slow, good people will walk, and it will be harder to grow.

To our thinking, the sea change required to implement disruption comes in on many tides, and needs to flow over every area of the organisation. Marketers are often expected to embrace change to get growth, but the disruptive mindset must be seeded *throughout* the business. The finance, legal and HR departments are, typically, more cautious and follow a more structured approach. However, with the growth of digital disruption, and a need to embrace the new forthcoming technologies, the challenge for these departments is every bit as huge as it is for marketing or sales. One defining characteristic of an organisation that possesses the disruptive mindset is that the executive committee down to the person on the factory floor, is engaged, on board and involved in digital implementation. Or, alternatively, within a startup, the whole team have got with the programme.

We like to say that everyone wanting to lead within the organisation must share the role of CMO: Chief Mindset Officer. Far from being a role for a single person, the chief mindset officer is a role that every board member should include in their title. Let us see that on your LinkedIn profile!

How to become a Chief Mindset Officer

Getting into a disruptive mode to enable long-term success requires a widespread collaboration, a shared sense of responsibility and a common purpose.

Below, we have identified the 10 most important characteristics of the disruptive mindset that underpin the Chief Mindset Officer's duties. These characteristics do not replace other commonsense notions that are essential for executives. Efficiency, effectiveness or strong decision making are all essential foundational principles to be built on. However, tomorrow's most successful leaders, be they startup founders or big business executives, will embody most, if not all, of these 10 characteristics in distinctly greater proportions.

> It is necessary to have voracious curiosity if you want to live a life of continuous learning.

The 10 most important personal characteristics

1. **Curiosity.** You do not know everything now, but you can always learn something new. Every. Single. Day. It is good to be curious, to experiment and to have new experiences. It is necessary to have voracious curiosity if you want to live a life of continuous learning.

2. **Openness.** Regularly try out new things and open up your thinking. Once the curiosity is triggered, be open to learn and accept challenging ideas and listen to contradictions. Look to meet people with unknown skills and different points of view and be open to change on an ongoing basis.

3. **Networker.** Be well connected to different groups both inside and outside your organisation. This is essential to expand your thinking, discover the best resources and to grow beyond your borders.

4. **Geek quotient.** Try and experience digital innovations *personally*. Let the change go deep. Improve your digital or geek intelligence quotient.[13]

5. **Jack of all trades.** Once it was important to have immense expertise in one area. Now, it is increasingly important to have multiple areas of expertise. We call this having a comb-shaped profile, rather than a singular, deep T-shaped knowledge.[14] Having a mixture of specialisms helps one leverage and find symbiosis between people and ideas. We believe that having new types of profiles, such as anthropologists, sociologists and journalists in the organisation can be beneficial.

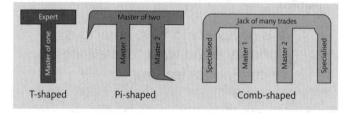

The three different expert profiles
Sources: Adapted from Classon, I. (2013) 'Stupid Question 218: What are T-shaped, pi-shaped and Comb-shaped skills, and which one should I aim for?, July, http://irisclasson. com/2013/07/08/stupid-question-218-what-are-t-shaped-pi-shaped-and-comb-shaped-skills-and-which-one-should-i-aim-for/; Hansen, M.T. and von Oetinger, B. (2001) 'Introducing T-Shaped Managers: Knowledge', *Harvard Business Review*, March, http:// hbswk.hbs.edu/archive/2235.html; and Dawson, R. (2013) 'Building success in the future of work: T-shaped, Pi-shaped, and Cone-shaped skills', 21 March, https://rossdawson.com/ blog/building-future-success-t-shaped-pi-shaped-and-comb-shaped-skills/

6. **Empathy.** If we listen carefully, we can discover magic in our customers' voices. People need to be heard, understood and responded to with empathy. By putting ourselves in our customers' shoes, we can create validated, meaningful and lasting experiences. What they think and feel must affect the design and overall customer satisfaction.

7. **Congruent.** In a world of increasing transparency, you must be open, honest and consistent. It is a risky choice for any leader to say one thing and do another. It will be unearthed. Eventually. Congruency is important for winning the loyalty of customers, the engagement of employees, and the respect of peers.

8. **Hands on.** All those in leadership need to pause the show, lose their egos and use their tech hands. We need a hands-on approach to taste, to test and experience the digital tools and devices that can otherwise feel too abstract. Being involved in the small details nourishes the vision for the big stage which, in turn, creates outstanding performances.

9. **Connecting the dots and the people.** Keep information flowing and communication open. Do not become an island, but commit to remain connected and help facilitate the exchange of information and business cards. There is nothing more harmful than the loss of information, lethargic communications and the laziness that follows. This can set in when people are not held accountable for their communications and, as a result, their actions.

10. **Focused.** Time is precious. Find focus and stay aligned both personally and professionally. This focus will give you energy to graft, courage to overcome and the resilience not to give up. Knowing your purpose helps you embrace opportunities, accelerate decision making and say kind, yet resounding, no's. There is always a surplus of new opportunities, but culture-changing people flourish as a result of their focus.

For each of the chapters we will be covering, we are going to look at some next steps through a three-way prism, which we have called The PIE Model: **P**ersonal, **I**nternal and **E**xternal. It starts with bringing the mindset and disruptive force into the personal sphere. First, without personal engagement, disruption remains just an intellectual exercise. Second, one must evaluate how the disruptive force should be baked into the organisation. Last, how can each force enhance one's position and outlook to the customers, partners, society and other external stakeholders? By adopting The Pie Model, you are able to grapple with and leverage these disruptive forces. It is also an important step towards having a more congruent and authentic presence.

One could dedicate a full book to explore the implementation of each chapter. We cannot. So, as well as inviting you to enjoy a slice of PIE, if you do not like eating alone, do not be a stranger. We speak, consult and work with businesses around these areas and you would be welcome to invite us in to enjoy some PIE with you.

A slice of PIE

Personal

1. When embracing curiosity, each day actively seek out a random new account on Twitter, look up a new tool on Product Hunt,[15] watch a TED Talk[16] or Bloomberg Technology[17] episode.

2. Be open to meeting someone new each day. You may be introduced, meet at an event or identify them on LinkedIn or Facebook. Find something interesting they have written or done. Put these rendezvous in a different colour in your calendar.

3. To get geeky, befriend a plugged-in teenager and watch them interact on a device, sign up for a educational session at your local Apple store, or subscribe to a course on Masterclass[18] or Udemy[19].

Internal

1. Who are the generalists within your organisation? Is their skillset and outlook celebrated and given space to grow? Establish a culture where staff are encouraged to learn a broader range of skills and develop deeper knowledge across multiple subjects. Identify existing areas of expertise and pursue new areas with intent.

2. To develop empathy, experience the customer's journey from beginning to end without letting on that you are from the company. If you work for a smaller startup, get a

close friend or relative to do it, and record the emotions felt at each stage of the customer experience.

3. Start with finding out what digital tools and platforms can augment your personal work projects or interests. Get hands on and pull out your debit card to pay for a trial yourself. It's important to get a feel for what different solutions could do for you, in your role.

External

1. Be connected to your customers by outlining a centralised list of engagement approaches in one place. Think through all the different disparate tools and platforms that you are using to engage with your customers. Even if you are not in the marketing department, by thinking through these steps it will influence your actions. A collaborative project management tool, such as Basecamp,[20] is a great tool to pull all this information together in one place.

2. Start with thinking through your purpose; both personal and organisational. What impact do you look to have on your customers? What do they believe and perceive your organisation stands for? Explore with your colleagues where there is a lack of congruency between what your organisation says and does. After all, actions speak louder than words.

3. As an organisation, be open to mutually beneficial partnerships. Not only can such a disposition accelerate your reach, output and growth, it gives your organisation the opportunity to learn and develop, with others who will have your back.

CLICK – the five key organisational principles key organisational principles

As a direct result of these new technologies, CLICK represents the five new principles that have risen in importance in the way startups, organisations, big businesses, founding teams and executives need to operate.

1. **Cooperation.** Work as a team. Many of the disruptive forces addressed in the following 15 chapters work best when applied together, and this requires people of different skillsets to work collaboratively. This may be in the office, working remotely or as an external consultant or supplier. We will explore this in greater detail in Mindset 3 Collaboration.

2. **Learning continuously.** We all need to be in a mode of constant learning. We are fans of the principles of Peter Senge's Learning Organization.[21] Much of the learning must occur by doing and experiencing for ourselves the user experience. Although we signpost this now, this will be unpacked in Mindset 2 as we explore responsibility.

3. **Innovate fast.** Not only has the speed with which one needs to innovate increased, the tools, options and models for innovation have multiplied. Thanks to new digital platforms, there are phenomenal new ways to enhance the *process* of innovation. For example, we see opportunities for open-source platforms, crowdsourcing, artificial intelligence (AI) and 3D printing. The applications for the new innovative mindset include research, data collection, communication, prototyping, testing and ongoing feedback. All in all, digital tools and platforms are revolutionising the way we innovate, not just the goods and services we create.

4. **Customer centricity.** It sounds obvious that the customer is important but, having a fully fledged, proactively thoughtful, customer-centric organisation is a distant reality for many brands. Businesses do not consciously think customers are not the most important thing. But all the barriers and lack of care means subconsciously customers do not *feel important*. Processes, people and promises need to be aligned to enable the customer to be at the centre. Importantly, each team member also needs to believe that this is true.

5. Kick bad habits. As creatures of habit, we take comfort in routines and customs. But in today's environment, this can lead to fatal flaws, both at a personal level and an organisational level. Although we are strong believers in aligning activity and output around strengths, this is no excuse not to take action to eliminate behaviour, actions that consistently produce poor results or experiences. As is contentiously attributed to Albert Einstein, 'the definition of insanity is doing something over and over again and expecting a different result each time.' Sanity is so underrated.

> Processes, people and promises need to be aligned to enable the customer to be at the centre.

There is a growing realisation that the pace of change is not only likely to continue incessantly for the foreseeable future but, in our business sectors, it is gaining greater and monumental momentum. Senior executives everywhere, with the likes of Bill Ford (the executive chairman of Ford) and Francisco González (the CEO of BBVA), express the refrain: 'The speed of change is accelerating.' Mark Benioff, CEO of Salesforce, says: 'Companies are no longer competing against each other. They're competing with speed.'[22] Similarly, Brian Solis wrote in a seminal blog post about digital Darwinism, 'It's not survival of the fittest any more, it's survival of the fitting.'[23] And, in large part, the fittest must also be the fastest. For leaders in all spheres, niches and industries, the challenge is finding ways to select and optimise disruptive technologies, adopt the right mindset and bridge the strategic gaps. Again, we ask, are you ready for disruption?

> The challenge is finding ways to select and optimise disruptive technologies, adopt the right mindset and bridge the strategic gaps.

Has digital disruption already happened?

Somewhere, someone is probably scheming *at this very moment* at how to disrupt your business. Many sectors have been 'uberised;' but many more are yet to be. Will yours?

If you were to listen to some high-profile consultants, they are claiming that disruption is over-rated and an overused buzzword. IBM went so far as to suggest that, 'The digital disruption has *already* happened.'[24] With no small amount of shock and provocation, they shared the following:

- The world's largest taxi company owns no taxis (Uber).

- The largest accommodation provider owns no real estate (Airbnb).

- The largest phone companies own no telco infrastructure (Skype, WeChat).

- The world's most valuable retailer has no inventory (Alibaba).

- The most popular media owner creates no content (Facebook).

- The fastest growing banks have no actual money (SocietyOne).

- The world's largest movie house owns no cinemas (Netflix).

- The largest software vendors do not write the apps (Apple and Google).

Of all the above examples mentioned, there is probably only one of these you have not heard of: SocietyOne, based in Australia, is still tiny in terms of worldwide volume and underscores how immature the disruption has been in that space. Moreover, if Uber and Airbnb are the biggest in their sector, it reflects more, in our opinion, the splintered nature of the market. For example, the top 10 hotel chains, which continue to see widespread consolidation, own just under 5 million hotel rooms between them. This accounts for less than 30 per cent of the world's total number of hotel rooms.

Are there confines to disruption?

The approach in this book is to look at how disruption is occurring and the impact it can have on both large businesses and startups. Does this mean that everyone needs to concentrate on all these disruptive forces? Not at all. Some areas and industries are far more exposed than others. And, yet, all sectors, geographies and functions are prone to disruption. The question becomes: what does disruption mean or cover?

For the purposes of this book, we are focused on three areas of impact: the business model, process and innovation. Importantly, we are not uniquely concerned with the innovative product or service. As the *Harvard Business Review* (HBR) article entitled, 'What is Disruptive Innovation?' says, 'Too frequently, people use the term disruption loosely to invoke the concept of innovation in support of whatever it is they wish to do.'[25] We would agree. For sure, pundits, consultants and entrepreneurs liberally throw around the term of disruption. Often, the term is used to scare management who are stuck in their ways. Disruption, however, is not an all-or-nothing notion that encompasses only the change or destruction of a certain business sector. Disruption is also happening at the smallest levels. We experience it both on a personal level, in our parenting and schooling, as well as on a macro business level. Cities, law enforcement agencies and governments are also having to adapt at uncomfortably faster paces. Disruption stands at the door and knocks. Do we hear it?

In organisations, every department needs to draw on its interdependence with others. This not only brings greater efficiency and effectiveness, but also enables disruption to spur innovation and creativity.

As much as companies have considered innovation as the lifeline of sustainable growth, innovation has moved beyond the new products and services being offered. The disruptive forces that are unravelling businesses are, by their nature, innovative. However, they are not only about *new* tech, much less *high* tech. Some of these new technologies have been 'new' for decades, but have not yet gone mainstream. These include genomics, artificial intelligence and energy storage; technologies all on the cusp of a quantum leap forward. Other technologies have been predictably seeping into our lives and affecting or disrupting customer behaviours and expectations. Meanwhile, there is a set of other forces that we refer to as 'mindset shifts' that, like water, have a tendency to permeate into every aspect of the organisation.

At the end of the day, almost every type of organisation is being forced to reevaluate their strategy, manner of working and, even, their business model. National governments, city structures and political staff, no less than in business, are facing a tsunami of change. Last, but not least, the individuals, both as citizens and employees, are adjusting, often faster than business and government.

> To succeed in disruption we all need to adopt a state of mind, *enhanced* or *empowered* by technology.

Disruptive forces

To succeed in disruption we all need to adopt a state of mind, *enhanced* or *empowered* by technology. Many of these disruptive forces are interrelated. This has contributed to the confusion and difficulty for entrenched businesses to know how to embrace and integrate them. For example, artificial intelligence is being applied in big data analytics, 3D printing, genomics and self-driving cars. Smartphones pervade all areas of communication and interaction. Artificial intelligence and big data analytics are being applied to genomics. Big data needs and cloud storage are related to security, especially when there is sensitive information involved. Additionally, blockchain technology is being applied to the collaborative economy.

The purpose of this book is to map out these disruptive forces and illustrate them with some of the best or most insightful examples. We want you and your business, though the task is somewhat challenging, to last the test of time. That doesn't mean you can stop the waves that are coming, but you can learn when to paddle out beyond the waves and when to ride in on them. We want to help identify the sectors, professions and industries most likely to be affected. Not only do we want to explore the core areas of disruption, we want to suggest how we might apply these principles into our startups and organisations. We want you to futureproof yourselves.

As co-authors, we both come from different backgrounds, having spent the majority of our lives working predominantly with either large corporations or with startups. Both have advantages alongside huge frustrations. Naturally, coming together, we have discovered there are some disruptive principles that apply to both startups and established organisations, and other approaches that need careful application to one group only. We bring our professional and personal experiences to the table. Like many writers, we want to engage and allow our words to connect and stir you, so we have sprinkled stories and anecdotes throughout the book. Where we want this book to take you on a journey, we have not allowed ourselves to get in the way and therefore you will always hear stories spoken in the first person. We leave those of you who are interested to play the game of 'spot the storyteller'. We hold on to the shared drive and motivation we had when we first chose to write this book. We are committed and driven to see you both *be* the change and *create* the change the world is crying out for.

Digital disruption and transformation

It has been fascinating to see which companies have been taking the digital wave in their stride and how they have done it. Just five years ago, there were still major fast-moving consumer goods companies who were scrambling to *try* to spend 10 per cent of their marketing budget via digital channels. Often, the bigger the company the slower the speed we have seen that company, and entire sectors embrace digital. Between legacy systems, older leadership and corporate lethargy, there has been much resistance. Some sectors, like tech that were located in certain geographies, were quicker to realise the power of digital. There are still others today who have only reached the point of carving out digital as a strategic direction for the organisation.

As other thought leaders, such as Ian Cox,[26] Dr Dave Chaffey[27] or Jake Ward[28] have elaborated, there are various stages of maturity for a company's digital transformation. Especially in the larger organisations, the first stages are, typically, rather ineffectual. As the experience is acquired and progress made, the culture of the company always needs to adapt, starting with the behaviours and mindset of the C-suite.

However, it is important to signal that these levels or stages are not static. That is to say that a *determined* organisation very easily can fall back into a *programmatic* or *defensive* mindset if the progress is not satisfactory. It is not about keeping up with the Joneses (or the competition). It is about keeping up with the customers. Because some companies have considered digital transformation as a destination, the wrong processes and technologies are being installed. As a result, the 'transformation' inevitably falls flat as the carpet is ripped out from under their stationary feet. For all manner of companies, it is vital to consider digital transformation as a mindset and to expect further change. We would argue that the digital maturity of a company should be a supremely important part of a stock analyst's evaluation.

Complete digital transformation is neither possible nor, even, desirable. At the end of the day, it is about getting into a constant learning mode, looking at and assessing the new technologies and opportunities as they arise in accordance with one's strategic goals. As Tom Goodwin writes, digital transformation is 'a philosophy that all must adopt'.[29]

The concept that all of these disruptive forces may also be destructive or counterproductive to one's own business or industry can be somewhat exaggerated. Some of these disruptive forces actually have been beneficial to certain installed industries. For example, as recounted by Duncan Stewart, director of technology, media and telecommunications research at Deloitte Canada, the music industry that he describes as the 'digital destruction poster child'. If the traditional players have been shaken up, the underlying industry is buoyant. Stewart elaborates: 'The MP3 file didn't just change CD revenues into some other kind of physical format revenues, or even into digital revenues, instead the growth and ease of piracy has caused *all* music sales to collapse, right? In fact, between 2008 and 2015, one US live music company saw its concert revenues grow 23 per cent in constant dollars, or 2.8 per cent annually.[30] The digital trend that almost obliterated the CD industry a) didn't seem to hurt live music at all, and b) may in fact have freed up consumer dollars for spending on live concerts.'

If disruption is largely a question of scientific advancements and new technologies, we cannot make the most of these technologies without the right mindset. For many businesses, and we have seen our fair share, we see founding and executive teams operating with a mindset that is backwards. For example, they might think that it is all about investing in the *best* customer relationship management (CRM) platform to help bring them more business. However, in reality, a great system on the wrong mindset will not work half as well as the right mindset on a system without as many bells and whistles. With a little wink and a hint to turn this thinking on its head, we have broken down the mindset into three sections that spell out CRM backwards: Meaningfulness, Responsibility and Collaboration.

We hope you enjoy the adventure. It is our goal to help get you ready for disruption.

Part 1

The mindsets

Meaningfulness

The importance of purpose and values

> **The mystery of human existence lies not in just staying alive, but in finding something to live for.**
>
> *Fyodor Dostoyevsky, author,* The Brothers Karamazov

'Life is short' is, possibly, one of the world's greatest clichés. Yet, it is probably the most challenging to integrate into the daily grind of life. Generationally and culturally, people look at time differently. Yet, we would argue, there is a strong drive to find purpose in both what we do and how we spend our time that runs across generations and cultures. We call this the quest for meaningfulness.

What is it?

Meaningfulness is a powerful source of inspiration and energy. It costs you nothing, although the sacrifices you make to embrace it wholeheartedly can cost you everything. Each person will have both a different definition and relationship to it. Meaningfulness cannot be found easily in every task we shoulder, but the more it is sprinkled into our activities, the brighter and more rewarding our lives become.

We believe companies and the individuals in their teams need to fully understand and incorporate a strong sense of meaningfulness. This will give them the focus to power on through hard work, the courage to make tough choices and both the humility and empathy to lead well. As a result, employees are more fulfilled, customers are more engaged and, ultimately, shareholders will see better returns. As we explore the different disruptive technologies in this book, developing meaning provides a strong foundation to build upon. Meaningfulness is, arguably, the most disruptive of the mindsets, as it is so foreign for many business leaders and has a deeply grounding and transformative nature to it. With that in mind, we have outlined the five Ps of meaningfulness that we believe are central to those wanting to be ready for disruption: purpose, people, planet, prize and profit.

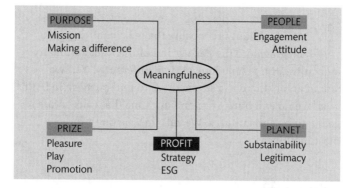

The 5Ps of meaningfulness
Note: ESG: environmental, social and [corporate] governance

Navigating the choices

Every day it seems like there's a new technology in the headlines:

Robots will destroy our jobs – and we're not ready for it[1]

Self-driving cars won't just watch the world – they'll watch you[2]

Australian entrepreneur says he invented bitcoin[3]

As a business leader, it's a balancing act exploring new technologies without succumbing to shiny object syndrome. Smart business leaders have learnt to discern which technologies bring value and which cause distraction. It is important to consider what makes most sense to the needs of the business at any given time. Additionally, what are the skills needed to optimise the implementation of a new technology effectively?

> As a business leader, it's a balancing act exploring new technologies without succumbing to shiny object syndrome.

Many companies have jumped on the bandwagon of digital transformation. Digital has become a term that more or less encompasses all that is involved in new tech. Although there are plenty of companies that have chosen not to become more digital, the success of those undertaking digital transformation varies hugely. Technology, fast-moving consumer goods, media and other similar industries obviously are more focused on digital than the likes of private banking and ultra-luxury brands. But everyone is concerned. At the heart of digital transformation is a key consideration: customer centricity. The customer needs to remain at the heart of the conversation for everyone. And if digital transformation is required to help this throughout the organisation, it needs to be a top-down focus. The conviction and drive needs to be carried through by senior leadership.

> Taking on board a disruptive new technology is, essentially, a question of mindset. It is less about the technology and more about the desired *outcome*.

Taking on board a disruptive new technology is, essentially, a question of mindset. It is less about the technology and more about the desired *outcome*. It is less about the specific platform than the *way* it is used. This comes with the presumption and recognition that such thinking needs to be built upon the core skills and understanding that all good leaders need.

▌ Since digital transformation requires experimentation, the culture must accept *trial and error*.

▌ Because new technology changes all the time, decision making must *speed* up.

▌ As the internet is visible for everyone, greater levels of *transparency* are required.

▌ Since it is impossible to be an expert in everything, *openness* and *collaboration* are key.

▌ Because the technology is created both by and for human beings, *empathy* and *social sciences* have a central role in design thinking, communication and business execution.

▌ To mobilise change at scale, everyone needs to know *why* the transformation is necessary.

> In reality, digital transformation acts as a litmus test because it easily exposes an organisation that does not have a clear vision.

As we will explore in Mindset 2, there is a huge need for *everyone* to take responsibility for the change they want to see happen. A seismic shift in approach is needed, but will not work if it is left to a few people or simply relegated to a chief digital officer. Digital transformation requires everyone to get on board behind a vision. In reality, digital transformation acts as a litmus test because it easily exposes an organisation that does not have a clear vision. In this context, leaders need the character and skills to fly the plane strategically at 30,000 feet and drive through implementation on the ground.

One of the major challenges to develop the disruptive mindset is the inherent conflict between vast choice and limited resources. A second major issue is the tension between driving near-term results and maintaining a long-term strategy. We like to refer to the need for each organisation to find its North*. What does this mean? It means creating a long-term direction for the brand, which includes the purpose that your organisation serves. The more clear and precise the northerly setting, the easier it becomes to work through the choices and to galvanise support amongst the team. This is why having a sense of purpose and meaningfulness is an important business dynamic in disruptive days.

It is worth noting that meaningfulness is not only important inside the company and for the employees. It is also a fundamental need amongst consumers and a strongly recommended part of the offering to customers. For example, in the world of travel, people are looking for meaningful experiences in their precious time off. A travel company that delivers and provides an amazing journey that creates meaning on a deeper level will also be more likely to create a committed customer for the next trip. Technology and data are both of importance, but it is how the product or service makes the customer *feel* that will shape long-term loyalty.

As we move through this chapter, we will explore the 5Ps of meaningfulness, when applied to an organisation. But, first, let us start with setting one's North, both as an individual and an organisation. Let us look at purpose.

What is your purpose?

Who am I and why am I here? These two questions, on a philosophical level, have been debated down the years. At the heart of these questions, for many people, is a longing for

---

*Refers to the philosophy/methodology of NEWS Coaching, pioneered by Aviad Goz. www.newsnavigation.org/

significance, and an exploration of identity and purpose. This applies to people from all walks of life. Whether as CEOs of large organisations or founders of startups, senior managers of blue-chip companies or startup interns, many of us want a sense of appreciation and respect, and to know that we are valued. We also want to be part of something we believe in.

Recently, I was talking to a friend who had just left what she described as a mundane, soulless job. She had worked for a reputable company, earning a good salary but, despite the strong career trajectory, it left her feeling dissatisfied. She wanted more.

In our conversation, she went on to explain that she had not seen significant value in what the company was doing. She knew she was helping the partners earn more money. But, unlike some of her colleagues, she did not have a husband or children and, as a result, work was her main focus for fulfilment. What she did each day, due to its lack of purpose, made her unhappy.

She mustered up the courage to leave the firm and join a startup. Why? 'Dynamic leadership, a clear vision, great ideas, and the team want to make a difference.' She believed in the mission and, for the first time in years, she felt alive.

Although, of course, it can swing the other way, with some startups lacking purpose or larger companies having an exceptionally clear vision, people are making a directional shift towards companies with purpose. As leaders within our organisations, if we want to have stronger chances of leading people to embrace disruptive technologies, we need to make meaningfulness a part of every day. When people can associate their tasks with the company's strategic direction and purpose, there is a natural desire to want to go above and beyond.

The expectations of millennials[4]

Millennials want a clear sense of purpose for their work. For many, it is more important than a higher salary. In fact, in a survey by Glassdoor, one of the fastest growing jobs and recruiting sites, 64 per cent of millennials would be happier making $40,000 a year at a job they enjoy, rather than making $100,000 a year at a job they find uninteresting.[5]

Let us start with the biggest question. 'Why are you and your organisation in business?' I'm sure, for many of us, it is a question we have heard many times. It is easy to repeat robot-like company mission statements and personal mantras; but it is crucial to allow space for a deeper response to arise.

My repeated and fully owned mantra is, 'I'm passionate to see people live incredibly, and I'm committed to ideas that can change the world.' Although, deep down in my core, I hope that reflects the work I do and the way I live, the truth is, I often feel in survival mode. Survival to finish projects. Survival to make things work. Survival to provide my family with all they need. I can feel like a dichotomy.

It is a challenge for many to hold on to big dreams, hopes and aspirations and, as a result, many, including myself, have, at times, resorted back to mediocrity. It is not an immediate decision but, over time, the compromises that were justified by the need for survival become commonplace. We have been hurt by our own failings, and the failings of others. This may range from pain on a political, societal, institutional or organisational level down to the personal pain of our family and friends. The idealism of earlier days gradually is replaced with cynicism. This is not necessarily deep-rooted cynicism. It can be subtle, a resignation to 'so-called reality', otherwise known as: 'just the way things are'. Even for glass-half-full people, continued failings, a negative environment and repeated painful experiences are hard to overcome. It takes determination to hold on to hope. But we need to. It is our lifeline.

You may not have experienced pain and untreated disappointment. You may read articles on technology and business and believe or, dare I say, even 'know' that you too will experience the success you read of. But how do both these sets of experiences and expectations marry together?

Are the poles too far apart or are there lessons that can be learnt? How does your organisation cater for those that have such huge hopes and longings, and yet empathise with those who have a lack of trust and a subsequent cynicism that so many of us have experienced in our hearts? There are three potential reactions, one of which we believe is optimal.

1. Be the calm voice of inevitable death, scorning others for not knowing how things really are and, in the process, lock yourself off from the opportunities that could come your way. Naturally, you will not attract talent or people around you that carry a DNA for making a difference and, most probably, it will be a self-fulfilling prophecy.

2. Throw caution to the wind, better engage with all the trappings and approaches that so many successful tech companies have, presuming that simply being open and exciting will get you to your goals. But do not be disappointed that, after offering happy-hour afternoons with free goji berry bars and bottles of beer, it does not translate to a guaranteed successful initial public offering (IPO). Thanks for the drink, though!

3. Use the past to inform the future, use the pain to build muscles of courage and use the anger to grow determination. But, equally, embrace raw enthusiasm to provide energy, live with openness to embrace new opportunities, and use the hope to provide fresh vision. Develop a context and an experience where the exchange of ideas build on the foundations of lessons learnt.

Number three is the reaction we like the most!

We have to learn to change our outlook, and to take on a viewpoint that encompasses multiple experiences and personalities, so together we can grow in wisdom and create greater meaning.

Of course, it is not just millennials who are longing for meaning. Deep down, we would argue that many people of all generations are looking for a sense of purpose at work; they may just be in the 'putting up with it' mode, having learnt not to risk their emotions in what they have come to call the 'pointless pursuit of dreams'. They have resigned themselves to the reality of what they experience. Worldwide, according to a Gallup poll, just 13 per cent of employees describe themselves as engaged, a level that has been stagnant since the poll was first made in 2000.[6]

A good question to ask is whether you display your mission and, if so, how clear is it? Would your team know it? More poignantly, what part of each person's work is related to fulfilling that mission? People want to have clarity of what is expected of them by the organisation and how they fit into the wider picture. As an indicator, 72 per cent of highly engaged employees understand their importance or role and how it contributes to organisational success.[7] It is one thing for teams to have purpose, but what would they describe as the reason the company exists? Does your team know the *why* of the company and, if so, do they care? If not, are you prepared to invest the energy and personal integrity to create a mission people can believe in?

Paradoxically, many larger corporations struggle to communicate their purpose, though they have the resources to do it. Although the original company will have begun as a startup, that may be in the distant past and there will be layers of bureaucracy that prevent and stunt creativity. We believe one of the key roles of the CEO is to be the chief storyteller, reinforcing, role-modelling and repeating the company's purpose. When it comes to startup companies, one has to ask: what is it that makes so many of them appear so compelling? Is it simply down to a strong emphasis on branding and design? Is it the apparent flexibility and freedom to do anything? Is it an idealistic vision and a dream that gathers people around it? A startup's simplicity is easier to communicate and there will always be people who can get behind a rallying call to action by an impassioned founder.

When you combine dynamism with strong experience and focus on a problem that brings positive transformation, you will find a deep sense of purpose at its heart. People are the key drivers of that.

When you combine dynamism with strong experience and focus on a problem that brings positive transformation, you'll find a deep sense of purpose at its heart. People are the key drivers of that.

Finding the right people

Good businesses create the right context where people can find true meaning in their work. Work at times is, however, exhausting and competitive, and demands a huge amount from people. Many startup founders suffer with depression and anxiety, with 72 per cent of entrepreneurs reporting mental health concerns.[8] Many high-flyers within established businesses are driven to the point of burn-out. If it is all grind and no kind, employees and the companies they work for suffer. It is important for people to know how they find and create meaning and what they need to do to flourish. But, often, it is people who can be major contributors to the strain. First, it is important to have the right people on your team. You will not have time to be a full-time counsellor.

Good businesses create the right context where people can find true meaning in their work.

Jim Collins, in his book *Good to Great,*[9] outlines the need to '[g]et the right people on the bus first, and the wrong people off the bus, then figure out what direction to drive the company.'[10] This has never been more important as you embrace the mindset that enables you to get ready for disruption. Some people are just not suited to an entrepreneurial or intrapreneurial environment. As well as the standard necessity of shared values and appropriate levels of skill, it is a challenge to identify people with the right emotional temperament to flourish in this context. There is a lot of uncertainty, and trial and error. Having to switch between attention to detail, whilst straddling blue sky thinking, can be uncomfortable for some.

Do not waste time, energy and resources on people who are not the right fit; otherwise known as, 'Don't cast your pearls before swine.' It is likely, if you are embracing a new project with disruption at the heart of it, that you will be working with some existing team members, recruiting others, and working with external consultants and partners. To help get the right blend of team members on board, consider carrying out psychometric personality tests to understand the people involved. Eighty-nine of the Fortune 100 companies in the USA are now using personality tests, valuing the industry at $500 million a year.[11] There are many to choose from and Myers Briggs and Belbin are the most popular and well known. We are also advocates of the Enneagram[12] and Strengthsfinder[13] because people who use their strengths every day are six times more likely to be engaged on the job.[14]

The problems entrepreneurs and innovators bring

Some of the biggest influencers of people are the innovators and entrepreneurs themselves. By their very nature, these people often can be task-focused and overly intent on getting the most out of those around them. There is a fine line between motivation and taking advantage of someone. Leaders often have a vision and a compelling sense of where they want to go. But how do they best balance this vision, whilst opening up space to effectively carry other people there with them?

It is common practice for leaders to focus closely on how to manage others in order to get the most out of their team. They tend to approach it based on productivity and efficiency: 'This amount of sausage meat into the sausage machine produces this number of sausages.' That is great if all you want to do is make sausages. Lots do not. And, if suddenly there is a need to do something differently, it can cause friction. Hence the challenges elaborated in the charming *Who Moved My Cheese?*[15] by Spencer Johnson.

Many people find the management style of their bosses problematic. In some contexts, this can be more than someone thinking, 'My boss is a Muppet', to being a highly destructive and dysfunctional way of management. In a robust 2015 US Gallup survey,[16] about 50 per cent of the 7,200 adults surveyed left a job 'to get away from their manager'. In this book, we have not got time to explore all the typical flaws managers show, though, if given time, I am sure you can reflect on a number you have experienced or, perhaps, even demonstrated. But John Maxwell's book *The 21 Irrefutable Laws of Leadership*[17] acts as a good antidote to these.

When it comes to disruptive projects, unless the culture looks after its people and welcomes learning from mistakes, there is going to be trouble. When things go wrong, which they will, it is severely dangerous if companies fall into the shame and blame game. This drains energy, kills creativity and stunts a company from being innovative. It results in everyone watching their backs, taking no risks and doing what they can not to be publicly shamed. It stands in direct contrast to creating a meaningful environment. Sometimes, we believe it is easy to overlook and excuse the behaviour of leaders, because of the power they hold and a belief that the end justifies the means. It may come from a lack of awareness, but many managers and leaders cause immense destruction to their team. This needs to be addressed to create space for meaning.

Positive cultures are essential, and people who are fortunate enough to have such a working environment often produce great work and find meaning. How transparent a culture do you create and model? Are you upfront, consistent and clear with people or are people often on edge around you? Do people play to their strengths and, as such, are they given the environment and opportunity to do so? Or do you feel the need to pull people down on their weaknesses? However much focus one puts on the stimulating nature of work, if the culture is negative and the leadership is destructive, you will hit the biggest reason why projects do not succeed. In our experience, time and again, leadership plays *the* critical role in defining change and driving long-term success.

So what brings people meaning?

When working with disruptive technologies, a combined creative and analytical team is essential. A good team provides a great context for belonging, meaning and friendship and 67 per cent of employees say friends are a reason to stay in an organisation.[18] When working on incredibly complex matters, if team members are skilled, competent and approachable, people learn to rely on each other and it helps make the difficult possible.

Challenging projects are immensely rewarding for team members when the creative force of the human being comes into full effect. As disruptive technologies are new, many of the people in your organisation interested by them will be early adopters. They are motivated to explore ground-breaking areas of work. Tackling the 'new' is incredibly stimulating and brings great satisfaction, especially where there is the space, resources and backing to help the project succeed. Many do not describe this opportunity as work, but rather enjoy spending time on it, both inside and outside 'working' hours.

It is easy to overcomplicate the ways that people find meaning through their work. Some of it is based around what the company stands for, and some is based on what the individual is involved in. Sometimes, there are simple ways that people feel valued and find meaningfulness in their work. They want to be heard, help people, learn and be useful.

When it comes to personal values and company values, do your team members find alignment? Do they belong to a community where they feel at ease with the people and the *existing* ethics? In what ways can they be part of a mission that will improve the world in some manner? These are helpful questions to consider in your relationship and engagement with others in the organisation.

The planet – how can we look after it?

In the past, many companies used to create sustainability initiatives whilst dragging their heels. Often, they would allocate the lowest possible associated resources. But, for the more enlightened, it has now moved from being a burden to being seen as good business sense. Corporates can legitimately convert sustainability into new opportunities. An Accenture study from 2013,[19] identified that more than 90 per cent of CEOs believed that sustainability was important for the future success of their company. Moreover, in 2015, 81 per cent of S&P 500-listed firms published corporate sustainability reports in contrast to just 20 per cent in 2011.[20] Why and how is it in the interest of companies to be more attentive to the planet? Deep down, we all know that the Earth's resources are finite. The only *real* difference in opinion is on the time horizon. For the more optimistically inclined, the belief is that human savvy will find a solution in due time; but, for many, there is genuine concern. Whatever sustainability actions your organisation takes, it is important that the company retains a legitimacy. Anything less and the initiative will either peter out or be considered as greenwashing.[21]

So what does that mean for your business? What steps should you take? You could engage your staff or customers and ask them to vote on which charitable initiatives they want to support each month. In the process, you could consult with and explore the different ways you can support this charity. It may be more than a financial donation. Opportunities could be created to offer support by giving time and your expertise.

Having a meaningful focus on the planet is, however, more than just supporting a charity. The mindset shift means thinking through the organisation's relationship with resources and energy. How can you change your consumption patterns personally *and* throughout the business? As well as the day-to-day work you do, you might consider ways you can reduce your organisation's carbon footprint and educate those around you. Many simple ways exist for businesses to do this. You could reduce face-to-face meetings, connect through online meeting tools, or choose to do all your reporting of projects online. You could even organise a company-sponsored car pooling scheme. Naturally, with this mindset, you will be able to identify all manner of environmentally friendly approaches, from choice of suppliers to energy consumption and everything in between. A key question to explore is what disruptive technologies your organisation could embrace that could have a significant impact environmentally, in a cost-effective manner so as not to impair shareholder value.

Through all of this, the adoption and commitment to the planet starts with each of us at a personal level. Many senior executives have their environmental bells rung by their earth-conscious children. As leaders, we get to decide how loud those bells sound. In reality, so much of the time, we set the tone. We provide the example and we, in turn, take responsibility and must be held accountable. We need to be the first to turn off the lights, set the temperature and sort the rubbish, in order to change the culture and to find the solutions. On this, there is still much work to be done.

Profit – it is always going to be needed

As much as any business must continue to maximise profits, the underlying long-term consideration is that the goal of business success cannot be done without the finances to do it. The relationship between economy, society and environment is more than ever a focal point to safeguard a firm's long-term strategic interests. Allocating significant resources to the environment can be sensible only if it is not at the expense of the long-term financial health of the company.

> The relationship between economy, society and environment is more than ever a focal point to safeguard a firm's long-term strategic interests.

The stock market now buckets these notions under the acronym ESG: environmental, social and [corporate] governance. Attention to the ESG weighting in mutual funds has become far more commonplace. Even the investment management titans that are renowned for a more ruthless quest for returns, BlackRock (Impact[22]) and Goldman Sachs (that, in 2015, acquired the specialised ESG advisors, Imprint Capital Advisors) have launched ESG funds. Despite the intangibility of social responsibility, Wall Street now talks freely about the triple bottom line: profit, people and planet.

Although it remains difficult to quantify the benefit, there has
been a fundamental shift in consumer habits and concerns. It
is often hard to gauge social responsibility at the product
level, as marketing claims tend to be poorly regulated and
confusingly different. Nonetheless, there is growing attention
being given to a company's ethics and to the integrity of its
supply chain and this is aided by initiatives such as
Sourcemap.[23] There is also focus on a company's production
methods and the transparent and responsible nature in which
this is conducted.

Given the ever-growing level of transparency and important
need for congruency, green PR spin is being washed out of
the system. Green initiatives can be a difficult subject to raise
in front of shareholders, particularly when the stock price
languishes. To what extent does 'green' turn into bottom line
profitability? The cosmetics giant L'Oréal was founded in
1907 by a brilliant chemist and its laboratories have always
sought to create the best products that chemistry can provide.
When the company endeavoured to be 'more green', there
was at first dismay both internally and externally. In the UK,
during the 1990s, L'Oréal often was targeted by activists for
its animal testing. It is a matter of record that, as early as the
1980s, L'Oréal had invested to find ways to avoid animal
testing and to viably test final products on synthetic skin.[24]

Then, in a need to accelerate its exposure to the 'natural'
trend, it announced in 2006 the purchase of The Body Shop.
This purchase was not just a way to learn about creating
'natural' products, it was also a way to learn first-hand the
business of retail. However, it was criticised by many as a
cop-out by the founder, Anita Roddick, and a rather
incongruent step for the world leader of chemical cosmetic
products. In this context, many years later, it comes as no
surprise that The Body Shop has not flourished within
L'Oréal.[25] Body Shop customers who were not aware that The
Body Shop belonged to L'Oréal, presumably blindly

continued to purchase. However, for those who knew, the fit was, at best, awkward. In their quest for transparency and congruency, customers want to learn which brands belong to which corporations. As a result, there can be an uneasiness knowing that one expensive product has a list of ingredients that looks remarkably similar to another product in a different brand, at a fraction of the price.

Similarly, employees, especially millennials, are acutely aware of corporate social responsibility (CSR) and many consider it as a necessary condition before they join a company. We need to make sure that when CSR is referenced in everyday functions of the company, it is both deeply understood and highly meaningful for the corporation, its history and its culture. Companies can no longer make grand claims about their CSR that cannot be tested. We can see now first-hand data from the Great Places to Work[26] list, the American Customer Satisfaction Index[27] or Glassdoor.[28]

The prize – the additional wins

We have outlined purpose, people and profit in our quest to explore meaningfulness. But, as much as these areas provide meaning in and of themselves, others work for 'prizes'. We might call these pleasure, play and promotion.

Once, in our jobs, the focus was solely on hard work; but now there is a greater emphasis on pleasure and enjoying work. Previously, our ambition was to work up until retirement and then to enjoy ourselves. Now, people take extended holidays or opt in for sabbaticals. Up until a retirement age of 65, working 40-hour weeks, with 4 weeks of holiday per year, people will spend one-third of their life at work. As brilliantly exposed by Ricardo Semler in his TED talk,[29] people do not want to live their prime years, only to 'enjoy' themselves at the end of their lives when they are less physically able to do so. Therefore, pleasure needs to be built into the organisation, as a clear way for people to find meaning. Many want the flexibility to live outside of work or have their jobs held open for them as they take extended holidays. If we do not consider how people find both pleasure inside and outside of their work and create the right context for this, it will be harder to get people to engage. Offering them more money simply will not be enough.

Additionally, many want to play at work. People want to explore and experience new technologies both in the pleasure of their own company and through playing with others. That is considered a good day at the office. Teams want their working environments to invite discovery, as opposed to leaving them feeling caged in a cubicle. Many offices now reflect this recognition of the need for play in the way they are designed and the space they give for creativity. Some provide alternative working spaces, and others give time to allow people to work on projects that interest them.

Promotion and pay are other important areas through which people look for meaning. Employees want the recognition that comes with increased authority and pay. And, as is clear in Maslow's Hierarchy of Needs,[30] the meaningfulness found in self actualisation, esteem, love and belonging are all built on the foundation of someone's physiological needs being met. A reliable, good income helps provide that stability.

For others, having a good profile within the industry is important to them. They want the respect of their peers and to establish themselves as an expert in their field. Increasingly, organisations are recognising that it is not enough to have a department solely promoting the business brand. Companies are aligning themselves to the reality that employees want to have their personal brand promoted as well. We will develop this point in Mindset 2.

As we embrace the need for our organisations and those individuals within them to find meaningfulness, we become more equipped for implementing disruptive technologies. It is essential to capture the hearts and the minds of all the staff. We need to map out the vision of where we are going. There is no point expecting people to give themselves wholeheartedly to something, if we are not giving them something to believe in. Initially, the financial investment, time and energy involved to embody meaningfulness may not seem possible. But you cannot flourish successfully over the long term, as both a significant and disruptive business, unless you have built this into your organisation. And that path has got greater financial significance.

How to bring meaningfulness into the business

Both within your own life and that of the organisation you work for, how is meaningfulness demonstrated? Whether meaningfulness is a mindset that you have grown already, or is something that you have not given as much space to, here is your slice of PIE to reflect on.

A slice of PIE

Personal

1. Meet with a friend to talk about what is meaningful for you. Discuss together where you each find purpose and help each other to condense into no more than 120 characters your personal mission statement.

2. Start a journal to explore your values and bring clarity on what is important to you. Are you aligned with your company values? We would recommend using Evernote as an online multi-media note-taking tool.

3. Reflect on ways you expressed creativity when you were younger. Take a few hours out to indulge and be creative again. Do not take on a pressure to perform, but allow meaningfulness and joy to find a home with you.

Internal

1. Why does your organisation exist? Host an internal day of reflection for formulating vision together and use a listening approach like the Samoan Circle[31] to open up each person's response in different scenarios. Work to find an agreed 'why' that is clearly understood by everyone.

2. If your organisation has values written down, do people live them out and hold each other to account on them? Can these values be expressed as recognised behaviours and expectations? How do you create a context that creates meaning for them?

3. Consider carving out a time each fortnight where those in your organisation are able to work on projects that excite them. It may be exploring a new product or service, functioning in a different internal role or coming up with some new marketing ideas. Each quarter, showcase some of the ideas that came from this time.

External

1. Using lanyrd.com or meetups.com, find a corporate social responsibility event and invite key individuals along to it who already carry the meaningfulness DNA.

2. Is there a charity that is relevant and congruent with the brand, who would like to receive a day of support from your organisation? Align your support with a tangible project that is focused on making a difference, and capture on video the lessons learnt and experiences shared.

3. Host a roundtable event with similar leaders working in the same sector and explore ways your companies can work together to have an impact on both people and the planet.

Responsibility

Why do I personally need to bother with learning, ethics or cyber security?

> **The question isn't who is going to let me; it's who is going to stop me.**[1]
>
> *Paraphrased from* The Fountainhead, *Ayn Rand*

'Remember. It's the most dangerous weapon you'll ever touch and you could easily kill someone with it. Be alert. Be careful. And make sure you take responsibility.'

I was 17, and my dad was talking about the family car he was letting me take out. I'd passed my test and, like a number of 17 year olds, I definitely thought I was a badass rally driver the way I took those corners. Truth be told, I wasn't 'subconsciously competent' at driving, and my driving wasn't based on years of good experience. In fact, both my age and road time put me in the high-risk bracket, especially when it came to insurance company premiums. If you are familiar with the Four Stages of Competency model, you would know that, as someone who was 'consciously competent', I felt ready, able and uncrashable. Not only was that cocky, it was dangerous. But my dad's constant ongoing reminders to take responsibility in this area has been one of the reasons I have never had an accident driving. The other reason is I am an older, slightly wiser badass.

What is it?

Responsibility is woven into the fabric of our society and our personal experiences at a young age, and we all make hundreds of decisions each week to demonstrate this. 'Put clothes on before you leave the house. Drive on the correct side of the road. Don't shout (even jokingly), "I'm going to cheat" when you are entering an exam room.'

As much as these eccentric examples highlight that we know how to take responsibility in areas of our lives, the reality is that there are vast areas of life where we do not take responsibility. It seems so obvious, and almost trite to hold responsibility up as a reminder, let alone a core mindset. But we would argue that failure to take responsibility, especially in the face of the complex demands on our time and energy, is one of life's greatest causes of pain. Whether it is world leaders evading responsibility for their words, or everyday individuals being thoughtless with their actions, the need to take greater responsibility for what we say and do confronts us all. To be responsible is to act with a sense of accountability. It means holding ourselves to account before blaming someone or something else. It means walking the talk and modelling the behaviour that we want to see demonstrated in others.

> To be responsible is to act with a sense of accountability. It means holding ourselves to account before blaming someone or something else.

With disruptive technologies, there is much to take responsibility for. A lack of it will certainly cause ineffectiveness but, through the impact of the technology, it could also create significant problems for others. We will explore this further in later chapters. The set of four areas where responsibility needs to be taken, as identified in the figure below, is not exhaustive. Yet the four offered are those we believe to have high priority: learning, personal branding, ethics and cyber security.

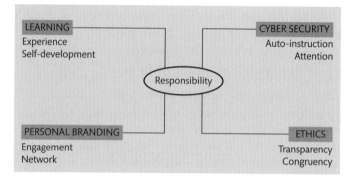

The four areas of responsibility

These four areas have all been brought to the fore because of the internet. Each has a direct link to the power of the internet, allowing the individual to become substantially more responsible for his and her own actions.

The new mindset – a question of accountability

From an early age, many of us were taught to respect hierarchy and obey those in authority. Teachers set homework. The Government laid down laws. Bosses gave objectives. As a result, we have become pre-conditioned to wait for orders. Some would call this the 'assisted mindset'. This need to do what others have told us regularly follows through in our behaviour. Often people do not do things to benefit themselves, but carry out actions in order to satisfy other people. In our early years, this obedience is important, as we learn and develop healthy boundaries, along with patterns of interaction and communication. If we did not receive this input and learn from others, our patterns of behaviour, communication and relationships would be poorly developed.

Sadly, some people have not graduated to take responsibility for their own learning, development and behaviour, and this has major repercussions in areas of their lives.

First, for those not yet in the workforce, a lack of taking responsibility can hinder personal growth and thinking for oneself. Second, it can result in a failure to grow habits of initiative and self-management. Employers, understandably, often look for self-starters. Those who need direction and the approval of others require more management time and energy. As for those who want to set themselves up in business, an inability to take true ownership of their thoughts and actions is going to produce a struggle. A keen sense of responsibility must be brought into the very fibre of a business; it will influence the ultimate purpose, the ethics and the means of achieving the goals.

A big consideration for many of us (one that we cover in Force 6), relates to artificial intelligence (AI) and the reality that so many people will lose their jobs. If people do not take responsibility for their own personal development, and grow creative-thinking skills, they may find themselves out of work. On the other hand, business owners must heed a vital call to take responsibility for the incredible losses of jobs and livelihoods that come in the wake of AI.

In the past, it was the commonly held belief that the CEO had to have the far-seeing, all-knowing vision to set the strategy. Yet, in today's muddied and fast-changing world, that is no longer feasible. Bosses cannot know *everything* that is happening. They are no longer beacons of vision and many executives feel well behind the eight ball. Different times call for different behaviours.

Different times call for different behaviours.

If there is one thing that the onslaught of new disruptive technologies has taught us in the writing of this book, it is that, despite our curiosity, we cannot be experts in everything. We have relied heavily on our network to help us, but we have also taken responsibility for our own learning to make sure that we are as up-to-date as possible. It has taken a measure of humility. But we have also held one another accountable for both our thinking and our contributions.

With all the developing technologies, new usages are being invented, resulting in business and operating models being turned upside down. This requires a shift in mindset. Inevitably, change is difficult. We are all creatures of habit and subject to long-standing attitudes. For those of you who have been in business for a long time it is likely that, through your experience and success, you have, perhaps, built up some entrenched beliefs about what it takes to succeed. Some of these thoughts will always last the test of time. But, in today's fast-paced world, many old beliefs and behaviours do not work. To succeed in today's business environment and to adopt a disruptive mindset, we might have to break down several old paradigms. We are not saying that everything outlined in the old mindset is no longer relevant. Of course each business needs to make a profit, have crucial areas of control and plan effectively. Crucially, however, we must make room for a new mindset to have space to grow and challenge the ways in which we are currently ineffective.

The shift from old to new mindset

Old mindset	New mindset
Professionalisation and specialisation	Multidisciplinary and collaborative
Profit	Purpose
Shareholder return	Customer/Employee centric
Directive and authoritative	Opt in, empathy and humility
Control	Empower
Hierarchy	Decentralisation & networks
Privacy & confidentiality	Transparency

Old mindset	New mindset
Information is power	Sharing is power
Perfection	Imperfection
Permanent education/ Learning for development	Continuous learning
Planning	Experimentation
Finance & marketing	Design & coding
Classic PR	Influencer marketing

In order to make the transition from the left-hand column to the right-hand column, there are two important concepts that need to be addressed:

1. It is no longer possible to separate the professional from the personal.

2. One must learn by doing.

Merging the professional and personal

> We must seek to bring our full personality to work. Real engagement happens when we get personal.

Why is it no longer possible to separate the professional and personal? First, it should be pointed out that by 'personal', we make a distinction between what is personal and what is private. By personal, we mean our full person, including our sense of humour, our values, our history and eccentricities. The private zone, which may include intimate details of our relationships or information about our children, should be given the right to remain off the grid or to be shared solely with our meaningful others.

We must seek to bring our full personality to work. Real engagement happens when we get personal. Your brand's first and biggest fans need to be your employees, especially in an era where good talent in specific fields is hard to find. For employees to be fans, they need to love their team. Teams are soulless without passion. Passion without personality is impossible. People need to be personal and, in doing so, the team can confidently perform to the raucous cheers of commitment.

Good pay is obviously essential, but the real motivator and performance enhancement comes from personal engagement. Additionally, a brand grows in power and attractiveness the more it connects with emotions, an area that is accessed only in the *personal* sphere.

Finally, the vast majority of these new disruptive technologies require a deeply human connection. We see this in the empathy that is needed in great design, where a good designer puts themselves in the shoes of the customer. It is remarkable how many senior executives ignore their own personal experiences on a smartphone, social media or an eCommerce site when it comes to overseeing company sites and applications. Instead, they create or approve interruptive, unfriendly and awkward user experiences for their customers. Yet, they would be the first to moan dramatically to family or friends, lambasting brands who give them a poor user experience or service in their personal lives. For all the above reasons, we need to be both professional and personal at work.

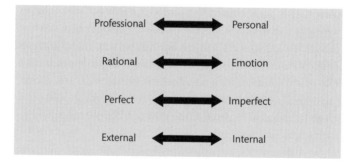

Break down that wall between professional (left side) and personal (right side)

What does that mean? It means creating an environment in the workplace where it is not just OK for people to be themselves, but it is actively and wholeheartedly encouraged. In effect, this means giving more space for emotion, so people can, indeed, begin to be wholehearted. If adding a ping-pong table or table football (aka foosball) is a wink in that direction, an even more powerful approach is to foster a culture where one can express oneself, and people feel safe to laugh and cry. In business schools and, historically, in senior management, the focus has been on providing strategic rationale, leading with authority and hitting the numbers. The rational side is not to be diminished. On the contrary, it is to be done in connection *with* the emotional side.

At another level, it is about accepting imperfection as well. Some high safety-conscious environments like laboratories or factories demand that everyone follows standard codes but, for the majority of companies, there must be room for imperfection and for making mistakes. There are many organisations wishing to be more 'agile' or to adopt an entrepreneurial attitude. However, this cannot work without the opportunity to err or fail. And, if there is failure, the goal is for fast failure so lessons can be learnt quickly.

Finally, in the crossover between professional and personal, we like to talk about congruency. On a personal level, is who you are on the inside, the same as who you are on the outside? For an organisation to optimise engagement and energy, there must be consistency between the external projection and the internal mechanisms. When one accepts the presence of such a wall between the professional and personal spheres, disorder sets in. Breaking down that wall liberates the energy and births creativity.

Continuous learning

This year we started homeschooling our daughter. She had started school the previous year and we saw a change in her that was not positive. The energetic, confident girl, hungry for learning, seemed tired, anxious and lacking energy for anything. We discovered she had announced to her school friends at the end of term that she was not coming back to school. It had not been our decision, but we had to consider it.

We were nervous, nevertheless, about making the change. We had questions about early education in the UK, yet appreciated that school worked well for the children of many of our friends. We now feel that homeschooling was one of the best, transforming decisions we made, providing a context where she loves learning, and can gravitate towards areas that really interest her. Because she is hungry to learn, she is excited to absorb so many new things. Often, she will teach us, excitedly: 'Mum, did you know that …' It is probably not too early to say she takes responsibility for her own learning. And, in that process, she is educating me and my wife to do the same.

Many people have an experience where they do not develop the habits of learning. Instead, they have been trained to do what is required of them to pass exams, to get to the next stage in life or to prevent them from getting into trouble. I do not think it was until my early twenties that I fully developed an appetite for learning. By this stage, I had finally picked up self-selecting and focusing on areas that really interested me.

Given the rate of change and the potential for decay in the information we are absorbing, it is our conviction that, for our professional development, we need to take learning into our own hands. When we rely on organisations to deliver this for us, there is a danger we may end up sluggish. We should understand what we most need to learn. The model of corporate learning, where individuals are invited to sign up to courses from a catalogue, is in need of a change. If someone needs to know about artificial intelligence, they should not be waiting up to three months to learn. We are not going to have the cajoling of teachers, professors or managers to help. We either take responsibility to learn or we miss out. People must get into a mode of continuous learning, so they develop muscles in self-development. When you apply this into your own situation, how do you embrace this approach to discovery?

To start with, we must think through what we want to learn and what is of current primary importance for our development, our organisation and the opportunities that lie ahead of us. For many, there is a need to fill in the gaps of knowledge. As a result, during conversations or meetings, it is easy not to 'share an opinion', because an opinion has not been formed. However, it is not enough to hope we do not get called out. Instead, as a result of taking responsibility for our learning, we can communicate the position at which we have arrived. It is in this context that we can grow further as others reflect on our views. Conversation is the bedrock of social learning. In areas where people feel embarrassed about being uninformed, often there is not the humility or nerve to ask for input from others, or to be signposted to resources that will bring knowledge. Many people who love to learn also love to share their understanding. We just need to ask and act on that.

Having discovered what you want to learn, it is essential to understand your best ways to do this. Here are eight different learning styles:

1. **Visual (Spatial):** you learn through images, pictures, videos, presentations, diagrams and spatial understanding.
2. **Aural (Auditory):** you learn through hearing, often with sound and music.

3. **Physical (Kinaesthetic):** you learn through using your hands, body and having a sense of touch.

4. **Verbal (Linguistic):** you learn through using words both in speech and writing.

5. **Logical (Mathematical):** you learn through logic, systems and reasoning.

6. **Social (Interpersonal):** you learn in groups and with other people.

7. **Solitary (Intrapersonal):** you learn working alone and using self-study.

8. **Immersive (Practical):** you learn through immersing yourself in intensive learning environments.

Knowing your learning style gives you the insights to find the best tools, resources and approaches to accelerate your learning. You could take advantage of video tutorials on Lynda.com, or subscribe to audio podcasts via services such as iTunes or Spreaker, or read blogs using an RSS reader like Feedly.com or the Flipboard app. Additionally, you could access meetup.com for social learning, lanyrd.com for conferences and listen to audiobooks on Audible.co.uk. You can work through tutorials, or get access to experts through mavyn.com.

We will be making suggestions about these approaches through the PIE Model at the end of each chapter.

When it comes to these disruptive technologies, one other approach to learning is the need to learn by doing, which can tap into a number of the learning styles above.

Learning by doing

The old paradigm was that an MBA and access to the *Harvard Business Review* were sufficient to stay ahead of the competition. Nowadays, businesses and schools have been

overtaken by the consumer and what is happening in the
startup field, university research centres as well as in big
tech companies. Here is an example of why this model no
longer works.

An advertising agency, eager to recuperate its lost mainstream
media business, proposed to its client a 'blended' campaign,
including repurposing its 30-second TV spot for YouTube,
Snapchat and Facebook. The ad agency touted large 'additional'
viewership that could be targeted and cost effective. The
C-suite immediately adopted the plan as 'intelligent and
efficient'. However, whilst they did get some additional
viewership numbers, they were surprised and disappointed by
the lack of additional sales. What the C-suite lacked was the
customer insight that each platform requires adaptation.
Without the appropriate content delivered in the relevant
context, engagement (not to mention conversion) will be weak.

With the arrival of the internet and the smartphone, there is
an inherent pervasiveness of technology that seeps
throughout organisations. The internet is constantly present
in our thoughts and conversations. Our phones accompany
us everywhere, literally attached to us at the hip. Like water,
connectivity flows into every nook and cranny of our
organisations. It is now implausible, if not undesirable, to
distinguish 'digital' marketing from 'regular' marketing. They
are officially one and the same thing.

> **It is now implausible, if not undesirable, to distinguish 'digital' marketing from 'regular' marketing. They are officially one and the same thing.**

As we will explore later, the smartphone is, increasingly, the
main gateway to the web. In October 2016, in a study by
independent web analytics company StatCounter,[2] it was
reported that mobile and tablet web traffic surpassed desktop

traffic worldwide for the first time, hitting 51.3 per cent versus 48.7 per cent. As brands continue to battle to gain visibility on the mobile, the challenge will be doing so in a way that is both successful in the eyes of the customer and effective for the brand. Learning by doing, being a practitioner and personally understanding great user experiences is the single best way to help drive and execute a superior mobile experience for your own initiatives.

As we will explore for the rest of this chapter, responsibility and ownership must be applied to a number of areas, including managing one's own personal brand, defining and living one's ethics and securing one's data.

Responsibility with personal branding

We believe a brand is constructed throughout the customer journey and, therefore, the individual employees are, at least in part, also representing and carrying the brand. How employees behave can have a direct impact on the brand. This is seen in how they handle customer complaints, provide service in a retail store or interact through social media. Depending on the industry and corporate culture, there will be different levels of strictness as to how employees are to behave online. Some senior executives struggle with the idea that individual employees should have the right and/or liberty to promote themselves online and develop their own personal branding. But, if a lack of self-expression and engagement is enforced, many opportunities will be lost. Ideally, it would be far better if the entire C-suite sets the tone and leads by example with a highly thoughtful and valuing-adding professional social presence.

Employees who are both allowed or encouraged to craft a personal brand must do so with responsibility. At a minimum, this means having a properly constructed

LinkedIn profile. It should not be written as an online CV, but instead as a tool to reach customers, partners, new recruits and other influencers in the industry. This has become a huge focus for many organisations. Taking it a step further, it could be advisable to have an active Twitter account that shows the executive's human side. The third level might be to have a blog where the executive expounds on his or her expertise or passion. Finally, thought leadership videos will be important and, where video services and content is expected to account for 79 per cent of global internet traffic by 2020,[3] this is going to be an essential area to look at.

In all cases, the maintenance of one's online presence is the individual's responsibility and, arguably, cannot be delegated to a third party without the risk of being revealed as inauthentic. As with all social media, the landscape is forever changing. No amount of company protocols or training will suffice to cover the evolution in social media or rein in employee errors of judgement.

At a deeper level, as we discussed in Chapter 1, it is about finding meaningfulness in one's job. When tasks at hand are energy-giving and the individual's values are appropriately aligned with the brand's values, there is a form of productivity and synchronicity that can step-change the growth of the organisation. That is when engagement is optimised and individuals are prepared to go above and beyond the call of regular duty. This, too, is part of making sure that one's personal vision and brand are aligned with one's organisation's vision and values. As Robin Sharma[4] likes to say, individuals must make sure that their audio is in tune with their video. Congruency is built individual by individual. And each person must be responsible for defining and applying their personal brand in line with the corporate brand.

The responsibility of ethics

Additionally, each person must take responsibility for their own behaviour and ethics. At times, it has been possible to hide behind the wall of an organisation, to hide flaws in its ethics. Within some organisations, there can be a great pressure to behave in certain questionable ways. In moments of stress or when facing requests from those in power, some people are tempted to give in and step away from their principles. In such instances, those people may prefer to buck the blame and refer to a manager or boss who may have established unhealthy habits or behaviour. It is our contention, however, that everyone throughout the organisation must make sure their own behaviour is congruent to the organisation's values. If the boss is bad, maybe you're in the wrong place?

It is so clear that we are living in a greater age of transparency. It is not possible to run your organisation in a way that is ethically challenged without it being called to task at some point. Current or past employees, customers or partners are likely to speak out. It will not be possible to abdicate responsibility and it is essential to learn from helpful feedback. Ensuring that businesses remain ethical is the responsibility of *all* within, and especially those in senior leadership.

Equally, there will be those who intentionally and maliciously look to damage the reputation of some individuals and organisations. They could be competitors, customers, activists or disgruntled staff. Sometimes, there is little in the way of protection for those who are targeted in this way. Our advice is to maintain dignity, respond non-defensively, act with integrity, communicate quickly and clearly, address any dishonesty head on, and not allow yourself to be burdened under any shame or inaccuracy. These issues are unpacked brilliantly in Jon Ronson's book *So You've Been Publicly Shamed.*[5]

With technologies like autonomous cars, AI, robotics and open-source software, ethics is a centrally important consideration for us all. But, it starts with the daily choices that we make. We cannot clearly see the bigger picture unless we live to the same standards ourselves.

Taking responsibility for your security

A core area where individuals must take personal responsibility is in cyber security, a topic we will cover in far greater detail in Force 4. No amount of firewalls or antivirus software will protect an organisation sufficiently. Each person ought to be in control of their own data, know what is distinctly important and understand the risks. The issue with cyber security is that hackers and cyber criminals are, generally, a step ahead of the industrial security platforms. When a hack is identified, software needs to be rewritten, an update needs to be issued, and then it must be downloaded and installed on each device. In the gap between identification and installation, a lot of damage can be done. So, the important and sensible approach is to prevent the virus from getting inside in the first place.

Even for companies that institute strict policies about bring your own devices (BYOD), vetting incoming personnel and policing activities through spyware, ultimately many of the hacks occur because of an error by an individual. It is reported that around 90 per cent attack volume is done via phishing.[6] Individuals need to keep up-to-date about the types of vulnerabilities that exist and the new cyber tricks being concocted. They also need to be aware of the basic 'healthy' practices with regards to foreign USB keys, suspicious links in emails or communications from unknown sources. Everyone needs to take responsibility for their own security. This attentiveness extends, of course, to third-party suppliers and partners. Cyber protection is only as strong as its weakest link.

A slice of PIE

When it comes to our need to take responsibility, change always starts with the individual. Organisations are made up of individuals. Without a strong personal conviction that is followed through in one's actions, it will be impossible to move an organisation to take responsibility.

It is easy to look at some of these areas and put them down as a lower priority when compared to financial priorities or wherever you are feeling most squeezed. We would argue that, if you are looking to help lead your organisation but especially in taking advantage of these disruptive technologies, each one of these areas of responsibility is of significance. The further challenge may emerge when, as a result of not embracing this mindset and the subsequent forces that follow, AI puts you out of a job. And, by that stage, it will require much more effort and pain to upskill and find new roles.

Prevention is better than cure. Get ahead of the curve. Take responsibility.

Personal

1. Buy an Audible[7] subscription and create a list of audiobooks to listen to. Double up and get the Kindle versions, so you can follow and create highlights and, at the end of each book, write a one-page book summary outlining what you learnt from it.

2. Arrange for a personal Facebook security audit to eliminate cyber vulnerabilities by using the checklist of actions outlined by Ian Anderson Gray.[8]

3. Carry out a Google search of your name and the company name. In what ways could you improve your own personal brand so it represents the organisation's brand well? If you do not have one, order a professional headshot, and make sure the cover images on Twitter and LinkedIn represent you well.

Internal

1. Throughout the organisation, create small learning circles where those who want to learn about a similar subject get to meet regularly to share experiences and compare notes.

2. Are there any ethical areas where you or your organisation are compromised? How can you resolve these?

3. Organise a small team within your organisation to have a residential bootcamp. Hire an Airbnb or Onefinestay house and, as well as the work-based activities, find ways where people can contribute to the wider group. They may be responsible for doing the cooking, organising some group entertainment or picking up a guitar for an evening's song around the fire. The one requirement is that everyone brings their full selves away.

External

1. Invite a random selection of your customers and pay them to attend a listening day, where you intently look to hear and understand how your customers perceive you. Ask them, amongst other questions, how they would describe your brand and the ethics of your organisation.

2. Send an email to your customers with the subject line saying, 'I wish [YOUR COMPANY] would take more responsibility in . . .' Make it clear that you are simply wanting their direct feedback and nothing more. Without any long preambles, enable them to read and reply to the message within 60 seconds. (only single space in between).

3. Grab an hour. In the first 30 minutes, see how many spreadsheets or Excel files of your customers' data you can find. In the second 30 minutes, set out and distribute a clear policy on how people can use and store prospects' data in the future.

Collaboration

The way some organisations collaborate, you wonder who the enemy is

Alone we can do so little; together we can do so much.[1]

Helen Keller

I grew up with jumble sales as a major part of my childhood. It made perfect sense to me not to spend the full price on something when, with a bit of extra work, you could get it at a fraction of the cost. I first explored the idea of doing a startup in what was then called the Sharing Economy with my friend Ben in 2011. The aim was to help people rent out their spare rooms online. Host meet guest. Guest meet host. I'd grown up my whole childhood travelling to different cities. Staying over at people's houses was always normal. I'd been enamoured looking at Couchsurfers with friends in 2006, and surfed a fair share of my own friends' houses without a platform. Enabling people to earn money renting out their room each night seemed like a great idea that would catch on. We were right. It did. In a very big way. The winner in that race was called Airbnb. You may have heard of them.

Why is collaboration important?

It is neither possible nor desirable to be an expert in *everything*. Once, knowledge was power, but with the democratisation of information through the internet, effectiveness now relies on being able to see how things fit together. Openness and collaboration are essential in order to cross-fertilise and operate with greater agility. Some organisations and individuals within them struggle to create a collaborative spirit. But to survive and, more importantly, to thrive, we must shape and develop a new mindset. This includes:

▎ seeking out and accepting different viewpoints

▎ taking advantage of shared and different skills, both inside and outside the organisation

▎ being prepared to share your own knowledge and content openly

▎ showing willingness to work in new ways and use different technological platforms (video conferencing, WhatsApp, Google Drive, Basecamp and the plethora of other tools).

▎ being able to make decisions faster (especially for large organisations looking to work with startups)

> Openness and collaboration are essential in order to cross-fertilise and operate with greater agility.

The strength in collaboration

In the not-so-distant past, it was common to believe that a great CEO had to single-handedly determine the strategy, carry all the knowledge, know all the moving parts of the business and have all the answers. Tough gig.

Needing others, especially if they were consultants or coaches, often was perceived as weakness. For many companies it still is. Today, as CEOs seek to act nimbly in the face of the mounting pressures and rapid changes, it is more important than ever to develop powerful networks. A business leader needs people who will inform, cajole and even rebut them, whilst additionally watching their back. One might call it 'tough love' but at its heart, it is about developing a trustworthy and diverse network you can work closely with. Significantly, a trustworthy network must be built as a two-way street. This collaborative spirit is behind the need to dismantle silos, break down walls and embrace a wider group of people. One of the keys to bringing the collaborative mindset into fruition is to share a common vision and set of values. In business, we are gradually moving away from the singular profit bottom line and the sole objective of shareholder return, to a more broad expectation and triple bottom line, as discussed in Mindset 1.

> Today, as CEOs seek to act nimbly in the face of mounting pressures and rapid changes, it is more important than ever to develop powerful networks.

It is in this context that we wanted to dive into what originally was coined as the Sharing Economy as the most symbolic of models and activities for the collaborative mindset.

From where did the collaborative economy emerge?

On the one hand, sharing is nothing new. For years, many of us have experienced what it means to lend money, let someone stay over at our house or pick up a hitchhiker from the side of the motorway. On the other hand, we have seen the growth of a new socio-economic ecosystem, with businesses valued in the billions and individuals making their livelihoods through these 'sharing' platforms. Sharing, as they say, is caring … but it is also big for business.

> Sharing, as they say, is caring ... but it is also big for business.

A key tenet of the collaborative economy is the lack of permanent ownership. Many new businesses are growing through the ability to rent, borrow and share. There are cost-saving and economic reasons that businesses share property, open up skills and share knowledge. There are also huge mutual advantages to those they collaborate with. Organisations need to get an understanding of the underlying force of the collaborative mindset in order to better take advantage of this change.

Here is what you need to know

At a basic level, collaboration is about sharing and partnering. Cities and governments have a deep need and unique opportunity to support the collaborative economy, as it compensates for expanding budget deficits. As writer and speaker Lisa Gansky said in an interview, 'The Sharing economy connects us in ways that make a tighter weave within and between our communities that goes far to creating ... resilience.' Further, she says that, 'cities are really a dialogue between citizens, businesses (for profit and non) and governments, therefore partnerships are a way of solving problems.'[2]

> Cities and governments have a deep need and unique opportunity to support the collaborative economy, as it compensates for expanding budget deficits.

When looked at from an aerial view, there is a sense that the collaborative economy could be a way to render our energy consumption more efficient, resulting in the reduction of waste.

Jeremiah Owyang, founder of Crowd Companies Council,[3] created a superlative 'honeycomb' of the collaborative economy that, unsurprisingly, we are encouraged to share.[4] Through Owyang's mapping, it is possible to see the collaborative spirit being applied to a whole suite of areas that will concern business and governmental leaders. In the following figure, we have simplified it down to the key categories. How could your organisation learn to develop a collaborative mindset, working in any of these areas?

> At the heart of the collaborative economy, the most precious currency between the members is trust.

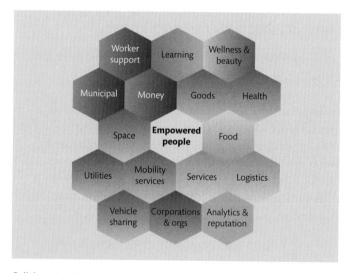

Collaborative Economy Honeycomb Version 3.0 by Jeremiah Owyang (simplified)

What is the DNA of the collaborative economy?

At the heart of the collaborative economy, the most precious currency between the members is trust. BlaBlaCar, the ride-sharing app, has gone so far as to create a blog, entitled *Being the Trustman.*[5] An elemental part of the collaborative economy, powered and, of course, empowered by technology, is the ability for *both* sides of the equation to rate and evaluate one another. Trust is not something you can command. It must be shown, experienced and earned.

> Trust is not something you can command. It must be shown, experienced and earned.

As declared by Rachel Botsman in *Fast Company*, many companies involved in the sharing economy have an ethical mindset. They 'should have a clear values-driven mission and be built on meaningful principles including transparency, humanness and authenticity that inform short and long-term strategic decisions'.[6]

Lisa Gansky wrote in a *Huffington Post* article, 'How the Sharing Economy Can Create Value from Waste',[7] that this sharing 'mindset' is like a new social contract. She writes, 'All of this marks a profound shift in our social operating system, or our social OS, in how we value and trust the people and "things" we would in previous eras have fought to control or own. We are only at the beginning of redefining our social OS, as it's baked into our institutions, practices and software.'

> In this transparent world, where both the supplier and the client get to rate each other, unethical practices may be easily outed.

In this transparent world, where both the supplier and the client get to rate each other, unethical practices may be easily outed. What if people within organisations were able to rate each other? What impact would that have over the long term? How does collaboration challenge our need to control and own, and what impact does that have on our social OS?

Why do you need to worry?

For some, the impact is financial. 'Show me the money'[8] is a phrase you would hear for different reasons. Taxi drivers lose. Spare room owners win because of rent gained from an underutilised asset. We see a strong economic message. The underlying principle against buying and owning property should be a wake-up call for many companies creating and selling hard goods. There are many initiatives around renting goods as opposed to buying them. Whilst these remain fringe when compared to the total industry, there can be no denying the interest now and the potential in the future.

> The underlying principle against buying and owning property should be a wake-up call for many companies creating and selling hard goods.

Whether it is a car, an office space or a luxury dress, the desire to own has diminished in favour of a more practical use-it-when-I-need-it model. In the fashion industry, we have seen multiple initiatives around the older idea of renting high-end clothing and accessories. For example, there is Rent The Runway,[9] Chic By Choice,[10] Rentez-Vous[11] or Bag, Borrow or Steal.[12] In each case, the marginal value for the renter and rentee is a win-win, especially without an expensive broker or legal and tax complications.

For many, the collaborative economy has been wonderful news. Especially for those renting their rooms: 'How renting my room on Airbnb helps me travel the world'[13] and 'How renting my place on Airbnb is funding my startup.'[14] It's likely that you know someone who is either renting out their room or has stayed in an Airbnb property. I still remember the conversations of naysayers convinced it would not work. Closed people often struggle with letting go of control in collaboration.

Underneath the economics of the sharing economy, there is a foundational need to collaborate. Sharing, after all, was at the heart of the internet at its birth. But, more fundamentally, digital technologies have a tendency to cut through silos and exhort more collaboration. The comment by Francisco González, chairman and CEO at BBVA, sums it up, 'Collaboration is the essence of successful digital change.'[15]

> Underneath the economics of the sharing economy, there is a foundational need to collaborate. Sharing, after all, was at the heart of the internet at its birth.

Being empowered by digital technology and finding strength in the power of human networks, there are many indications that the collaborative economy will compete with and beat traditional business models and current market offerings.

The majority of challenges the Collaborative Economy faces apply to the goods and services being offered to customers. But there are other questions raised. Should an employer accept Airbnb or Uber as part of an employee's expenses? Typically, we would imagine the answer here to be a simple yes. A more complex question would explore workers' rights. Should an employee be allowed to outsource their repetitive tasks overseas so they can spend a lot of their working day as they please (as one programmer did for a fifth of his six-figure salary)?[16] Companies may need to loosen up their processes to accommodate these new services.

Intellectually, many executives have heard of the Sharing Economy. However, few senior executives have truly adopted the collaborative practice and mindset. This can include the existence of middlemen that are not providing sufficient value for a slice of the pie. Even 'newer' startups like PayPal can be considered to be lagging when compared to crowdsourcing and crowdfunding platforms. Céline Lazorthes, founder and CEO of Leetchi[17] and MANGOPAY[18] stated in an interview, 'PayPal wasn't made for retaining its customers, it was made for eCommerce, but not for this kind of crowdfunding platform.'[19] In these new collaborative initiatives, there is both cost efficiency as well as value added through the more direct digital user experience.

> In these new collaborative initiatives, there is both cost efficiency as well as value added through the more direct digital user experience.

How will collaboration have the most impact on your business?

The Collaborative Economy does not necessarily directly impact everyone. The sharing driving force has to be the *mindset*. Again, like with so many of these new forces, we find a crossover and complementarity with one another. For collaboration, the values of diversity, transparency and openness are essential ingredients for developing trust.

As Jeremiah Owyang's Honeycomb establishes, there are many sectors where the collaborative economy is visible. We can see that the first port of call is to examine where there are unused resources. Second, there is a question of third-party brokers along the value chain, at which point there may be unnecessary friction or unreasonable complications. Here is a way to evaluate the exposure of one's industry to the force of the Collaborative Economy.

Collaboration externally – the role of the brand

In the search for collaboration and partnership, the brand name plays an important role in the inferred confidence. Scott Monty[20] wrote:

> 'Having a trusted and well-known brand – even when competing with well-liked startups – is an advantage.

*There's a close relationship between brand recognition
and market dominance. Most people have heard of big
collaborative economy players like eBay, Craigslist, Etsy,
Uber and Kickstarter, and many of the top-sharing
players have positive reputations. Yet more than 25% of
would-be sharers will consider traditional buying if it
means doing business with a reputable brand. The role of
brand in the collaborative economy presents an
opportunity for large companies to take advantage by
marketing on trust or partnering with sharing services to
leverage their brand.'*

The impact to your business will be significantly different,
depending on whether it is an established organisation or a
fledgling startup. It will be affected by your response, based
on how much you currently share goods and services. It
would be useful to look at these broad groupings from a
sharing perspective.

There are three possible ways to approach collaboration from
an organisational standpoint.

> We all need to attach the right *meaning*
> to exploration time, so that it is valued
> appropriately.

First, organisations find it hard to create the culture, space
and environment to fully explore and hear from those who
have something of value to share. The pressure for many
younger team members is 'just to grow revenue'.
Organisations need to be more intentional about listening to
the up-and-coming staff members. We all need to attach the
right *meaning* to exploration time, so that it is valued
appropriately. It is also essential to establish the right format
to encourage ideas being shared. This could range from
questionnaires or face-to-face meetings at one end of the
spectrum to round table discussions, conferences or World
Café-based[21] events on the other.

Second, brands must look at how their business model could be disrupted or augmented by the collaborative opportunity. In the automotive space, we have seen significant efforts to take on board the sharing movement. BMW has created a car-sharing scheme, called DriveNow[22] (a joint venture with Sixt), which it hopes will create one million new customers by 2020. Avis also bought Zipcar. In the lodging area, Hyatt Hotels is responding by establishing agreements with sharing companies and investing some $40 million in the British luxury home-share company Onefinestay.[23] Product designers are launching products on crowdfunding platforms such as Kickstarter and Indiegogo as a way to test the market with an idea before putting it into production.

Third, from a logistics standpoint, there may be opportunities to collaborate with different groups to find synergies, share burdens and optimise resources. This could be, for example, making use of excess office space.

As part of developing the collaborative mindset, we suggest organisations explore and experiment with collaboration. Next, it is important to engage with a project to further develop the thinking and, lastly, to execute the project details.

Explore and experiment

Like so many of these disruptive forces, their 'novelty' cannot be understood from a textbook alone. Lots of inspiration around collaboration will be received from reading articles on your Flipboard app or RSS reader. What collaborative ideas excite and stimulate you? What could bring about change within the business? We recommend you set up a project to understand and explore the potential impact collaboration can have in your organisation. This may be solely an internal-based collaborative project or something you work on with another organisation.

Within your organisation, it is important that the relationships between workers and management, founders and board are one of cooperation and trust. If there are areas of mistrust, guardedness or a lack of needed vulnerability, this can cause potential friction when working with others. When exploring ideas, enabling an environment where everyone can communicate well is going to be central. Different people bring different perspectives. It helps if there is visibility across the organisation of expertise available, where there may be knowledge gaps and who naturally has a collaborative mindset. They may be key to helping your project work.

Be aware of the areas in your business that might profit most from partnering, whether these are efficiency, growth or learning. If you want to work with an external collaborative partner, assess what you can offer them, what you will receive from them, and whether it would be a good partnership. They might be partners to help you scale, open up new networks or be able to work with you longer term on mutually beneficial projects. As you think through what collaboration could look like, start to build further bridges with specific people and companies.

Not all collaborations, internally or externally, are easy to establish, and you may find it helpful to consider what the main challenges are when forming partnerships. Where trust needs to flourish at the heart of this collaboration, how do you deepen the experience of mutual trust?

Engage – build vision and plan how to leverage this disruptive force

When it comes to integrating a collaborative initiative or seeding the collaborative mindset into the organisation, the most effective approach is to link action to a strategic objective. If you want to see change happen, strong momentum starts with intentional embryonic activity. For the activity and mindset to grow throughout the organisation, it will need the support and engagement of senior leaders. Similar to learning by doing, change needs to be activated and old habits need to be corrected. New approaches need to be created and then practised. In order to embed the underlying collaborative mindset into the organisation, a broad cross-section of individuals will need to become engaged in both the thinking and the project.

> If you want to see change happen, strong momentum starts with intentional embryonic activity.

With the project you are creating, one of our own valuable insights gleaned from working with clients has been that there are three keys to aligning the team:

1. Make the project not just strategic, but linked to a meaningful objective that resonates (see Mindset 1). The less trust there is in top management, the more attentive management must be to making a difference.

2. You will need a respected leader or senior sponsor actively involved, showing and setting the example.

3. Build the project around the customer. Make the client the centre of the story. For an example of how powerful this exercise can be, try making or calling the client a partner.

Your strategy will develop in relation to people, targets, resources and technology:

▌ **People.** Identify the project leader, project members, external consultants and experts. You want to have the right people engaged to embrace the project. Depending on the nature of the project and the size of your organisation at a minimum, it is vital to consider including HR and IT. If there are legal questions that need to be addressed as well, you will not want that to hold up the project, so think ahead.

▋ **Targets.** Think through what would make the project a success. By knowing the objectives and goals you are setting you can gather the key metrics. During the planning phase, it will be essential not to get caught up in a short-term return-on-investment argument because the experimental nature of collaborating makes any firm numbers unlikely and/or unachievable. If the key performance indicators are not aligned with the collaborative mindset, failure is an inevitability.

▋ **Resources.** If there is no immediate payback, often it can be difficult to allocate funds, given budget constraints. Nevertheless, it is important to know what resources will be at your disposal, as misaligned expectations are likely to cause problems and frustrations. In the case of collaboration and to get inside the mindset fully, generally, budgets are bootstrapped by definition.

▋ **Technology.** Think through what technology you will need for the project. Typically, collaboration involves third parties and either party may have a strong opinion on this. It is helpful to work with cloud-based technology to enable a greater flow and accessibility of data. Speed and agility are important in these projects. Assess the security measures that are in place to avoid unwanted cyber attacks and thefts. Good project management software like Basecamp, Slack[24] and Trello[25] fosters collaboration, ensuring people have access to the information they need and activity is kept away from emails.

Execute – say what you do and do what you say

If, as the inestimable Peter Drucker allegedly said, 'culture eats strategy for lunch', execution is wrapped up in culture. With poor execution, even a great idea will fold. With good execution, a mediocre idea can work. In other words, execution is entirely strategic.

> With poor execution, even a great idea will fold. With good execution, a mediocre idea can work. In other words, execution is entirely strategic.

Are roles and responsibilities clear? As we mentioned in Mindset 2, responsibility is a key ingredient to taking on these disruptive forces. If roles and responsibilities are vaguely defined, the net effect will be, at best, confusing, and at worst, completely counterproductive. With the collaborative mindset, there is a tendency to operate with 'openness' and sometimes amorphous groups (such as with OuiShare 26). As a result, accountability can be more difficult to gauge and monitor.

Part of the collaborative mindset is also volunteering information, *especially* when it is relevant to others. One should evaluate how well and at what times the project has been communicated to other parts of the business. At least at the outset, this can be on a need-to-know basis. However, one ought to try to avoid opacity, where those working on the project sense others around them will misunderstand their activity. Each person should be encouraged to 'share' appropriately the project with those around them. As with the complication of having a watertight approach to cyber security (Force 4), when information is kept too close to the chest, it is not an environment favourable for collaboration.

During the execution phase, therefore, it will be important to allow the team to proceed without being held back by bureaucratic policies, controlling individuals, or excessive demands on their time in other areas of the business. If a boss commits with his or her word, the best way forward is to follow through. We like to insist on saying upfront what you are up to and then delivering on what you say you are going to do. That is the cornerstone of a proper execution.

We live and work in fast-moving environments. As a result, even the best laid plans can be undermined by changes with competitors, new legislation, or other external forces. As part of any experimentation, learning is as important as the results. In this case, some may argue learning is more important. As part of a fluid and developing organisation, the key will be having the compassion and flexibility to adapt and improve, especially when errors are made.

> As part of a fluid and developing organisation, the key will be having the compassion and flexibility to adapt and improve, especially when errors are made.

A slice of PIE

Personal

1. How are you demonstrating or modelling the behaviour you want to see happen in terms of sharing, openness to new ideas and fluid communication?

2. Attend a conference, such as the OuiShare Festival[27] to understand better and imitate the collaborative mindset that reigns.

3. If you have not explored areas of the Collaborative Economy, spend a weekend in an Airbnb, rent a Zipcar or try Uber. Experience first hand the 'spirit' when both client and supplier are rating one another.

▶

Internal

1. What mixture of talents and/or resources will be needed to deliver the best performance?

2. To what extent is expertise and knowledge grouped together and shared throughout the organisation?

3. How will the learnings from tests and experiments be shared and embedded back into the business or the next initiative?

External

1. Look to build bridges with third-party suppliers, distributors and independent influencers to create open and transparent partnerships.

2. Invite customer feedback and criticism. View it as a gift.

3. Publish your mission statement and hold yourselves accountable every day.

Part

2

The forces

1

The web

What's so important about social media, eCommerce, eLearning and peer-to-peer?

> The web is more a social creation than a technical one. I designed it for a social effect — to help people work together — and not as a technical toy.[1]
>
> *Tim Berners-Lee*

Accessing the internet was once laborious. The experience started with dialling in through a modem and hearing the famous ping pong ping sounds. Many minutes later, a browser loaded up, then the destination of the hyper-linked document needed to be typed. This is far distant from today's experience. Now, we get irritated by a website that makes us wait two seconds to load.

The world is increasingly measured in milliseconds, especially on the web. We live in fast times with ever increasing expectations. In this need for speed, we expect immediate access to information and rapid responses to requests. Development lead times and product life cycles have shrunk; the way we work, learn, communicate and sell continue to need dramatic readjustment.

> Development lead times and product
> life cycles have shrunk; the way we work,
> learn, communicate and sell continue to
> need dramatic readjustment.

What is it?

Let's state the obvious. The web is an abbreviation for the world wide web. You have heard of Sir Tim Berners-Lee 1991? He invented the web. Or was it the internet? People often mix up the web and the internet. Without getting stuck on pedantics or wanting to be the definition police, here is the difference:

▌ **The internet** links your computer to a collection of computers globally, and is a method used to transport content. Some liken it to the postal service, as it simply gets the post into the letterboxes. Its early signs date back to the 1960s.

▌ **The web** is software that enables you to view, use and create your own content. When you use your computer's browser, you are accessing the web, whereas, when you are downloading emails onto your desktop computer, you are using the internet.

It would be simple to leave it there, except people are now familiar with accessing email through the web by using platforms like Gmail. So it should come as no surprise that people mix up the internet and web; they neither understand the difference, nor do they particularly care. They just want the thing that works. But *you* understand now, so you have no excuse! Now you can look smart at a dinner party (and can thank us with an invite to that dinner party if we're in your neighbourhood).

Within the web, there are an enormous number of different applications. We do not consider the website as disruptive. Web101 understanding is that every company must have a website. We have been there, done that and bought the domain. It's no big deal. It was great when lots of additional domains were sold and, of course, specific websites can be incredibly disruptive themselves. But we want to highlight four areas that have been, and we believe will be, the most disruptive forces for business in the web. These applications often require significant changes in mindset *and* organisation for full implementation.

▌ Social media.

▌ eCommerce.

▌ Peer-to-peer (P2P) marketplace and funding.

▌ eLearning.

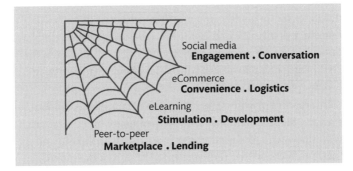

The four most disruptive web applications

Social media – what is new to know here?

Over 3.7 billion people are on the internet and, by 2020, an estimated 2.95 billion will be active on social media.[2] Social media is a dominant force, led by titans: Facebook, YouTube, WeChat, Instagram, Sina Weibo, Twitter and LinkedIn. Yet, with more than 1.2 billion *not* joined or submitted to social media, it has critics. Why? Security, privacy and lack of time are often cited. Many social media users are also on the dark social, using applications like Snapchat and WhatsApp, where messages are not in the public domain and are under the radar, thanks to end-to-end encryption. Dark Social, coined in 2012 by Alexis C. Madrigal, a senior editor at *The Atlantic*, refers to social sharing of content that occurs outside of what

can be measured by Web analytics programs. Facebook, with
1.86 billion users worldwide,[3] and its encryption on Messenger,
is still the go-to site amongst those aged 18–29, with a
penetration equating to 82 per cent.[4] The penetration drops
with each age bracket, falling to 48 per cent for those over
65 years old. The majority of social media users visit daily.

Usage of social media differs between countries and is
dependent on culture, behaviour and the governments in
which people are based. Facebook communication was key
during the Arab Spring in 2010/11. Users sharing the same
account details were able to write and read messages saved to
draft and set up clandestine meetings without having to send
them across the network. In the UK after the terrorist bomb at
Manchester's Arena in May 2017 and attack in London in June
2017, Facebook played key roles. The platform helped re-unite
lost people with their families, enable people to mark they
were safe and provide offers of practical support like places to
stay and blood donations. They helped many of us to mourn
with those who mourned in the face of such great pain and
tragedy. In Brazil, the indigenous Orkut site, at one point,
became the communication tool of reference for criminals. In
India, the 'matrimony' site, Shaadi, was used to foster millions
of 'real love' relationships in reaction to arranged marriages.

Social media has created a space where ordinary people,
without access to mass media channels, can communicate
easily and openly. This means that conversations about
brands, business and government can occur all the time, often
out of earshot, and without participation from concerned
parties. Messages can spread insanely far, and incredibly fast,
with organisations no longer able to control what is said.

> Messages can spread insanely far
> incredibly fast with organisations no
> longer able to control what is said.

If social media was born out of the free movement of the web, it remains *free* for the user, only in that they are not paying upfront to use the platform. However, as Andrew Lewis (aka blue_beetle, who first wrote on the website MetaFilter) says: 'If you are not paying for it, you're not the customer; you're the product being sold.'[5] Free is not necessarily free for the consumer, much less for brands.

> Free is not necessarily free for the consumer, much less for brands.

It is media; forget the social

Widespread and growing personal consumption has made people familiar with social media. Platforms and the experiences on those platforms are changing constantly. If social media still offers some free earned media for brands, marketing departments now know that social media is largely a paid media. The exposure that 'earned' media earns has been on a steady decline, as social media platforms eke out revenue in exchange for views. The earned media brands get tends to be relatively insignificant and unpredictable.

Businesses need to be selective and strategic with social media, not relegating it solely to the intern, because both time and money are at stake. Your brand, seen globally, needs to be in experienced hands. Words like viral or organic are no longer realistic when it comes to setting expectations with 'free' social media marketing campaigns. You are unlikely to develop a video that goes 'viral' without significant advertising money and a detailed plan behind it, especially if you are focused on the more established platforms. As a business, Facebook is unlikely to become a lead generator unless you are willing to pay for advertising. Brands must use these social media with their eyes wide open to the cost/benefit ratio. In any event, a brand's use of social media must be embedded in the core strategy.

Businesses need to be clear on their acquisition costs, the purposes and contexts of the different social channels and what content and engagement produces the greatest impact for them. It will become second nature for firms to address what is the lifetime value of a client found on LinkedIn, in comparison to those found on Facebook. Rather than waste time baulking at having to pay to appear in someone's social feed, brands need to put in the hard work getting accurate pictures on their return on investment (ROI), and not resist what makes commercial sense. Businesses must stay flexible on how they invest in social media. Operating and business models will continue to shift. As a result, there are no pre-fabricated recipes for success.

Regardless of the technological changes, some principles pass the test of time. You do not quite need to throw the rule book out yet. Businesses need to enable potential customers to receive content that will engage, educate, entertain and empower them. Multiple media forms include, amongst others, blog posts, podcasts, adverts, snapchats, videos, vlogs, lipsync videos, infographics, Q&A responses, images and social posts. It is essential for businesses to be where their customers are, rather than on a platform that is popular and expensive but their audience is nowhere to be found. It is noisy and crowded on these platforms, and you can quickly be paying inflated prices to be seen and heard by the wrong people.

Businesses need to see and be able to analyse their data to have a clear picture of the content to produce, the platforms to be on, and the strategy to deploy. Note the old saying that marketers ruin everything. It is, generally, always more cost-effective to be on platforms earlier. Once sites become vastly popular, agencies direct their clients towards growing platforms and they become noisy and costly. The smart businesses look out for new, emerging channels, to market to their customers before the channels become expensive.

Additionally, with a plethora of tools to choose from, it is important that social media is not in its own silo, but is integrated instead as part of a full marketing stack. This is especially important, as we look to place the customer at the centre of engagement.

Consider the following 10 questions for how your business might use social media.

1. How are you exploring and deciding what content works best with your audience and how can you create this consistently and efficiently?

2. What platform or channel currently gives you the greatest return on your investment?

3. How are you partnering with other organisations looking to reach the same audience?

4. What lesser-known platforms should you be moving your attention to, and what message or content would work well there?

5. How are you growing trust and credibility with your audience?

6. Is there any expertise you need to bring in to avoid learning through expensive trial and error?

7. How are you appealing to those customers who do not want to be social or who are on the dark web?

8. How are you observing where people's attention is going online and what are you learning from that?

9. In what ways are you wowing people through your social media?

10. Based on the lifetime value of an average client and your current acquisition costs, are there any changes you need to make?

eCommerce - show me the money

The second disruptive area of the web is eCommerce. Electronic and online commerce is projected to equal $2.5 trillion in retail sales in 2017, up 22 per cent. This represents 10 per cent of total retail worldwide.[6] As a result, no business can afford to ignore eCommerce. Yet, growth and profitability can be elusive and vary tremendously from one sector to another. Two alluring components to eCommerce arise from a business perspective. First, there is sense of control. A brand can own its distribution via a self-managed eCommerce site (as opposed to going through a third-party retailer, such as Amazon). Second, is its *apparent* profitability.

However, both 'control' and profitability can be difficult to achieve. Controlling one's distribution depends on how the remainder of the retail channel and the logistics are organised. A brand running its own eCommerce site whilst distributing through wholesalers, creates an inherent and sticky conflict. Moreover, with the power and influence of social media on business, building brand awareness, driving traffic and growing sales are far from easy tasks.

Regarding profitability, margins are slim, as with offline distribution in general. Different accounting methods for activities allocated to eCommerce may produce the difference between profit or loss. Profits are naturally squeezed, online, because of the ubiquity of price comparison sites that help display price discrepancies transparently. Additionally, as the purchasing process appears deceptively simple, it is easy to overlook the offline logistics that are needed for the distribution of goods. Though eCommerce is done through a digital interface, the offline world problems of branding, notoriety, HR issues and customer service weigh heavily on eMerchants. Businesses wanting to grow their eCommerce platforms often need an offline presence as we have increasingly seen with rise in physical stores for the likes of Amazon, or pop up stores for Ebay.

What does the customer want?

Consumers often are looking for convenience. Companies often are looking for efficiency. Buying online through an eCommerce environment provides both. However, it would be short-sighted to ignore other motivators that drive people to purchase. Too many companies may focus on short-term profit, at the expense of a longer-term gain. Lots of people within businesses discount branding when it comes to eCommerce. Therefore, the style of the platform or product display looks relatively sparse and basic. Customer service is often poor and, with razor thin margins, the management forget to look after their staff. A lack of resources often denies the customer the right experience and the staff member appropriate job satisfaction. So where eCommerce feels simply transactional, the experience needs to be humanised and people enabled to find connection and resonance with the business.

Whether your firm is looking to build out your own eCommerce platform or feature your products and services on other eCommerce environments, do hold on to what customers are looking for. Even in eCommerce, price is not the only thing that customers want.

What your business needs to consider

Clearly, trust and credibility are needed for people to purchase from anywhere, and this is even more the case when it comes to eCommerce platforms. The trust is threefold: in the eCommerce platform, the products being sold and the distributor or company selling the product. Of course, this may often be the same company.

Whether you are building your own eCommerce platform, or selling your products on another platform, similar challenges need to be addressed. Consider the following nine ways you might sustain high levels of trust and credibility.

1. **Brand.** Ensure people receive an experience fitting to your brand.

2. **User experience.** Make sure that descriptions accurately describe the produce, keep the visuals attractive and be careful to answer questions promptly. Pay particular

attention to make sure products are properly tagged to make the search function effective.

3. **Customer service.** Put a high priority on customer needs, for example in making customer returns policies transparent.

4. **Reputation.** Reviews are important, so it is worth spending time chasing good, credible authentic reviews for your product listings. Make sure to follow up on customer comments, especially those that are critical.

5. **Resource.** Give appropriate resources to handling questions and enquiries speedily.

6. **Trust.** List all the steps you can think of that will help create and maintain trust with your customer base.

7. **Engagement.** Look carefully at the products and services on offer and review the extent to which customers interact (view, click, like, share, etc.).

8. **Communications.** Focus on creating a clear message with which customers will be able to connect both emotionally and rationally. Look to create content alongside the merchandise that educates, entertains or engages your customer.

9. **Customer delight.** Reflect on what else you might do to ensure that the purchasing experience from the eCommerce platform is satisfying.

> Focus on creating a clear message with which customers will be able to connect both emotionally and rationally.

eLearning – the opportunities for development

Like eCommerce, eLearning is key for businesses keen to push employee development plans. Offline learning is expensive, requiring training facilities, transportation, accommodation and speaker costs, not to mention the opportunity cost of not being at work. eLearning on-demand costs scale easily at a fraction of these.

Like eCommerce, eLearning growth has been at a sustained double-digit level for a decade, though it has been slower recently. As a relatively new field of expertise, best practices and appropriate budget allocations are generally more difficult to find. Work becomes more distributed, so employees need to be kept engaged, inspired and connected to the organisation. Corporate eLearning is strategic to keep people at the top of their game.

In fiercely competitive hiring spaces, like developers and designers, the best employees need constant stimulation. Continuous learning helps build competitive advantage. The greater the learning experiences, the greater the likelihood that employee motivation and belonging will remain at peak levels.

> **In fiercely competitive hiring spaces, like developers and designers, the best employees need constant stimulation.**

eLearning has huge potential to engineer great learning environments, tools and curricula, but requires work. Users need better user habits and methodologies. Businesses need the right mindset, an appropriate corporate culture and the right blend of on and offline learning. Crafting learning paths that are user and human-centric are essential. Yet tools (augmented reality, virtual reality, artificial intelligence…), methods (social learning, serious games) and platforms (Coursera,[7] Khan Academy[8]) are being developed at speed and are changing the learning experience and eLearning opportunities.

> **Real learning happens only with learner-owned development.**

The biggest challenge lies in fostering learners' accountability for their own learning. Real learning happens only with learner-owned development. The company's role is to provide impetus, an appropriate sets of tools and open attitude that encourages initiative and self-learning.

The expectations of millennials and Generation Z

The aspirations and expectations of millennials (those born between early 1980s through to mid to late 1990s) and Generation Z (those born mid 1990s to early 2000s) have changed. Where previously there was an expectation amongst baby boomers (those born early to mid 1940s through to 1960–1964) that a job was for life and you would find stability and security within an established company, many millennials and those in generation X (those born mid 1960s through to early 1980s) have grown up experiencing a distrust of the establishment. Companies no longer show loyalty and employees are quick to reciprocate. A report by Gallup in 2016 indicated that 21 per cent of millennials had changed jobs in the last year and 60 per cent were open to new job opportunities. With the growth in businesses formed each year and the rise of the freelancer market, people are putting increasing importance on personal development. Companies are having to show a commitment to invest in their talent if they want to keep them.

> Companies are having to show a commitment to invest in their talent if they want to keep them.

Do you know, right at this moment, what you need or want to learn next? Do your team members have knowledge goals? Do you know where to go for the world's best training in those areas? Different levels of approach can be applied to these questions. On one end of the budget scale, for small startups, a company-wide access to an Audible (part of Amazon) account can enable people to listen to audiobooks that you collectively purchase. (You may also choose to access iTunes

University (iTunesU[9]), and make a shortlist of helpful courses there.) Some may prefer to learn through video tutorials so, if you do not have the budget to provide access to learning platforms like Lynda.com[10] (owned by LinkedIn), you may create a library of helpful YouTube channels and videos around specific subjects or areas of learning.

As well as recommending specific resources, with a directory or easy access for core areas of your business, you can make additional direct investment in your team members. Providing them with a budget they can spend in the eLearning environments of their choice gives them the possibility to choose and prioritise what is important to them.

Additionally, creating the space and support for deep thinking and reflection is powerful. Cal Newport, in his book *Deep Work*,[11] explains the difference between shallow work activities (checking emails, updating social accounts, attending meetings, providing updates) and deep work pursuits (thoughtful reflective work etc) What percentage of employees' time do businesses want spent on deep work? In transitioning to a four-day week, Basecamp[12] allowed more time for reflection, which resulted in greater bottom line performance and a more productive learning and development environment. It is great to be committed to providing opportunities for people to learn, but expecting people to slot it in between 7 pm and 8 pm on Friday evening after a frantic week is not a good idea. Regardless of the platform, the learning at those hours will not generate the best results. Better at that time to have an earthy, peppery discussion over a few drinks after work. Mine's a single malt. Nothing like a Friday night chat to see into the future.

How to implement eLearning into your business

Here are 12 ways to think about the development and learning for you and your team.

1. Consider people's different learning abilities. Give your people the chance to identify how they best learn and absorb information. Refer to Mindset 2 and the outline of learning styles. Options could include reading, video tutorials, audiobooks, Ted Talks, books, group discussions, conferences etc.

2. If not already in place, initiate a learning plan. Encourage, if not allocate, a reasonable amount of time for learning.

3. Explore the best eLearning environments, websites, software and devices to make available for your team.

4. Check out how new technologies such as augmented reality (discovery) or virtual reality (simulations) are being used to enhance the learning experience.

5. Research the best source of reliable teachers and communicators. Not all online education is created equal.

6. Create an environment where the team are encouraged to share learning with others. Encourage peer learning and discovery. Embrace social learning.

7. Provide financial support for your team to learn and find out where they would most prefer to use that resource.

8. Support your team and encourage from the front, to show how important learning and personal development is for you.

9. Evaluate the best learning platforms to invest in. Creating an in-house eLearning site can look like a short-term saving, but we believe online education is better suited to being outsourced to stay fresh and fluid.

10. Check out how new ideas and learning are disseminated through the organisation. For example, do you have an online ideas board? Do you respond to all the ideas?

11. Consider creating content for others to learn from to show your industry expertise.

12. Develop core habits of learning within the organisation. This can include scheduling mealtime 'byte size' sessions. What do you applaud and celebrate? Create an internal *return on education* (ROE).

Support your team and encourage from the front, to show how important learning and personal development is for you.

Peer-to-peer – the two worlds

Peer-to-peer could be considered the original evil of the web as well as its most liberating force. In literal form, *peer-to-peer* describes the initial premise of the internet where individuals share files with one another in remote locations via connected nodes. Between music and video file-sharing services, peer-to-peer took several industries by storm in the 1990s, impacting other sectors and verticals, little by little, not just with digital assets. We want to highlight two important peer-to-peer (P2P) areas that have an increasingly important role in business today:

▌ **P2P marketplaces** – where goods and services are traded between two individuals, an individual and a company, or a company with another company, all without third-party involvement.

▌ **P2P lending** – the practice of lending and borrowing money between individuals or between an individual and a business.

Decades of hyper consumerism have left households with an abundance of second-hand goods. As and when economies suffer setbacks, households naturally look for ways to supplement their finances. The adopted peer-to-peer marketplace represents a particularly efficient and effective channel, supported by strong fundamentals. New business models have been born and the distribution landscape has been materially impacted. Almost by definition, the peer-to-peer lending services take their cue from the collaborative spirit discussed in Mindset 3. Additionally, clothing brands, such as Patagonia, similarly look to participate actively in the second-hand clothing market.

Car manufacturers are getting into the car-sharing space. As well as BMW's DriveNow,[13] Daimler launched car2go.[14] At the higher end of the market are Mercedes-Benz Rent[15] and Audi on demand.[16] Meanwhile, and more saliently for this force, there are also manufacturers investing in peer-to-peer platforms such as General Motors' Flinc[17] and CarUnity.[18] The largest initiative, Ford's Peer-2-Peer Car Sharing programme, allows customers to rent their Ford Credit-financed vehicles for short-term rentals – explained in their 2015 press release:

> 'Ford Credit is inviting 14,000 and 12,000 customers in six U.S. cities and London, respectively, to sign up to rent their Ford Credit-financed vehicles to prescreened drivers for short-term use, offsetting monthly vehicle ownership costs. U.S. customers participate through the Web-based, mobile-friendly software of ride-share company Getaround, while London drivers connect through a similar rental system of easyCar Club.'[19]

Peer-to-peer lending – how we have reacted to the banks

Peer-to-peer lending (P2PL) online, meanwhile, is also on the rise, cutting out the banks that have been asleep at the wheel. The first ever P2PL site, Zopa, started in 2005 in the UK. The practice then spread quickly to the USA. Industry leaders now include big league unicorn players, such as Funding Circle, Lending Club and RateSetter. Some of the space-carving players lend to individuals and small businesses, though the market remains very small and profitability elusive in comparison to the entire lending market. In terms of P2PL business generated, the cumulative

total amount of money lent will soon exceed £10 billion, according to figures from the P2PFA industry body.**
Amongst the leaders, Zopa[20] and Funding Circle[21] have lent close to £2.5 billion since launch whilst RateSetter[22] has lent close to £2 billion since launch.

In China, where P2PL had been particularly strong offline because of the lack of easy access to funds via state-owned banks, there are over 2,000 P2PL sites in activity today.

In the peer-to-peer area, whether it is distribution or payments, there are tangible opportunities that businesses can take advantage of.

The peer-to-peer marketplace

Many businesses may regard selling their services through marketplaces as a cop out. They like to control the complete customer experience, have access to all the data, and not give away commission to other companies. However, we would argue that it is an opportunity not to be missed: additional platforms generate new clients and good customers. Many businesses, whether B2B or B2C, have embraced marketplaces and peer-to-peer platforms and taken the opportunity to launch their own niche marketplace, and find new clients through links with others.

As always, there are trade-offs. Profit margins may be reduced through paying commission; but there is a lower level of marketing costs, improved timeliness and confidence in receiving payments.

What is needed to succeed in this environment? It is essential to be intentional, quick, responsive and offer your services in such a way that clients will want to buy from you. We have

----

**Footnote - http://p2pfa.info/data

seen this spring up for all professional services and multiple business niches.

1. Explore which marketplaces exist for the area of business you are in.

2. Evaluate your positioning on these websites. Do you look credible with reviews and early testimonials against your name and work? Peer validation makes all the difference.

3. Brainstorm with staff, influencers and customers how you could get a larger share of the business on these marketplaces, and how, where appropriate, there are further upsell opportunities and/or the ability to maintain reinforce the loyalty of ongoing customers.

4. Review and measure how quickly you respond to questions. Identify bottlenecks that hinder quicker responses.

5. At a set time, evaluate the return on investment made through these marketplaces and compare to your other routes to market.

Considerations for a peer-to-peer funding campaign

Similar strong advantages exist in lending from the P2P network. You can road-test both new product and marketing message to detect any appetite for it before it goes into production. You can source and identify adopters, supporters, partners and advocates.

Naturally, this is a strong alternative for startups and scaleups who are looking for alternative routes to finance. With £10 billion lent, banks either need to partner with existing platforms, as most have chosen, or create their own, as Goldman Sachs did.[23]

P2P funding offers advantages for both established businesses and startups. If you are looking to raise additional revenue for a product or service, or trying to identify key influencers to support your business, careful planning will help you to apply successfully for P2P lending or funding. Some P2P lending partners focus less on marketing a campaign than on a good business plan and following due process. For other P2P funding platforms like Kickstarter, marketing is a core component of the chances for success.

1. Brainstorm the advantages and disadvantages of a P2P-based funding campaign for your business.

2. Weigh up the benefits and challenges in having one lender or backer (a bank) compared to multiple lenders or backers (P2P funding).

3. Ponder what would happen if your business venture did not succeed and you were unable to repay the loan. How would working with a commercial bank differ from a P2P funding platform?

4. Ensure you have a compelling story, clear metrics on customer acquisition, and the traction you have been able to generate and a detailed expansion plan laid out.

5. Explore investing in other people's ventures to understand more fully what the experience is like when you are on the receiving end of news, updates and possibilities.

Why do you need to worry?

The landscape has changed dramatically. The web and the use of social media, eCommerce, P2P marketplaces, P2P lending and eLearning are central issues to many businesses. And, if not all are equally relevant or pressing, it is highly likely that businesses should be paying close attention to two or three of these.

These are no longer *new* areas to be 'excited' about. First move advantage has been taken. These are areas that businesses need to seriously grapple with to avoid losing major competitive advantage. Whilst some businesses still are sadly stuck with arguing over what external websites employees can visit and others are getting hung up on the need for face-to-face learning environments, both the sleeping giants and the slow-to-react SMEs will face repercussions if they do not respond quickly.

What should you do about it?

Whether you call it the web or the internet frankly does not matter. The web is moving fast and has made such a deep impact on the lives of so many on the planet, that it is impossible to oversell its importance. Where some of these areas are still less than a decade old, regardless of the four areas that we have explored in this chapter, we all know there will be other disruptive forces springing up out of nowhere. The question remains: will we be able to move our organisation fast enough to take advantage of these opportunities?

> Whether you call it the web or the internet, frankly does not matter. The web is moving fast and has made such a deep impact on the lives of so many on the planet, that it is impossible to oversell its importance.

A slice of PIE

Personal

1. How could you find more meaningfulness in your personal use of social media? For example, do you use social media, to intentionally follow, engage or further your interest in a personal hobby?

2. What eLearning platforms and sites do you use? If you are looking to learn a new language, we recommend the crowdsourced and gamified Duolingo.[24]

3. What peer-to-peer marketplaces can you find for your industry that you could generate leads from?

Internal

1. Organise a LinkedIn training day to enable your sales team to know how to use LinkedIn Sales Navigator, provide engagement and generate leads. Gamify and set out a competition for the best and most improved social selling index score, resulting in prizes for the best performers.

2. Are there any areas of expertise your organisation needs that could be found in a peer-to-peer marketplace? Take a look at Talmix,[25] Clarity.fm[26] and Upwork.[27]

3. Do you have any products or services that could be tested through a peer-to-peer fundraising project? Take a look at Kickstarter[28] and Indiegogo.[29]

External

1. Assess the App Charts and see what social platform apps are currently popular. Sign up to a new social platform and spend 10 minutes looking to discover if your potential customers are on the platform.

2. Using Buzzsumo,[30] carry out an audit of your website to see which pieces of content have been your most popular and well received. Carry out the same analysis on your competitors and use this information to shape your monthly content plan.

3. Do you have an eCommerce strategy to sell your products or services? If not, what products or services are your priority to sell? Using Google Search, research and see what suitable marketplaces exist.

The smartphone

I wouldn't say I'm *really* addicted to my phone

> I get text messages on my cell phone all day long, and it warbles to alert me that someone has sent me a message on Facebook or a reply or direct message on Twitter, but it rarely ever rings.[1]
>
> *Susan Orlean*

I remember riding in the back of a friend's car with a telephone console as armrest. It felt ever so sophisticated to be able to call ahead to the store we were visiting to advise them of our arrival. Unlike the walkie-talkie, this felt like science fiction. Today, the phone is variously more important than the wallet, ID or even a toothbrush when travelling. The reflex to recharge the phone battery is becoming almost obsessional. Yet, for all the time I spend on my mobile, I have two observations:

1. 95 per cent of the time I spend is on the home screen.

2. It is not yet half as smart as it or will be.

What is it?

The smartphone is a mobile phone that can connect to the internet. There were 1.5 billion new smartphones purchased in 2016, with many people owning two or more.[2] Some

91 per cent of online users have a smartphone, which is higher than PC/laptop ownership.[3] The smartphone is rapidly becoming the device of choice to connect. Media consumption on the mobile surpassed desktop computer consumption for the first time in 2016[4] and, with so many objects now being connected to the internet through the internet of things, the smartphone will be a hyper important gateway into the connected objects. It is only a matter of time before the term *smartphone* will be replaced by another name that de-emphasises the telephone feature and takes for granted the internet access. For the sake of this chapter, as well as smartphone, we will call it mostly what we all call it anyway: the phone.

Thanks to advancements in computing power, battery endurance and functionalities, the phone is tending towards becoming a mini-computer. We choose to exclude tablets from the smartphone category because of the lack of standard telephone functionality. However, since many communication and VOIP messaging services like Skype, WhatsApp and FaceTime can be found on tablets and the difference in size is shrinking, the line between phone and tablet is ever murkier.

In the USA, a survey by the Pew Research Center found that smartphone penetration is reaching saturation in several groups, notably, '86% of those aged 18–29 have a smartphone, as do 83% of those aged 30–49 and 87% of those living in households earning $75,000 and up annually.'[5]

It is clear that the app is superior. As a portal into the internet, the mobile browser experience has taken a backseat to the app. That said, the average phone user uses only 27 apps, whereas the average phone has over 90 apps installed,[6] out of an estimated available 2 million apps (according to the OS). Across the board, app downloads are hovering at around 0.5 and 1 app per month. In a comScore survey (comScore is

a US global media measurement and analytics company)
conducted in June 2016, half of the phone owners surveyed
had, on average, downloaded zero apps over a three-month
period. One of the big challenges for businesses looking to
capitalise on the smartphone is not only creating a value-
added app that is worthy of being on the homescreen, but it
is in being discovered, downloaded and activated.

The usages of the smartphone that have only just scratched the
surface include:

▌ mobile commerce which already accounts for 20 per cent
of eCommerce sales in the USA)[7]

▌ mobile payments, where you use the phone to pay in stores
with a mobile wallet)

▌ geolocated and personalised messaging

▌ augmented reality

▌ virtual reality using the smartphone

▌ hub for the smart home.

How important is your phone to you?

For many, the phone is their most important possession,
and this is the case for me. It goes with me everywhere I go.
I can access almost any data or information I need on a
daily basis from it. To put it bluntly, it would be the
equivalent of my defibrillator for a work or personal
emergency. People carry their phones close to their heart,
check them on average 140 times a day and even settle
down to a night's sleep lying close to them. As the phone
has permeated into the inner circles of our lives, we need to
allow ourselves to critique and question whether they are
always a good fit for us. Will future generations look at us
and think we have lost the plot? Phones are such a normal
and ubiquitous part of our lives, but let us take a moment to

ensure we are getting the best from them, as opposed to being possessed by them.

The dangers

I am someone who has to work hard not to be wired in. In the morning, I would reach for my phone to turn my alarm off, only to be lured immediately into early email checking. In fact, so strong was my addiction to email consumption that, for a while, I would find my weekends hijacked by reading a work email, thinking of something I still needed to do and, as a result, not mentally and emotionally being able to switch off.

There were two major impacts with this working habit. First, there was the obsessive need to please others' flawed mindset. After all, the quicker the response, the shinier the halo. Sadly, messages and alerts release a huge endorphin hit. Repeatedly, I succumbed to the addiction and it grew. Before long, you set up expectations that are not realistic, healthy or enjoyable and find yourself in a hamster wheel trying to meet them.

Second, the quality of my work was affected. Sure, I could multi-task, work from four screens and be incredibly quick in my work. As soon as I needed to do some deep work, which required a good level of thinking and didn't allow me simply to rely on my experience or ability to think on the spot, I was distracted. The deeper and more focused work became a real challenge to get to grips with.

We know that this pattern of getting distracted significantly affects productivity. Unfortunately, it is common to see people in small team meetings checking their phones and causing others to wait. 'Sorry, please can you hang on a moment whilst I just … um … check my … um … yeah, one second', as they look down at their phone, oblivious of the irritation that others feel from the lack of respect for their own time. Bosses often think that they can get away with it. To the contrary, such behaviour causes more of the same throughout the organisation. Where's the efficiency there? Is there a need for a greater level of humility and appreciation of others?

Being socially mobile

In relationships, couples also complain about their partner's use of their phone, with it's constant beeping and checking cutting across quality time together. Not using the silent mode is a constant interruptor during a movie or face-to-face time with others. Being out socially, groups of friends sit in pubs with their heads down looking at screens. In restaurants, it is easy to see someone take a rather too frequent trip to the toilet mid-course to check their phone. Is the company they are with not enjoyable enough? Or do they need to learn to let go?

I have two young children and the use of our phones raises a number of questions for me. I want my children to know they are the priority when we are together. They do not play second fiddle to a phone. It's challenging juggling work pressures. But after all it's better to be 100 per cent attentive, 30 per cent of the time, then be 30 per cent attentive 100 percent of the time.

The intelligent phone

Despite the negative ways that the phone is disrupting family, friendships and work, the phone is still my most important possession with all the incredible things that can be done through it. It is so easy to be familiar with the phone that we have lost sight of how much it has changed our lives and our work.

At the heart of a phone is the need for a personalised experience and, therefore, the issues of individualisation, customisation and privacy are important. But, additionally, we expect immediate intelligent responses when we look to our phones. We want to be provided with the solutions we need and the connectivity that enables us to be close to loved ones. Smartphones have changed our workplaces, enabling people to work, communicate and function flexibly. There are important considerations for businesses to reflect on.

The need to be mobile first

With more than 50 per cent of page views now done on mobile devices, the question of having a mobile *first* strategy is central. Not only do company websites need to be developed first for the mobile and then adapted to the desktop, the development and deployment of effective mobile apps is challenging for marketing departments. The app needs to be created for different operating systems, and be desirable to users found in the different app stores. Additionally, brands must be aware of constantly providing value, finding ways to render the app both indispensable and fluid in a multi-channel environment.

The process to create a mobile-first website is more easily said than done. A non-negligible challenge is finding a good development partner. Second, because of size and bandwidth limitations, apps require a radical streamlining and reduction of your messages. Third, the app must exist as part of a non-linear, multi-channel and multi-device customer journey. App creators need to keep in mind the interplay with relevant staff like instore personnel, customer service, sales and social media teams. The app must evolve, both with the operating systems and the business needs. Ultimately, you also need to consider when and how to sunset your app, rather than leave it as an out-of-date relic. In today's world, it is still rare to find traditional companies other than new pure players (e.g. Uber, Snapchat, Instagram) who have operated on a mobile-first basis. And, even when companies declare they have a mobile-first strategy, the result, quite often, is still anything but user friendly.

> And, even when companies declare they have a mobile-first strategy, the result, quite often, is still anything but user friendly.

Mobile in retail

Going into a store clad with a smartphone is about as normal as going outside with an umbrella when it is raining. Of course, you can do without it, but the experience is not half as good.

Retail stores have long been battling the smartphone. It is often viewed by store personnel as the opposition, if not an unpleasant weapon in the hands of the customer. Of the many scenes you can still find in retail stores, here is a list of sore spots:

- No (free) Wi-Fi for customers.

- No permission to take photographs.

- Inconsistencies with pricing or messaging on the eCommerce site in comparison to what is on the shelf.

- Google (on my smartphone) knows more than the store personnel.

- No digital recognition (e.g. NFC or QR codes) on the labels; or worse, QR codes that no one understands.

- Store personnel do not know how to approach a digitally connected customer.

- A blue letter F stuck on the window that is supposed to incite you to check out the store's page on Facebook – because, of course, when was the last time you did that after seeing a sticker?

The customer journey from smartphone to showroom has plagued the bricks and mortar store. Whilst some retailers may be trying to find ways to fight against the smartphone or to cut costs, others are dedicated to enhancing the connected consumer's shopping experience. Amazon Go and Apple Pay are two examples of how the smartphone can become an ally both to the shopper and to the retailer. But, as with most technology, the winning combination is when both human and machine interaction are optimised. If banks follow the customer trend to shun the local branch, a majority of people still want the option to go and speak to someone. This is as much a function of the poor mobile experience and the unsatisfactory distance of customer service, as it is a part of the social element of doing business.

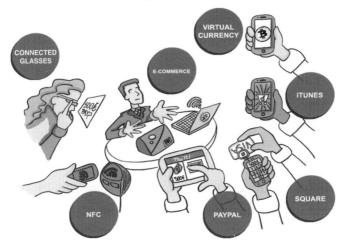

The many ways to use your device to settle your shopping
Source: Drawing by Antonio Meza (http://antoons.net/), commissioned by The Myndset

I used to work in the professional haircare industry. A distributor I worked with in Canada, run by a bastion of the industry, looked with a crooked eye at the role of the internet and smartphone in his retail space. One of his big questions was how to manage the eCommerce opportunity with the instore experience. Instead of making the internet and smartphone the enemy, methodically he tested out new approaches. Specifically, in half of his stores, he added a computer terminal that allowed customers also to shop via their eCommerce portal. Many questioned his approach. But it became clear within six months that, on a like-for-like basis, the stores with the eCommerce terminals won out. The key to success was that he involved the store personnel in the tests and decision making. Why did the stores with eCommerce terminals produce more aggregate sales than stores without eCommerce? Because the staff were trained and motivated to work *with* the eCommerce terminals. And because the option of having big items delivered at home was a bonus for customers. Additionally, when a client whips out her smartphone, the store staff are encouraged to interact with the client, not take umbrage behind the counter, making the instore experience comfortable for everyone.

Finding your mobile SPACE

We have created an approach that helps you to find your mobile *SPACE*. A mobile phone strategy is smart, productive, adaptive, customer-focused and has etiquette.

Smart

> How are you solving their pain points and how could your app or the mobile version of your site bring value to them?

As you look to engage with your customers on their phone, it is not acceptable to provide a website that does not work well on a mobile device. What may have engaged people on a desktop will not be enough and the starting point needs to be the best experience people could have using their phone. Before you start building your technology, it is important to understand what your customers need. For instance, how are you solving their pain points and how could your app or the mobile version of your site bring value to them?

It may be that they are looking to receive quick answers and information, knowledge and entertainment, engagement and even access to data. You will need to ensure that your app will be smart enough to satisfy these needs. Consider the value you will provide them in exchange for collecting their data, and whether your app will be static or evolving as you gather data on what they want.

Building your app requires extensive experience and skill and, as we will discuss, there are multiple areas in which the developers need to be proficient. Make sure you are clear about the criteria you are using to choose your development partners.

Productive

With apps and cloud-based software syncing with the rest of your team, you are able to work closely with everyone whilst on the move. Everyone can track tasks in the project management software, sign off work that is completed or put through sales information. Some will be checking finances or managing cashflow. Others will be editing a video clip for a social post, whilst many will be managing client communication through email, phone, text and social media.

Additionally, education, learning and development is a core way for businesses to support their teams in productivity. People are able to take advantage of commuting times to learn through reading books and articles, listening to podcasts and audiobooks, and watching tutorials and videos. These areas of learning are then grounded through app-based coaching and habit-forming solutions.

Staff productivity is a key consideration for every business so it is understandable that many businesses encourage people to catch up in the evenings, when so much can be done from the phone. Is there a danger that this approach is a quick win for the employer but costs the relationship longer term? Having the appropriate care, compassion and respect for others' time is important. But, equally, you would be shooting yourself in the foot, if staff were not able to access the software they need from their phones.

It is important to know what apps, tools and patterns of working could help people be more productive. Often, company data and information is needed, and vast amounts of time would be saved if this was set to be visible at appropriate times. Furthermore, knowing the basics of the phone settings ensures you are getting the most from your phone. Many have not mastered their phone settings, missing out on many streamlined approaches. At a minimum, make sure that the messages that pop up in the lockscreen are curated to reflect what's truly important to you.

A phone can make someone more productive. The irony, however, is that the biggest productivity boost for many would be *not* to check phones or emails so regularly. This would give the head space to concentrate on important work.

> The irony, however, is that the biggest productivity boost for many would be not to check phones or emails so regularly.

Adaptive

It is essential to be able to adapt to the changes we see in the ever-evolving world of mobile. Customers need to access you wherever they are located. This may be on their phones using your apps or the mobile site. It could also be on social media or via a messaging service. What happens if the adaptivity that you need requires a move away from the phone itself? We are experiencing the beginnings of a time when you are utilising this data on your watch, Alexa, Echo, Smart TV, Fridge and a plethora of IoT devices. Where does the adaptivity begin and end?

Always check that, when the size of the screen changes, the content is optimised to fit the appropriate sized images, and work on different operating systems and devices. Look at the additional devices or platforms that your content could be a part of and ensure you are creating content that can adapt to future mobile solutions.

It is clearly essential to think of your audience who are using multiple devices simultaneously, as well as those utilising features like augmented reality. What experience do you want to give them?

Customer-focused

As well as being mobile first, you need to create an app that adds incredible value. You want it downloaded by a customer, in a prominent 'phone homescreen' location and for it to be used regularly and repeatedly. To achieve this, we need to put ourselves into the shoes of the customer. We need to understand their pain points, engage with empathy and grasp what they need.

Make sure the videos, podcast and written materials address the customers' needs and look good. Reflect on the context that mobile plays in the customer's journey. What can you help them with? As a result, can they learn to trust you?

Additionally, as important as it is to have your own app or mobile version of your site, what other apps would it be essential for you to be on that would extend your reach?

Would partners bring additional value to your customers to allow for cross promotions? How can you reach these partners? Part of considering how you market your app, services or products is to understand on what apps or sites your customers congregate, and what are the best ways to reach them or advertise to them there. Checking the app store regularly to assess which apps are growing in popularity is a good approach. Different apps will have different mobile marketing opportunities and, as with Force 1, the lesser known apps, though popular with potential customers, often will provide a stronger ROI for advertising spend and make it easier to target the influencers on that channel. Be strongly intentional before the marketers discover the audience.

Etiquette

Let us put it bluntly: as phone users, we can be incredibly rude. Behaviour we would have taken offence at 10 years ago, is often our own behaviour today. People are blithely unaware of the impact, frustration or irritation their mobile habits can cause others. Not only does it show a lack of respect and empathy, but it can become a considerable blocker to good communication and relationships.

> People are blithely unaware of the impact, frustration or irritation their mobile habits can cause others.

As a result, there is a great opportunity to go against a culture that has emerged and show good etiquette as individuals. stand up against the trend of bad manners. Poor etiquette in a business probably will chip away at your brand image and the trust that customers may have had in you.

Privacy is also crucial and the phone requires a more sacred approach. People have zero tolerance for businesses 'space invading' and sending spammy text messages or making unsolicited calls.

Security is important to factor in, as a phone accesses sensitive data. To lose your phone could result in security issues. By using software accessed in the Cloud, when a device is stolen or lost it gives you the flexibility to suspend the account so others cannot log in. You can even delete the data that is on the device. It is often a good idea to simulate losing your phone to see what you would do to protect your data. Companies do fire drills, but data drills are not common. The risks of a data breach are more like to impact your organisation than a fire on your premises. Some companies allow staff to 'bring your own device', which generates significant ergonomic benefits for the user, but also carries security risks. Naturally, people tend to know their own devices better and, therefore, will be quicker on them, but you will need to put measures in place to ensure that your IP and data are not compromised. We will address more security-related issues in Force 4.

A slice of PIE

Personal

1. Fed up with the phone dominating social time with friends? Next time you go out with friends for a meal, get everyone to put their phones in the middle of the table. The first person to pick up their phone to check their messages picks up the bill.

2. Develop a daily learning ritual you can stick with, using your phone. Choose a TED talk, your favourite podcast, an in-depth blog or your Flipboard account.

3. Where there is only so much energy each day for willpower, make life easier by developing habits. How could your phone help you develop healthy habits? Try the Way of Life app[8] and take satisfaction each day by marking off actions to turn them into habits.

Internal

1. Get access to company-wide learning materials. Try out a Lynda.com[9] subscription and map out the courses your teams would benefit from.

▶

2. What software and productivity tools does your company provide access to? There is a plethora to choose from, but we would recommend Basecamp, Slack and Trello.

3. Do you have a clear time where you are able to switch off from work communication? Make a decision if you want to have a clear cut-off time. Consider encouraging people to leave phones outside of bedrooms when charging overnight.

External

1. How have you built mobile first into your web strategy? Test how mobile friendly your site is using Google's 'Test My Site.'[10]

2. Consider creating video content for your mobile audience around a theme. For a B2B series, you could create daily themed Q&A videos, a series of recorded interviews, regular tips on your product or industry news updates. Do not forget to explore advertising on YouTube where advertising costs are as yet comparatively low.

3. Especially if your audience skews younger, take a look at buying a Snapchat geofilter[11] to raise visibility of your brand and reach your potential prospects through their phone.

The cloud

What happens if the cloud disappears?

> **The cloud services companies of all sizes; the cloud is for everyone. The cloud is a democracy.**[1]
>
> *Marc Benioff Founder & CEO Salesforce*

What is it?

They sold it to us. The chance to work from a café overlooking the beach. The world is your office and all you need is at your fingertips. Team members work from their own location and apart from the expected: 'Sorry I was having problems getting into the video conference room' we are more adept at working remotely. We have got the cloud to thank.

The cloud may sound ethereal and abstract but, in reality, the cloud is made up of fixed hardware and server farms located firmly in regions throughout the world. The cloud is a way to store, manage and work with data using computers and memory that is located elsewhere. Rather than having the data resident on your phone or laptop, computer or local server, the data processing power is delegated to a remote location where it is accessed through the internet.

For many companies, the cloud moves data storage from local hardware to more efficient locations. This lightens the processing load on the local machines, and increases both space and speed. As the server hardware is not needed in the office any more, the cloud enables us to be mobile. Many of us are familiar with this as we are used to working from home, hotels and cafés. Some may even be forgiven for thinking that coffee companies have had a part to play in the cloud, somehow being behind the technological drive. After all, it has been some time since the coffee shop became the temporary office space of the masses, and who knows how many lattes have been consumed as a result.

One of the major benefits of the cloud is the ability to store data backups. This relates to a business that has an archive of records, but could just as easily be relevant for a smartphone accessing photos and videos that are synced up to cloud storage accounts. A second great opportunity of the cloud is the ability to run software across an entire organisation that can be distributed, maintained and upgraded in unison from a central point; otherwise known as Software as a Service

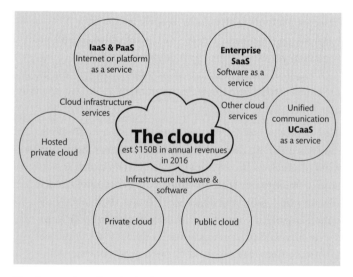

Cloud segments and market leaders
Source: Synergy Research Group

(SaaS). A third great advantage is the processing power. With the ever-increasing amounts of data and the need for speed, access to vast computing power allows for greater velocity and data analytics. In sum, the cloud provides accessibility, more space, processing power and the assurance of backed-up information.[2,3]

Why do you need to worry?

The truth of the matter is, for many of us, the cloud is becoming a standard experience. It is a normality and a major advantage that does not give us cause for concern. Perhaps a decade ago, the philosophical and deep-thinking Spock from *Star Trek* may have said: 'It's life, Jim, but not as we know it.' Yet, the truth is, most of us now accept the cloud as part of our daily existence, even if we may not always be fully aware of the extent of its usage. For those who have come to understand the cloud, what is not to like about it?

Of course, as with many breakthrough technologies, there is still plenty of resistance to the cloud, mostly in enterprise organisations. Some overly zealous or highly controlling IT departments, under the threat of an expensive hack, would prefer to abstain from the cloud as much as possible. We have good reason to overcome that caution, and we will explore more sensibly some of the challenges they face in a moment. But, for many of us, the cloud is a daily and positive companion to our lives.

We listen to podcasts, audiobooks and music when we are working out in the gym. We look at photos, files and videos whilst riding in the back of an Uber. We access spreadsheets, reports and emails when we are on the toilet. Toilet waiting times have definitely gone up! For work, for play – it is our constant resource. The cloud is ours. We harness the power of technology and make it bow to our every whim. Flexibility, control and efficiency. Multi-tasking, fiefdoms and creativity. Just give me a dongle, 4G or Wi-Fi and watch me roar. We are Titans of technology, masters of destiny and Kings and Queens of the Cloud.

> The cloud is ours. We harness the power of technology and make it bow to our every whim.

And yet we are stretched. And stressed. After all, too much of a good thing can make us sick. And it seems like some of us have become very ill.

It is all about the work

Working well is not easy. The danger of always being plugged into the cloud, despite not being connected with cables, leaves us feeling frayed. And afraid. It once seemed exciting to be able to access everything on the go. But now we are at the point where we cannot switch off from the demands and shouts for our attention. What message have we forgotten about? We waste time on unimportant and seemingly *urgent* work, losing the space to do significant work. This is not the work that delivers great results, helps us grow exponentially or creates a positive legacy. This work is often tedious, mundane and distracting.

> The danger of always being plugged into the cloud, despite not being connected with cables, leaves us feeling frayed. And afraid.

A manager responding to an email within five minutes may seem impressive to a lazy and poorly organised director wanting a quick response; but, more often than not, it shows the manager's inability to distinguish between urgent and important, short-term and long-term issues. Resorting to an immediate focus of pleasing others is an easy trap many of us fall into. One of today's biggest strategic challenges, due to our lack of time, is the inability to focus on deep, significant and challenging work. Just as the phone makes us always available, the cloud makes everything always accessible. With both, we need to impose times of being off the grid. It is like the analogy of water to which we referred in Mindset 2. Water has a way of seeping into everything. If we are not mindful, everything becomes wet, which is just not desirable. As much as 'always on' and 'always available' can seem like enhanced competitivity, 'never off' is corrosive to long-term productivity.

> One of today's biggest strategic challenges, due to our lack of time, is the inability to focus on deep, significant and challenging work.

We are writing today from the Barbican Cinema café in London. I am reminded again just how addictive email is. Only by switching off our phones, closing down emails, turning off all notifications and having out-of-office alerts on (yes, at the time of writing, these do still exist), have we found a mutual rhythm that works. The urge remains strong to check emails mid-way through paragraphs ('Give me a minute Alex, I'll look over your book in a bit'); and, unless, we are careful, the work that we deliver could end up being splendidly average. I would prefer to be disconnected with the ensuing cold turkey that this brings, and have a better chance of writing a chapter of a book, than producing a whole slurry of non-important emails. Clearly, responsibilities cannot be ignored, but do our tools serve us to be more effective, or do we end up serving the tools? Do we even become slaves to them?

I believe there are two areas to consider here. Forget work–life balance. It has become such a cliché that we have become completely desensitised to it. It is too easy to blame the evil tyranny of work, where, for many, work brings them a lot of joy and life. Instead, how do we manage to do both: work *and*

life to an exceptional standard? How do we experience what
we call work–life brilliance?

> Instead how do we manage to do both:
> work *and* life to an exceptional
> standard? How do we experience what
> we call work–life brilliance?

Is it time to live a little?

When it comes to life outside of work, many have become
numb to the true pleasure and delights of life. The transition
catchphrases at the end of a long day do not mean the same
any more. We cannot 'leave it all behind', as there is no office
to leave it all behind in. We *are* the office. It comes with us in
our pocket. And we cannot just 'switch off', as the devices we
use for both work and pleasure rarely experience us sliding
our fingers across their 5.5 inch screens to power them off.
We get in a panic if we cannot access our phones. We feel a
compulsion to stay connected for the fear of missing out.[4]

> We *are* the office. It comes with us in our
> pocket. And we cannot just 'switch off.'

So, what level of quality time do families and friendships
truly get in this culture? How do we relax, blow off steam
and enjoy ourselves when the odds are so stacked against us?
Is it too easy to rush to the endorphin release of an email
response, which results in a level of impatience when our
children ask us to read the book again? Is it too easy to be on
a meal out, sneaking a quick peek at our phone to see if there
are any messages, only for others to know we are now
distracted and emotionally checked out? The message
reminds us of work not completed. Guilt follows. Another
night, if not totally ruined, is relegated to the forgettable and
low levels of simply being … all right.

Should we feel obligated to check and respond to our messages last thing before bed? Is there an incessant pressure to be plugged in? With the plethora of platforms, is it really bad form to simply ignore some channels? Many attempt to carry out their responses in any spare moment; in between underground stops or whilst walking up the stairs. We have lost sight of the wonders around us and bump into others on the street with our eyes down. We are frenzied and hassled as a result. We do not think well, prioritise and learn to organise our lives effectively. It may seem like a company owner's dream to have someone as attentive to their work that they respond to an email at 1 am; but, when someone is not resting or enjoying a brilliance in both their work *and* life, the lack of downtime is not serving them or the organisation they work for.

It is clear, despite all this, that, for the vast majority of us, we consider the technological advancements of the cloud to dwarf the potential cost it has on us. Whether as a founder of a tech startup, a freelancer who works remotely or a company employee in and out of the office, aside from the challenge of working habits, the cloud is considered good news.

Why do some companies struggle with the cloud?

There is a major shift in mindset still needed for many corporations. Lots of individuals and cultures are reluctant to embrace the cloud. For years, these businesses have had complete control over all their data stored in local environments and in their own premises. It is tangible. They own the servers. They employ the IT directors. Why would they even entertain exploring a less tangible and visible solution when data is one of their organisation's most valuable assets? With reports of hacking and data breaches, one would be a fool to give up local control when it has, arguably, worked for years? Perhaps, as a kick back, one could also argue that you would be a fool not to capitalise on the true value in this data when others have now done so for years. Without bringing it into the cloud and having it analysed by people and tools created to extract additional value from it, precious resources and opportunities are being wasted.

It is a major psychological shift to move from owning servers and having the software and data stored inside the building, to moving towards storing your material in the cloud. There is a loss of control and a perceived greater vulnerability. For many executives, they are rightfully concerned about the risks they face with their data being stolen and hacked. By having data stored in the cloud, it is seemingly easier for people to attempt foul play. With the cloud there are two sets of security issues that they consider: access to the farm of servers and access to the business' data itself. Losing control over that is, understandably, concerning. It does not take long to look at how vulnerable data solutions have been. Not only have we seen large databases of private contact information stolen, we have seen hundreds of millions of dollars worth of Bitcoin and ongoing credit card theft. With the advancement of the internet of things, it is now easier to access and hack into these applications. Thanks to the cloud, a group was able to hack a Tesla to open its sunroof, unlock doors and even use the braking systems. We explore this more in Force 11. If the data was not stored and accessed in the cloud, the Tesla would not exist in the way we know it. The blessing is also the curse.

Naturally, we can be protectionist and, for a time, feel safe and secure. But will this last? I am reminded of one of my children's favourite films, that often gets a viewing during Friday family movie time. *The Croods* are a prehistoric family living in a dangerous time. Grug, the caveman father, has successfully managed to keep his family alive, by keeping them safely tucked away in the cave. His approach up until now has been understandable. All the other families have died. But, as the story unfolds, there is a bigger danger ahead. If they do not adjust their ways and venture into new places, they will certainly end up dead. The exasperated daughter says in her defeated moment of frustration:

> 'Anything new is bad. Curiosity is bad. Going out at night is bad. Basically, anything fun is bad. Welcome to my world!'[5]

Perhaps many employees within highly constraining companies experience a similar level of frustration. For some is it now a time to embrace a different approach? Or, put less politely, do we need to come out of our caves?

In an article by Glen Gilmore, it was reported that Huawei's rotating CEO, Ken Hu, said this about the cloud: 'The cloud is our shared, digital brain, always getting smarter.' With the surrounding new tools and devices, the cloud continues to evolve and become more powerful, more intelligent, as an ally to your strategy. Gilmore continues, 'As [the cloud] evolves, so must we to tap its great potential.'[6]

What should you do about it?

The distributed office

In a world of long commutes, dwindling fossil fuels and high office rental rates, the cloud is an indispensable asset to allow people to work together at a distance. The cloud can be used to share software services and store all necessary documents to be shared amongst colleagues. As a result, individuals can work from any connected location, using teleconferencing services for the face-to-face meetings and avoiding the unnecessary expense of office space and the waste of time in long and unproductive commutes. Many startups now operate in this mode, especially where the variety of workers ranges from employees, contractors and freelancers spread throughout the globe. The challenge for big business is to move from a mindset of needing to be present and overseeing everything to delegating and operating in confidence with a distributed network of employees.

> In a world of long commutes, dwindling fossil fuels and high office rental rates, the cloud is an indispensable asset to allow people to work together at a distance.

There are five keys to moving towards a more distributed network of employees:

1. Establish how and why this will be more effective for the customer. What initially can feel like a deterioration (with different or missing features and functionality) is usually a question of transitioning and learning the new ropes.

2. Involve the employees in the process and understand the best practical details about how and where people want to work.

3. Be vigilant about the clarity of goals and objectives as well as working out clear roles.

4. Be prepared for upheavals and teething challenges by creating contingencies.

5. Set the example from the top, to show how you can work efficiently, effectively and with empathy when working remotely.

From Microsoft Office to Google Suite

For many companies, especially big business, Microsoft Office remains the top choice for corporate software. However, there is a myriad of alternatives and these have brought with them a host of new services. The ability to mix and match is now more accepted. The locked-in subscription model with a hard-to-extricate software is no longer as appropriate. Yet, for many Microsoft Office users, even if Microsoft now has a suite in the cloud, the key element is that the software continues to be *resident* on the local computers. This can be a headache to maintain and keep up-to-date. It also tends to be more expensive. The migration from Microsoft Office to Google Suite across the range of services can feel like a quantum leap of faith with many functions generally inextricably tethered to the heritage Microsoft solutions (e.g. finance with Excel, legal with Word, sales with PowerPoint).

The Fairfax Media Company, based in Australia with over 10,000 employees and 400 media titles under management, was one such company that made the migration back in 2012. Andrew Lam-Po-Tang, then chief information officer of Fairfax Media, said, 'We saved well over half a million dollars a year in licensing fees, but the real benefits were intangible in that ultimately it helped render the culture far more collaborative.' As Lam-Po-Tang recounted, to begin with, it was a mighty battle to get everyone out of the comfort zone and move them to the Google Cloud Platform. No one likes change. There were hitches and glitches but, ultimately, the cloud services presented benefits well beyond the cost savings. If there were initially also concerns about security and privacy, it proved that the cloud is actually more secure. Lam-Po-Tang continued, 'Even our journalists, who had legitimate worries about anonymity and confidentiality for their investigations, ultimately felt comfortable. Moreover, the fact that all the software and data was in the cloud, made it easier for everyone to work together and from a distance.' For Lam-Po-Tang, the biggest win was in how the transition, including the installation of video conferencing capabilities at every desk and in every meeting room, made collaboration so much more fluid. It also helped that the software can be upgraded or patched with the click of a switch.

Amongst the keys of success in breaking through the cultural resistance to change, Lam-Po-Tang added, were the 'get out of jail' cards given to the different functions. People never felt stuck in a corner if the new solutions were to prove ineffective.

The advantages of working in the cloud

There are clear opportunites that all firms can take advantage of. As well as software and overhead cost savings, there are also the benefits of optimised operations, faster turnaround times and more collaborative ways of working.

Running a marketing agency, a lot of our work comes from two extremes on the spectrum: fast-growing tech startups and slower moving large corporations. We see the best and worst of both worlds. More often than not, we find ourselves using different sets of software solutions for the relevant organisations, but the same issues come up each time. With startups and some forward-thinking corporations, we have to ensure they are maximising their marketing stack to help them scale and move quickly. With corporate clients, we demonstrate patience, persistence and influence, recognising there is a level of resistance to working in this way. Budgets, prior work and even job security can be tied to specific software for some employees, so one always needs to show patience and empathy to understand what is needed for everyone.

Just because an IT department can be a stickler for their rules, the logic does not always follow that the more security-conscious larger organisations are are more sensible in their security than startups. Often, in reality, these companies lose pen drives, laptops and Blackberrys brimming with confidential data. Some employees in any company can lose pen drives, laptops and phones brimming with confidential data. But with larger companies there's often more people to lose the data, more data to lose and the data has a greater value attached to it. If I was a thieving data junkie, I know who's laptop I'd want. With the software we use and recommend, we could wipe the data on a lost mobile phone in a few minutes and close down access to emails and confidential information in a moment. So, much of it comes back to mindset. Work in the cloud collaboratively, be responsible with security and have the right tools at your disposal to respond quickly.

All the tools exist. But moving over to them requires change management, especially for a larger more conservative organisation. In 2008, I started using a Beta version of what is now called Google's G Suite. At the same time, I started working with Basecamp (a project management tool), HubSpot[7] (a marketing system), Xero[8] (finance software) and Salesforce[9] (a CRM system). Of course, along with the rest of the world, we were familiar with working on LinkedIn, Twitter, Facebook and YouTube. All of our client-based communication was always in the cloud. I couldn't imagine being able to work without these solutions and ones like them.

We are now in an era where internally within our organisation we have a clear reporting dashboard that enables us to be email free. Some of the benefits that I have experienced each day include:

▌ The choice for my team to work remotely from anywhere in the world, so they can live and travel where they like and not be tied down to a physical location. This gives a wider cultural understanding of the different countries our team are based in, and for those who want to travel, it beats getting a bar job in Fiji.

▌ A greater flexibility in the areas of work that different team members can and want to cover. This enables an easy way for team members to play to their strengths, and for work that is more administration-based to be outsourced to other team members who are more competent in these areas of work.

▌ With the integrated software solutions working in sync, the right people have visibility to the right information at the right time. No longer are spreadsheets or word documents emailed backwards and forwards, with people looking for the latest version. Instead, teams and clients work collaboratively and in real time on the same document.

▌ We are able to work around a 24-hour time span with different team members picking up work in different regions. One region clocks off for the evening and passes it on, to find the work completed when they wake up.

▌ The customer remains at the heart of the business and we are able to identify and track the work that is necessary to them. Everyone is always up to speed with a project without needing to request further input.

▌ The onboarding of a new team member or client is easily managed, with prepared folders, video tutorials, training manuals, processes, checklists and automated reminders. These are updated and evolved constantly as we learn more. There is an ability to scale team members more quickly as we can recruit from a wider geographic pool, aka the world.

▌ The ability to see in real time the progress on a piece of work, providing accuracy on how long it will take before a task is complete. Having data and reports always available enables better strategic decision making and a nimble and faster responses to situations.

▌ The opportunity to access skillsets that are not internally based. For instance, having AI scientists able to work on an efficiency project and for the team to have visibility and engagement around the project.

Taking your work into the cloud

There are so many benefits to working in the cloud. It is more efficient and collaborative, enabling both a faster pace of work and a higher quality of output. Alongside many millennials who have grown up cloud-native, I could never work in an organisation that did not embrace this way of working. Increasingly, we will see more ambitious and sophisticated plug and play solutions, with integrations between different cloud-based software solutions. This will enable a greater flow of data, communication and, therefore, productivity.

Zapier[10], sits in the middle of many applications and generates 'Zaps' connecting through each software's API. An application programming interface (API) is a code that allows computers to interact with each another. An API is a set of routines, protocols and tools designed for building software applications. This API access results in an action from one piece of software, resulting in a new action in another piece of software. For instance, someone who watches a video past the halfway mark, receives a different follow-up email from the person who did not watch the video at all and is, instead, added to a private Twitter list to engage with on a personal level. Not only do these 'Zaps' save incredible amounts of time, but we are seeing more intelligent applications as big data and AI overlap when working in the cloud. Now it's not just being able to access the data but, as will be explored in Forces 6 and 7, what you can do with this information that causes seismic shifts.

The irony has been that whilst corporate IT departments have discussed whether specific websites were allowed to be accessed from their premises, startups without these limitations were busy disrupting their industries. If ever I have seen the need to respond to one of those get out of the cave moments, it is now. Time to reverse the old saying, and get your head off the ground and into the clouds.

> If ever I have seen the need to respond to one of those get out of the cave moments, it is now.

A slice of PIE

Personal

1. How are you managing the pressure of being accessible and 'on' the whole time? Develop a guilt-free ability to become intentionally disconnected to keep a healthy sense of equilibrium. Perhaps have it known that, one day a week, may be your tech-free day, where you can enjoy being fully present with those around you.

2. Amongst family and friends, what cloud technology enables you to streamline tasks and communication? We would recommend Nozbe.com[11] and Remember The Milk.[12]

3. There are times when you will need information for you and your family. Sit down and write it all out, and take photos of the necessary proofs of ID that may be needed. Create an Evernote 'Notebook'[13] dedicated to information you may need, and create a confidential information 'Note' for each person. For greater protection, highlight the confidential information inside the note, and encrypt.

Internal

1. What software solutions do you need to remove from a local host and put into the cloud? In what areas do staff get frustrated about not having access to data? We would recommend that your finance, marketing, document management, sales and project management software are all cloud-based.

2. What savings would you make if your office were distributed and you could combine remote working and in-office working? Consider creating a Typeform[14] survey to assess your staff's opinion to remote working.

3. Map out the work that could be outsourced overseas more cost efficiently. Start to build out the processes to ensure a high quality of work, enabling you to kick off with a small trial project.

External

1. Try collaborating and working with external partners and clients with Google's G Suite.[15] Work on tracking progress in spreadsheets or writing up minutes from a GoToMeeting[16] conference call in Google Docs. Use Basecamp's Clientside[17] to keep everyone updated with the progress. Remember to learn the collaborative rules and expectations of each platform.

2. What services can you offer to clients and customers through the cloud that you currently rely on face-to-face appointments to do? This could include meetings, video consultations or interviews. Additionally, you may deliver training webinars, group hangouts or online brainstorming sessions. It could be hands-on accounting work, content creation or executive coaching. When you put your mind to it, it's amazing to see that many businesses can carry out a lot of their work remotely.

3. What *Zapier* or *If This Then That*[18] integrations can your organisation take advantage of? These will help you set up automatic actions across multiple platforms or apps.

Remember to learn the collaborative rules and expectations of each platform.

Security

I've got security nailed: capital letter, familiar word,
two numbers and an exclamation mark

A password is like a toothbrush. Choose a good one.
Change it regularly. And don't share it with anybody.

Anon[1]

few years back, a friend of mine was warned that
he was under surveillance by Anonymous, a
leaderless consortium of cyber vigilante hackers
led by a more or less vague mission to protect the liberty of
the internet. He had allegedly aggrieved another member of
its sprawling, loose confederation of *hacktivists*. The friend
was given due warning that, under the circumstances and
depending on the outcome of the 'investigation', he was
likely to be outed or doxxed. To be doxxed is to have the
sum total of all your digital life displayed out in the open.
This isn't limited to the content of your emails, as was the
case with Sony Pictures, which we'll explore shortly. It
could include having all your personal details, photographs,
videos, private messages, browser history and [offshore]
bank accounts exposed. The threat of such a warning
weighed heavily. He turned to advice from a few digitally
switched-on friends, started to read about the different
options left and took steps to secure his devices. How on
earth was it possible to check on all the vulnerabilities,

shore up all the holes and stay vigilant 100 per cent of the time? The truth is that just the *threat* of being exposed was plenty of concern. He lived through some very difficult months before feeling that the imminent threat was averted, possibly because the threat was just that, or because Anonymous had found other better targets.

What is it?

Cyber security is the protection of computerised systems from theft, corruption or disruption. The enemy is malware, a bucket term that encompasses all forms of hostile software, 'including computer viruses, worms, trojan horses, ransomware, spyware, adware, scareware, and other malicious programs'.[2] Each year, that list will surely grow longer.

From individuals through to corporations and governments, the importance of cyber security cannot be understated. In a study entitled 'The Future of Cybercrime & Security: Financial and Corporate Threats & Mitigation 2015–2020', published in 2015 by Juniper Research,[3] it is estimated that the cost of security breaches will reach $2.1 trillion (£1.7 trillion) for businesses globally by 2019. Those who get access into systems, we call hackers. Hackers come in different forms and have different motivations. Some hackers may be operating as pure criminals: stealing money, identity data or engaging in corporate or state espionage. Some hackers have a purpose that is self-proclaimed as ethical. Others merely hack for the entertainment value. Many possess a great power.

To the extent that a device is connected to the internet, it is prone to be *hacked*. Cyber security is the new Wild West as far as the underworld is concerned, presenting plenty of legal, moral, technical and organisational challenges.

How would you like to be hacked?

The *vast* majority of people, whether or not they are in business, are vulnerable and not only at risk of being hacked, but are often entirely ignorant of what to do if and when they do get hacked. They respond in different ways:

▋ Put their head in the sand: 'It won't happen to me!'

▋ Buy the 'best' security software.

▋ Never use social media or USB keys.

▋ Never use any *public* Wi-Fi.

> Privacy, like the right to anonymity, is a defining principle of a healthy society and, by extension, a respectable democracy.

As an exercise to open the eyes, we dare you to watch this short movie, *Take this Lollipop*.[4] You will need to connect via Facebook, assuming you have signed up. This personalised movie is guaranteed to grab your attention and remind you that: 'When it's free, you are the media.'

Many smart people are asking whether a lack of privacy is the right price to pay for all these free services. As Alessandro Acquisti said in his stirring TED talk,[5] 'Privacy is not about having something *negative* to hide ...'
We, personally, believe that privacy, like the right to anonymity, is a defining principle of a healthy society and, by extension, a respectable democracy. Acquisti concluded his TED talk saying, 'One of the defining fights of our times will be the fight for the control over our personal information.' Moreover, the question of privacy is not just a personal fight. The ramifications are much broader and touch on commerce and politics. Dana Boyd,[6] from the Data & Society Research Institute[7] and a principal researcher

at Microsoft Research, said in an interview on Do Not Track[8] (4'00–4'17):

> *'It's no longer about you. It's about how what you put out here affects everybody else. When you become a part of the system of data, your data is used to judge other people. Your data is used to assert power over other people.'*

Why do you need to worry?

Businesses need to be seriously concerned about cyber security because it is a real source of risk. The blanket response that everything needs to be protected is not only highly expensive and draconian, but also it can have a debilitating effect on creativity, reactivity and employee satisfaction.

As an individual, you need to be proactive about the protection of your personal and private information. This includes your financial data and accounts, details of your family and sensitive health information. What you need or want to hide is largely a question of personal comfort and circumstance. However, once you choose to go public, it is near impossible to wind back the clock.

As a business leader or entrepreneur, the protection of your intellectual property, confidential business plans and clients' data are amongst the high-value targets that can be prone to outside interest. In business, employees will have a tendency to believe that the corporate system (firewall and antivirus software) will provide the necessary protection. As a result, they are liable to let their guards down. In matters of cyber security, the optimal solution is a combination of the best adapted system *and* an alert and responsible workforce.

In matters of cyber security, the optimal solution is a combination of the best adapted system *and* an alert and responsible workforce.

But, along with the risk that this valuable information can be stolen, damaged or manipulated, another real concern is the revelation of what could be called the 'gaping gaps'. These are gaps between what is said and what is done by the company. The gaping gaps exist between the internal discourse and the outside reality, the commercial message and the shareholder message, what the employees feel or know and what they say. The key concepts that underpin this further risk in cyber security are: *transparency* and *integrity*. In the case of transparency, there is a greater risk of exposure of what goes on behind closed doors. As we have seen time and again, many activities, including internal emails and 'private' text messages, can now be outed. Second, and somewhat related, a company's integrity has weight in the valuation of the corporate brand. Integrity is tied in intimately with trust. The wider the gap between what is said and what is done, results in a greater likelihood of one's integrity being called into question. The perceived character of the CEO and all the company staff will have a bearing on the brand's trustworthiness. Some hacks are designed to expose these gaps.

> A company's integrity has weight in the valuation of the corporate brand. Integrity is tied in intimately with trust.

The hacking of Sony

For a number of reasons, Sony has been the object of many cyber hacks. In April 2015, Sony Pictures Entertainment, part of the $72 billion Japanese firm, had 170,000 internal emails published on WikiLeaks. These emails not only revealed the acerbic, unsavoury and ethically questionable management practices, they exposed Sony's greater 'evil' in its links and ties to the Government. As Gawker[9] reported, 'The Sony Archives show that behind the scenes [Sony] is an influential corporation, with ties to the White House ... with an ability to impact laws and policies, and with connections to the US military-industrial complex.'

> The perceived integrity of the CEO and all the company staff will have a bearing on the brand's trustworthiness.

The Group in Japan has also been the subject of numerous attacks by Anonymous. Sony became a target because of its perceived ethical improprieties, dating back to the aggressive stance it took in 2005 to digital rights management. Beyond the victim that Sony has become to various hacking groups, the company has an infamously poor cyber security practice. Its internal culture seems to undermine any systems it puts in place. This is further proof that the healthiest of cyber security systems involves the people at least as much as the systems.

What should you do about it?

There are four key actions to be taken with your cyber security: core data, culture, contingency plans and communication internally.

1. First, and by no means the easiest, is to identify the absolutely *core* data that is truly strategic to protect and apply resources to surround that information. This is sometimes referred to as the *Crown Jewels* approach. Give all information and systems a hierarchy in terms of sensitivity and what you need to protect.

2. Second, whilst it is important to have someone centrally take charge of system acquisitions and integration, it is critical to develop a *culture* where *everyone* is held personally responsible for their security.

3. Third, develop a *contingency* plan for *when* your data will be hacked. Best practice would be to rehearse on a regular basis an attack via simulations or 'war games'.

4. Fourth, work intentionally and *communicate* internally to eliminate areas where you or your organisation's integrity could be called into question.

Needless to say, cyber security is an evolving feast and, therefore, individuals and businesses should not be relaxed about it. New cyber hacks are being invented and perpetuated daily. One cannot rely on a static defence. It is a generally accepted fact that cyber criminals are at least a step ahead of protective software. Moreover, with a seemingly unending pipe of digital innovations, the inevitable arrival of new devices, platforms and tools will mean new opportunities for vulnerabilities and openings. As a result, we must be in a constant state of learning.

Staying ahead of the tide

We need to be able to distinguish between what is fact and fiction in the risks and holes of cyber security. There are three harmful myths that make cyber security such a disruptive force:

1. By having a strong firewall, my system will be safe. *Wrong.* Your firewall is only going to be updated *after* the latest virus has been detected.

2. If I do *everything* I possibly can, I will be safe. *Wrong.* Your broader network, including your suppliers, are part of the security risk.

3. Nothing I do or have is worth being hacked. *Wrong.* Your naive computer and identity are entirely desirable, not to mention your personal data and financial assets.

Here are five other myths about cyber security that need to be debunked:

1. **Your Apple operating system is secure.** There was a time when it was considered that Apple had too small a market share and therefore was not worth the hacker's time. The second myth is that Apple's operating system is so secure that hacks cannot be made. Today, using Apple is no longer a safe haven from malware and viruses.

2. **If you have not clicked on a link, you are safe.** You do
not need to click on a link to get infected from visiting a
web page. Now just visiting a site can be sufficient to be
infested with malware.[10]

3. **Your mobile is safe.** Your smartphone is distinctly
vulnerable to malware, especially when connecting to
public Wi-Fi networks.

4. **Security is the same as privacy.** You cannot rely on
security software and systems. You need to have your own
privacy 'system' where you manage your own data outputs.

5. **Private or incognito browsing will hide your online
activity.** The terminology is quite deceiving. In fact,
incognito mode only helps keep one's browsing history
confidential from others who may use the same machine.
Outside of the porosity between private and non-private
browsers, one is still vulnerable in incognito mode to
many plug-ins with loose coding as well as malicious
websites that can steal data outright.

Does security stunt creativity?

> In the world of tech, it seems the cloak
> and dagger mindset is almost required as
> companies try to leapfrog one another.

In the world of tech, it seems the cloak and dagger mindset
is almost required as companies try to leapfrog one another.
They need to keep a distance between themselves and the
competition who are coming from all quarters, all the time.
Apple is famously guarded about its plans and has
organised itself in such a way as to disperse knowledge to
avoid a total break-in. Samsung, whose headquarters are
located near Seoul, has created a massive campus 13 miles
south of the capital, called Samsung Digital City. An area
covering nearly 400 acres, the Samsung Digital City hosts

about 35,000 Samsung employees. The complex provides, amongst other services and amenities, free healthcare, 500 shuttle buses and scores of sporting facilities for its employees.

The entrance to Samsung Digital City for employees is rigorously controlled. For visitors, the examination is fit for a maximum security prison. The first time I arrived, it took 45 minutes to get through. Once my ticket came up, all of my belongings were thoroughly searched and all of my electronic equipment was tagged and secured. Specifically, each of the USB keys were logged and put in a tamper-proof, unopenable bag. The individual serial number of each computer device and phone was also logged. All cameras and recording devices were blocked with a tamper-proof tape. The whole process took about 20 minutes. Every morning, I was subjected to the same search and lock-down process. On the fifth consecutive day, despite a number of the security guards recognising me, I found there were no pleasantries or relaxation in their communication. I think it is fair to say, things were lacking in the laughter department when I tried to crack an Apple-related joke with one of the big guys. Awkward.

Samsung's worry about leakages is certainly warranted, given its sensitive military branch and the constant risk of competitor espionage. However, do the effects of such a broad and thorough mania for secrecy have an impact on the creativity and fluidity of communications?

Looking at your security – where are you exposed?

From our observations, people fall into one of four camps when it comes to managing their online privacy, shown in the following figure.

Comfortably exposed (+/-knowledgeable)	Out there but not aware/concerned	Minimal or zero presence	Well protected (knowledgeable)
Naivexperts	**Vulnerables**	**Stayawayers**	**Pro-fessors**

The four categories for how people manage their online privacy

Pro-fessors

At the far end of the scale (far right of the figure), there are the *Pro-fessors* who are using the internet and mobile devices with a well-versed and purposeful system of protection. Typically, they might be white-hat or black-hat hackers. Maybe they are affiliated with the amorphous *Anonymous*. Their defining characteristic is that they have a superior understanding of the inner workings of the internet, cyber security and data protection. The motivations for these individuals to stay off or under the radar differ very much, from good to ill-intentioned reasons. The Pro-fessors are, by definition, at the cutting edge, able to bypass any line of protection, all the while protecting themselves from external threats.

Stayawayers

In the second category are the *Stayawayers* who prefer not to cultivate an online presence. Often, they do not even have one. Typically, they are far too nervous or suspicious. They might just not have enough reason to care about going online. They simply prefer not to be out there. They tend to have a negligible online presence, to the best of their abilities. Stayawayers might be senior executives of well-known companies, elder statesmen or high-profile bankers. The defining characteristic of Stayawayers is that they do not believe these new technologies will provide a net benefit to their lives or work.

Vulnerables

The third category, comprising the largest and most at risk set of people, is the *Vulnerables*. These *netizens* are using an array of free services and are either not aware or sufficiently concerned about the way their personal data is being monetised. At some level, they might be aware that their privacy is being violated but, on balance, they do not have the cynicism, knowledge or capability to do anything about it.

Naivexperts

The final class of people, we call the *Naivexperts*. They are comfortable with the notion of exchanging their data for a free service. Naivexperts are more or less aware of the level of privacy incursion and have a greater or lesser form of security regarding their online presence. The defining characteristic of Naivexperts is that they tend to be optimistic about the fundamental principles and ethics of the larger forces driving the internet.

The dangers of the lockdown mentality

There are multiple problems with applying a total lockdown mentality within a business. For starters, even in the most confidential of businesses, there is a need to maintain a healthy pipeline of ideas. Creativity and fluid communications are the lifeblood of innovation. Granted, constraints can be a driver of innovative thinking, but virtual handcuffs will tend to kill the creativity. Second, there is a patent war for the best talent and having working conditions that are uncomfortable will weigh on the attractiveness of that company. Third, and not least important, a business needs partners. These inevitably will include third-party suppliers and external associations. If a company chooses to tighten down everything, the flexibility and fluidity of relationships with external parties are likely to be severely compromised.

The five actions to be taken immediately

If you are the singular and dedicated object of an expert attack, it is unlikely that, shy of living in a cave, anything you do will save you. That said, to make it substantially more difficult and to cause your identity and online activity harder to hack than the next person's, these are the five most important actions to be taken.

> Since it is impossible to keep everything protected, focus your efforts on the most keenly sensitive information.

1. **Prioritise your most sensitive information.** Since it is impossible to keep everything protected, focus your efforts on the most keenly sensitive information. It is also a good idea to understand that *anything* you do that involves a computer can be subject to a hack.

2. **As an individual, review your own passwords.** Make them more complex and varied. Using a password manager can be a *better* solution, but one such service, LastPass, was itself the subject of a hack. Nevertheless, it's much wiser to use one as opposed to a password like Mushntgrumble2018!

3. **Enable double authentication.** Many platforms offer a system whereby a second and separate lock, like a text message to your mobile, must be opened to gain access. Just make sure you remember to update your number on any applications if you change your phone number. Doh!

4. **Ethical hacking.** For your business, consider hiring an ethical hacker or setting up a reward bounty for finding vulnerabilities in your system.

5. **Education and training.** Your people are by far your weakest link. Explore ways to enhance you and your team's understanding of how to best take care. 'It doesn't matter what firewall or intrusion detection you use if your employees don't understand the significance of data

privacy and protection,' said Anthony R. Howard, IT consultant and author of *The Invisible Enemy: Black Fox.*[11]

Other tips and tricks to stay safe(r)

When you look for online services for your communications, storage or payment services, make sure to use the more respected brands that have a reputation for being security conscious. If none is totally secure, there are still some brands that merit more trust than others. Today, those brands would include the likes of Amazon, Google, Apple and Facebook.

Whichever service you choose, take a close look at the company's privacy policies for their respect of, and efforts to, protect your data. Fortunately, there are investigative sites such as ProPublica[12] that are on the lookout for borderline practices. A Google scan is also a good starting point to see if they are in the news and outspoken in their position. Certainly, it is also worth evaluating the CEO's ethical track record. Another good indicator of a healthy application – although, admittedly, it can also be somewhat aggravating – is that there are frequent updates.

When using Wi-Fi in public, know that you are exposing yourself to the security of that location. At a minimum, do not use such hotspots for any confidential activities. Second, ensure that the sites you visit are preceded with the term HTTPS (the added S is for secure). When using applications like email that access the internet, make sure to enable SSL (secure sockets layer). This means that the data communications will be encrypted. A higher level of protection will be to use a reputable VPN (virtual private network) service, such as CyberGhost, that effectively scrambles your online activity. At home, it is a good idea to set up three different Wi-Fi accounts, one reserved for the computer devices (smartphone, computer and tablet), a second for guests and a third for other connected (e.g. IoT) devices. If hiding your router names is also a useful idea, there is nothing more vulnerable than an easy password.

Whilst these tips may already look like a long list and a burden to implement, we recommend you get used to it. Tomorrow's list will change and, in all likelihood, will be even longer. But putting the time and work in now will be a lot less painful than finding all your private and confidential information hacked.

You have been warned.

> Are there any personal 'gaping gaps' that you can take greater responsibility for, so your personal life and public persona are aligned?

A slice of PIE

Personal

1. Do you have the same password for multiple accounts? Consider putting aside a few minutes to go in and update your passwords using a service like 1Password[13] or LastPass.[14]

2. Are there any personal 'gaping gaps' that you can take greater responsibility for, so your personal life and public persona are aligned?

3. Have you set up double authentication on each of the sites you use that enable this? You can check on Two Factor Auth (2FA)[15] to see if your site offers 2FA.

Internal

1. Are there passwords that are stored on shared documents within your company? If you are a startup, how liberally do you share the company banking information with team members? You may trust them, but how careful are they with your data?

▶

2. In the UK, the Information Commissioner's Office (ICO) has a number of good training materials and videos. We appreciate you may not find data protection videos on the ICO exactly Hollywood material. But remember films on Netflix about data are typically focused on people, businesses and organisations being hacked. Want a drama of your own? Choose the ICO over Netflix for now, do the hard work and then watch the next hacking film reassured, and with (a little) smugness.

3. Is it time to close the gate to any possibility of 'Name The Issue' gate? Are you communicating internally and regularly to eliminate any areas where your integrity could be called into question?

External

1. Map out the most important customer data to protect and list it in order of priority. Ensure from the outset that only the right people have access to the data. Data protection and strong systems sit closely aligned, so you may want to consider working towards getting your company ISO9001[17] approved.

2. Who in your supply chain has access to any of your data and what service level agreements do you have with them on their security procedures?

3. In order to be responsible and to have your own peace of mind covered, build out a contingency plan and then run through the response steps after a 'pretend' data hack.

5

Internet of things (IoT)

Do we really get to have robots at home?

> As the internet of things advances, the very notion of a clear dividing line between reality and virtual reality becomes blurred, sometimes in creative ways.[1]
>
> *Geoff Mulgan*[2]

What is it?

The internet of things (IoT) or internet of objects is an umbrella topic for the connection and the connectability of the real world to the internet. Everyday objects in the workplace, at home or in nature will have sensors that can communicate both with one another and with us. 'The reason sensors are so important is because they provide context.'[3] The growth of these IoT devices, which are able to connect with each other, is predicted to expand exponentially over the coming years.

Data from Juniper Research[4] predicts that the number of IoT connected devices will increase by 285 per cent, reaching 38.5 billion in 2020, up from 13.4 billion in 2015. Other organisations have forecast anywhere between 20 and 50 billion for 2020. The numbers will vary according to the inclusion or exclusion of smartphones, tablets and computers using the internet. We have included these items in the numbers, as we believe the territories of these devices will evolve and the lines between each will blur.

Today, IoT is an abstract term for most companies as businesses continue to grapple with being connected through the internet and the smartphone. The pace of change is phenomenal. New advancements in miniaturisation and the promise of the revolutionary material graphene could see the proliferation of sensors and trackers in all forms of objects. We are already seeing connected cities, cars, homes, factories and offices. Tomorrow, there will be virtually no limit to what might be connectable. Businesses and governments are struggling to keep up. Regardless, technology marches on and IoT will soon be everywhere.

> We are already seeing connected cities, cars, homes, factories and offices. Tomorrow, there will be virtually no limit to what might be connectable.

Technologies such as LoRa (USA), Sigfox (France) and LTE-M[5] are working to wire the world with low-power, wide-area networks (LPWANs[6]), albeit in a fight to establish a standard. Meanwhile, companies such as Ayla Networks[7] (USA), Eurotech[8] (Italy) and Filament[9] (USA) are providing software and support for IoT related activities. As such, businesses will soon have all the necessary infrastructure, tools and partners to take advantage of IoT.

It will be key for businesses to upgrade their data analytics capabilities, since IoT will make big data a dramatic and dynamic reality. McKinsey released a study that projected that IoT could deliver an economic benefit in the range of $3.9 trillion to $11.1 trillion by 2025.[10] From a marketing angle, where there is a strong focus on getting to know your customers, IoT is an incredibly powerful force once the technology and approach to working with it are mastered. There will be ways to create a fuller picture of a customer, even to the point of providing a complete single-customer view. As a result, there will be opportunities to use IoT in order to provide and deliver more customised, contextually relevant content, offers and enhanced customer experience.

But it is not just in marketing where businesses will see the benefits. There will be innovative ways to create and provide new and improved goods and services as R&D will be improved with access to real time and increased data points. Instead of having to guess what customers will want, the data will provide much clearer insights. Additionally, we will see improvements to operations within a business. Whether it be in transportation or resource management, security or office facilities, management of stock and goods or human resources and many more internal workings of an organisation, there will be greatly enhanced data, enabling significant improvements to be made.

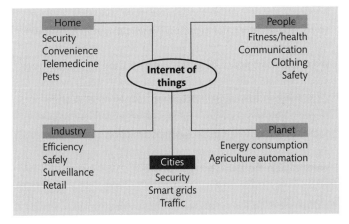

Everything is connected; internet of things applied to different segments

---

Imagine this . . .

Looking out of the window of her office, Kay Hinks was adding the final touches to her CEO address to shareholders as she made herself a cup of coffee. It was raining at last, and she was relieved to think that her sprinklers at home would have automatically turned off, thanks to the rain gauge. She was looking forward to a celebratory dinner, and was grateful the food delivery would be stocking her fridge back up with her favourite items. But before she went to the meeting, she had been nagged for the last 21 hours by her watch to hit the office's treadmill. After a 22 minutes workout, she knew she would be in optimum condition to deliver her speech.

The company she had founded, XSPARE ABC Inc., a leader in industrial spare parts, had registered strong double-digit growth again. The company's security index had been at 99.9 for 14 months straight since she had approved the plan for IDIoT-Proof installation. All heavy equipment was equipped to communicate with the other machines and the sensors in employees' helmets on the factory floor. The insight had been to insert the sensors in helmets because, previously, too often staff felt that a helmet was useless against falling debris. Now, they knew that the helmets served another more important purpose – to communicate with all the moving machinery and heavy crates. With the new tracking system, based on blockchain identification, the drone deliveries of XSpare's spare parts were now faster, more secure and efficient. Energy consumption metrics had shown considerable improvements thanks to the new flexi-weather sensors. Hinks was satisfied that her SSS approach, 'Smart Safe Steward', had borne its fruits. Her next ambition was to use the stockpile of data from the sensors embedded inside the spare parts to push the innovation labs further.

As illustrated in the case above, the application of IoT is by no means limited to consumer devices, such as the infamous wireless fridge. Yet, most media is focused on the consumer angle. The reach and sophistication of IoT is, possibly, seen as mundane, but we have high expectations to see wider networks and broad applications.

How will IoT affect business?

There are four core groups who are affected by changes with IoT and we refer to them as DDEC. Firstly, those businesses who work directly to develop IoT devices. Secondly, businesses who are focused on the data that come from the devices. Thirdly, businesses that embed the sensors into different products and then, finally, the consumers using the devices.

If the internet of (all) things is a long way off, little by little we are seeing different industries look to connect their objects to the internet. The opportunities to connect objects in the physical world for purposes of business are seemingly boundless. It is not a question of if, but how and when businesses will need to incorporate IoT into their strategic plans.

In the near term, where immediate payoff is likely to be greatest, the area we see a lot of growth is within health and fitness. Though the private sector is leading the charge, the ubiquitous nature of IoT requires a broader eco-system in order to have the greatest leverage and impact. For instance, the connection between doctor and patient is one of the more pressing issues of our world, especially where the age pyramid is top heavy, as is found in the likes of Germany, Japan and Spain. An initiative we find interesting is BodyGuardian[11] by Preventice Solutions, which allows patient monitoring by doctors at a distance. BodyGuardian Heart is a small wireless cardiac monitor that, once prescribed by a doctor, is designed to capture and detect irregular heart beats. The data is sent to a smartphone that transfers the information directly to the doctor's office. The Pebbell 2 GPS Tracker, is a handy device for those who have relatives with Dementia or Alzheimer's. When someone does go walkabout, you can see where they are, and can speak to them through the Pebble. If they're not likely to take their keys, the GPS Smart Sole is a sole insert that fits inside their shoe, giving you more reassurance. When you're out looking for them, it takes a lot less time to track them down.

The French company, Babolat, specialising in racquet sports, developed a connected version of its highest end tennis racquet. The Babolat Pure Drive racquet measures and analyses your strokes for power, spin, location and more. Synchronising via Bluetooth, the data can be read via an application for a better understanding of your tennis game. The key then is to use that data to improve your game!

> Companies are having to learn to organise and react to the massive influx of information.

We are also seeing IoT expand in industrial contexts. In the oil and gas area, IoT has made good headway in machine-to-machine data exchanges. Companies such as General Electric (Predix), Indian-based Flutura (Cerebra), Ambyint[12] and WellAware[13] provide state-of-the-art monitoring solutions. Sensors and monitors for wellheads and pumpjacks help to optimise the chemical mixes, reduce operating expenses and cut down safety hazards. Meanwhile, with all the new data being churned out, the analytics needs to be adapted to be 'smart' and companies are having to learn to organise and react to the massive influx of information. As with all data, it is what you do with the data that matters.

Why do you need to worry?

IoT will end up being a thorn in the foot for businesses who are laggards and do not anticipate the impact it will have in their sector. Where it may not affect all sectors, it will have a wider reach than many of us may anticipate. As seen with big data and AI, there is a lot of work that businesses need to embark on. Gathering the data is one thing, but leaders in business need to understand the data for research, data for relationships and data for revenue. As explored in Force 7 Big Data, we call this DataR3.

> As with all data, it is what you do with the data that matters.

Data and research

USA-based John Bean Tech, the world's largest manufacturer of airport equipment, has placed sensors and geo-tags on its machines to provide data. This data enables them to predict vehicle movement and operational bottlenecks and, as a result, it cuts down any delays on the tarmac.

The customer's physical journey around a retailer's store can provide a lot of background understanding about that customer. A smartwatch will pick up and gather data at points in the customer's physical journey. It is not inconceivable that, in the future, smartwatches, with appropriate permissions built in, will be able to provide biometric data to the retailer. The IoT device tracks what aisles the shopper visits, what products are picked up, how long they are held for and when they are put back down. The data could show they had decided to put something back at the last minute or they have tried the same dress on more than once. This information would be valuable to retailers wishing to sell new or additional products to their existing customers. Going even a step further, as the smartwatch picks up the heartbeat, could one imagine measuring and correlating excitement with purchase intention?

The role of IoT in healthcare will be both exciting and frightening, possibly in equal measure for some time. Geneticist Michael Snyder, a professor at the Stanford University School of Medicine, initially developed a way for the Apple watch to detect in advance (via a high heart rate and raised skin temperature) if someone was coming down with a cold. An in-depth study of 60 people wearing biometric sensors was able to establish baseline measurements and deviations that were symptomatic of other conditions.[14] They are currently building the algorithm to commercialise the biometric sensors. One can quickly imagine the impact for doctors and pharmacies. Going forward, what would be the usage of such data in all organisations? Will staff be invited to wear sensors to avoid accidentally contaminating their colleagues? Or, perhaps, to fight against absenteeism? Try pulling a sickie then!

Businesses will get left behind if they are not using data to research and gather information about their customers and internal operations. The challenge in all of these areas rests in having a standardised solution. Devices need to be able to talk with each other but, currently, due to walled gardens, there is a lack of open data available. Those who are able to move beyond this point and develop meaningful partnerships will have an advantage.

Data and relationships – the partners

Businesses need each other. Some businesses creating IoT products or embedding sensors into other products need larger data samples to test and grow their technology. Larger organisations typically have a bigger customer base, employment base and broader reaching data opportunities. Those within larger organisations need tech and IoT startups to enable them to gather and interpret the data, streamline their operations and create new market opportunities.

> Partnerships take both time and resources to become established but, most importantly, they require trust.

Partnership first movers typically have a strong advantage. Partnerships take both time and resources to become established but, most importantly, they require trust. Businesses need to develop strong levels of trust if a partner's data hose needs to be opened and research and development plans are discussed. Partners need to learn from each other and understand the opportunities that emerge from the collaboration. Firms do not tend to form partnerships with your partner's competitor. Subsequently, if you missed out on this opportunity, you may find yourself having to settle for less significant partners as the best relationships have already been formed. Remember the playground, back at school? You may have been the geeky one lined up against the wall, finding yourself last to be picked. Well now's the time to get ahead of the pack and do the picking. After all, the geeks will inherit the earth.*

An example of an effective IoT partnership would be PitPat's[15] relationship with insurance companies. PitPat can be described as a Fitbit for dogs, enabling dog owners to ensure their dogs get the right level of exercise. At first glance, one may consider it to be a niche product, and it is. But their partnership with insurance companies has opened up many more opportunities. With the animal health insurance market valued at a potential of £2.5 billion in the UK,[16] this enables insurance companies to charge less than their competitors for dog owners who can show through their PitPats that their dogs are healthy. The insurance companies have sophisticated data on the likelihood of claims based on the details of a dog. Now that they are able to cross pollinate this data with a dog's exercising habits, it provides a unique solution for being more competitive.

Data and relationships – the customers

Many companies are keen to get on the bandwagon of connected goods. Technically, all connected items, be they connected tennis racquets, cars or hairbrushes, are part of IoT, even if the smartphone is often the conduit to the internet. In

---

*reference 'The Geeks Will Inherit The Earth' song by 'I Fight Dragons' from their album KABOOM! http://www.ifightdragons.com/

the case of Babolat, the underlying Pure Drive racquet is a great tennis racquet. However, on using it, I found the reliability was not good and the synchronisation had lots of bugs. Additionally, the wired download failed to work when the plug broke. Taking a wider look, a number of new technological IoT devices that are launched on crowdfunding sites like Kickstarter, often have failings, but consumers still put up with them. We have a patience for Kickstarter launches and new innovations that we do not have for established brands. But that will not last as the market matures.

L'Oréal announced its connected hairbrush at CES 2017 (Consumer Electronics Show), which at £160, is not cheap and represents a move away from their typical products. Time will tell if the consumer is prepared to fork out such sums for a L'Oréal hairbrush and, more saliently, whether L'Oréal customer services will be able to manage the inevitable bugs and technical issues related to the connectivity.

Brands need to provide a good level of care and attention in their customer service. It is not enough to be proud of the technology, the customers need to be bowled over by the service they receive as well.

Taking responsibility for the security of data, as we discussed in Mindset 2, is an area of great concern when it comes to the connectivity of all objects to the internet. Breaches of private data, such as personal biometrics or home presence and activity, will not be tolerated. With the vast quantity of interconnected devices, data protection is a major concern for consumers and brands alike. We have already seen examples or threats of hacking into the Tesla car, drones, children's toys (the Cayla case)[17] and aeroplane controls.[18] Shodan[19] is an IoT search engine and it can show, for instance, where connected refrigerators that have not been secured or obscured can be found.[20] Shodan helps to expose and educate about one of the bigger challenges of IoT: security and privacy.

Data and revenue – the ecosystems

IoT devices and the data that comes from them provide an opportunity to create new and additional revenue. This can be related to those creating devices and those working with data, as seen with PitPat and the insurance companies. But, as much as health is one of the core frontiers for IoT devices, the home is where some of the biggest advancements have been made. Still the remit of a relatively exclusive club, Nest[21] is, perhaps, the most symbolic consumer application of IoT. Founded by Tony Fadell and Matt Rogers in 2010 and then sold to Google for $3.2 billion in 2014, Nest allows the homeowner to control their home from a distance. The power of Nest is found in the ability to connect all the devices at home together. Other companies, such as General Electric, Amazon, Whirlpool and Mercedes Benz, are able to tap into that network and there is a growing list of brands and products that work with Nest.[22]

> **The move into ecosystems is one of the most dramatic developments in IoT.**

The move into ecosystems is one of the most dramatic developments in IoT. Once you are tied into an ecosystem like Nest, it is hard to move to another company, because the ecosystem has your data conveniently in one place. Where heating may not feel significant enough to maintain historical and predictive data, if a device is tied into an Under Armour platform like MyFitnessPal, you may be far more reluctant to lose access to this data. Your training patterns, health and fitness statistics, and accountability and support network may have taken years to gather.

In some businesses we see people increasingly tied into these IoT relationships. If your office has developed a supplier arrangement where the supplier automatically knows and delivers your stock orders, through sensors in your stock room, it may feel like a huge hassle, risk and cost to consider moving suppliers. And people currently say it is hard to change banks!

What should you do about it?

For some organisations, there will be an understandable caution to embracing IoT. IoT devices, typically popularised by a Fitbit or smart fridge, may seem so alien to a company's core offering that there is not even a need to consider them. Stating the obvious, IoT does not need to be a core priority for some sectors. But it will certainly be more important in other niches.

> You may ignore IoT but other companies are still gathering data on your customers, talking to them in new ways and using it to their commercial advantage.

There will also be a level of fear that some leaders will have, which causes an inertia and a hesitancy to make the most of these opportunities. A consideration when forming partnerships is whether it will be detrimental to allow other firms access to the data you have. Businesses need to choose their partners wisely and, as we explore in Force 4, the security steps should be an essential requirement to have in place. As much as one can be cautious, it is going to be far more detrimental not to move quickly enough. There's rarely a prize called last mover advantage. Businesses had this same loss of control, as a result of the transparent nature of social media. Through our consultative work, the argument we have presented to businesses over the years would be: 'You may ignore social media but your customers are still going to be talking about you on it. The question is, do you want to be a part of that conversation?' The extra argument we present to businesses now is: 'You may ignore IoT but other companies are still gathering data on your customers, talking to them in new ways and using it to their commercial advantage. The question is, do you want to be a part of *that* conversation?'

When it comes to IoT, big data analytics and AI, the current central and most important question to ask is, 'Do you have the right experts and skills to gather, interpret and leverage the data?' To be able to understand the habits, rituals and movement of your customers is of immense value. It helps build a clearer picture of your customers and the decisions they make. But it is not just the external that is important. Internal data from within your organisation can bring increased efficiencies and improvements.

Where would the data that comes from IoT have the greatest potential impact on your business?

> When it comes to IoT, big data analytics and AI, the current central and most important question to ask is, 'Do you have the right experts and skills to gather, interpret and leverage the data?'

A plan for implementation

Step 1 Understand from your customers' perspective the different ways they interact with your brand. Allow the customer journey (a framework to help improve customer experience) to highlight the service, product delivery and ongoing customer care. How would you like to keep in touch with your customers and what data do you want at each of these stages? In exchange for requesting this data, it is important to consider what you can offer to your customers in return.

Step 2 Look at your staff and suppliers, contractors and partners, and the steps taken to fulfil their work. There may be different touch points, locations or data that would be mutually beneficial to all parties. As a result, there may be the opportunity to carry out a joint initiative around this.

Step 3   By building up a data action plan, outline the data you have around your customers and operations. This may help identify any data that is needed or missing. Think through how this data could help improve customer service, increase sales or improve innovation.

Step 4   If there are strong benefits, look at which devices, partnerships or services would enable you to get that data. What arrangements could you develop to grow in this direction? What obstacles do you need to overcome in order to forge a way forward?

Step 5   When you have access to the data, who will help make sense of it, detailing the commercial advantages? This may result in changing business practices, communication methods and operational logistics. As a result, there will need to be an evaluation of the ongoing improvements to your business built into the project.

A slice of PIE

Personal

1. You have seen them in feeds, noticed them in articles or have heard others talk about them. We imagine there may be some IoT devices that fascinate you. Go and indulge yourself, and look to understand more about the product and benefits it can bring to you.

2. With time at such a premium, it is time (pun intended) to find the single biggest time-saving device. Driverless cars not allowed, but everything else is up for grabs. Get your Flipboard app out, Google at your fingertips and get hunting for treasure.

3. Have you explored an IoT hub for your home to connect all your devices? We would recommend the Samsung

SmartThings Hub,[23] Amazon's Echo,[24] Google's Nest[25] and Apple's HomeKit.[26] Why don't you dive in, intrigue your friends and see what IoT can do for you and your household?

Internal

1. Smartphone apps and HR software can enable your remote team to work together and stay updated with tasks. How can you foster this communication amongst your team? Check out the HR platform, Namely.com.[27]

2. IoT enables smart labelling which uses printed electronic sensors. The smart labels are helpful for supply chain tracking, and give the opportunity for businesses to look at and analyse the transportation routes that are taken to streamline times and costs of deliveries.

3. Amazon Business[28] aims to deliver to businesses what it delivered to people through Amazon.com. There is a lot of time spent on restocking supplies, but using Amazon Dash[29] means your office supplies come your way with the press of a button.

External

1. How could your business take advantage of the opportunities that are present with Amazon Business? Have you thought of becoming a seller or an affiliate through this platform?

2. With whom could you enter into a collaboration either as a business creating IoT devices or a business with access to a large customer base?

3. Once you have the data you want through IoT, how can you use it meaningfully? What good could come out of such a project?

Artificial intelligence (AI)

What am I thinking now? And now?

> Numbers do not feel. Do not bleed or weep or hope.
> They do not know bravery or sacrifice. Love or
> allegiance. At the very apex of callousness you will find
> only ones and zeroes.[1]
>
> *Amie Kaufman and Jay Kristoff*

What is it?

Artificial intelligence (AI) is the development and use of
machines to function in ways normally associated with the
cognitive functions of the human brain. This human brain
functionality can include such capabilities as problem
solving, decision making, language translation, speech and
visual recognition.

The idea of robots with independent thought is far from new;
it has been around since Karel Čapek's play, *Robota*, in the
1920s. Moreover, the practical development of computers
capable of mirroring human intelligence began in the 1970s.
But things are now accelerating intensely. For example, we
are now seeing AI applications seamlessly embedded in our
smartphones (e.g. Google Voice, Apple Siri), in web browsers
(e.g. Google's RankBrain algorithm or Wikipedia's Objective

Revision Evaluation Service (ORES) that helps vet the new content, as well as in many call centres (voice recognition).

Thanks to significant progress in the science of artificial intelligence accompanied with access to the cloud and increased processing power, AI is truly on the cusp of becoming universally recognised. The scale and scope of what is possible with AI is vast, ranging from completing very elemental tasks, learning and self-correction all the way up to areas of autonomy.

Sophistication	Simple	Advanced	Future
State	Existing	Developing	Prospective
Application	Chatbots	Assisted driving	Fully autonomous
AI technology	If this then that	Deep learning	TBC

State of advancement in AI

In the figure above, the scale of AI goes from the simple on the left to the supremely complex and prospective on the right. The right side of the scale brings up many ethical issues and attracts much media attention. However, the true potential of AI is far more mundane and immediately relevant without even having to accede to the ethical frontier of autonomous cyborgs.

Artificial intelligence technologies include:

▎ **Logic programming:** using facts and rules to create logical formulas.

▎ **Bayesian systems:** using statistics and probabilities for prediction.

▎ **Expert systems:** using knowledge-based systems for decision making.

▌ **Semantic knowledge bases:** understanding language sets, identifying content by its type, meaning, metadata or tagging.

▌ **Deep learning:** using algorithms and artificial neural networks to create models of high-level abstractions. Deep learning comes from the use of multiple layers of networks that are able to improve with exercise (i.e. iteration).[2]

AI often is segmented into different technologies and expertise, with the inevitable mixing, merging and arrival of new techniques as AI continues to evolve. In any event, AI has a wide and vast number of possible applications. Opportunities abound. At a very minimum, AI is to be applied to alleviate tasks that are repetitive, where human value-added input is negligible. But, as AI develops, it will be useful to handle large, complex and unstructured data. AI will be able to outperform humans in physical labour as is seen with robotics. Additionally, it will both help and replace human beings in uncharted or hostile territories, such as space, deep oceans, nuclear waste or war zones.

There is little doubt that AI and robotics will result in many people losing their jobs. Even where this does not happen, people will need to adapt their skills to learn to work *with* AI.

> AI and robotics will result in many people losing their jobs. Even where this does not happen, people will need to adapt their skills to learn to work *with* AI.

Stick it to the man(agers)

Right now, for many mundane applications, AI already has its place. Wherever there are rules or regulations, AI is well suited to help analyse and make the best decisions. For example, whenever there is a lot of text in a legal document to be digested, AI can be used. It is also essential for use in more sophisticated automation, including in transport where not all patterns are easily predictable.

As an important tool in decision making, AI strips away the emotional factors that can cloud the thought process, crunching data in a methodical way. Linkilaw,[3] a legal tech startup that I am involved in, is planning work with AI to produce contracts that are accessible to the ordinary startup founder. Startup founders usually have lawyers draw up contracts, which can be so complicated to understand they need a law degree to make sense of them. We are building a contract with AI, allowing the contract to be written in plain English. Based on answering questions, it will explain the dynamics that are important to each founder, so it reflects what they 'really mean'. Standard clauses will appear and where there are differing views, areas of contention are easily highlighted and worked through. Subsequently, the contracts are simpler, the relationships are stronger, and the legal bill is greatly reduced. In healthcare, AI is already being used to help mine vast amounts of data and is being explored to help in patient diagnosis. Whilst it will not be able to replace a doctor, AI certainly will become a valuable tool to accompany the doctor's evaluation and to help make decisions.

In business number-crunching, where empathy is less a consideration, AI again has a place in assisting decision making. Perhaps as a sign of things to come, in early 2017, the world's largest hedge fund, Bridgewater Associates, announced its plan to replace managers with artificial intelligence. Bridgewater hired a team that is 'building a piece of software to automate the day-to-day management of the firm, including hiring, firing and other strategic decision making.'[4] However, as with many announcements in AI, there may be the ambition, there may be the development, but then there is the implementation.

Many managers look at AI as a cost-cutting tool in reducing workforce headcount and a rush to create chatbots seems to follow. Facebook now has some 40,000 chatbots at work in its Messenger app, handling communications for brands. In marketing, especially in the B2C space, given the number of comments and inquiries, it is clear that AI presents an important avenue to help handle the volume. With the need for marketing at scale, whether it is text or voice-based, human to machine conversations will be evermore present. AI will be able to assist in areas such as dynamic pricing, effective tagging online and production forecasting. There will also be a growing role for AI in customer service, especially thanks to the advancements in voice recognition.

In outsourcing, reducing headcount and handling communication, AI is clearly of enormous benefit, yet the signs point to optimal results when human and machine intelligence are combined. As Charlene Li, principal analyst at Altimeter, wrote, 'If we want our AI to truly understand and engage with us, it will need to develop "artificial empathy".'[5] We might reflect on the part AI could play in the transhumanist movement, which envisages the enhancement of our human bodies and abilities by sophisticated machines and technology. But, whilst we are waiting for our AI to develop 'artificial empathy', perhaps its ideal use is to eliminate human error in repetitive or mechanical activities, so the human being can work to add value in areas where machines are not as capable. Here, creativity, intuition and emotion can be used to maximum effect.

At the moment, the overall size of the industry producing cognitive software platforms (AI) remains relatively small and largely a 'start-up' space. It was estimated by Bloomberg that there were 2,600 start-ups in the space in 2015. However, companies such as Google, Apple, Facebook, Amazon, IBM and Palantir have been investing heavily in it and venture capital activity remains buoyant, with $1.5 billion invested by venture capital firms as at May 2016. There were

40 acquisitions of privately held AI companies in 2016[6] versus a total of 100 in the 5 years from 2011 to 2015.[7]

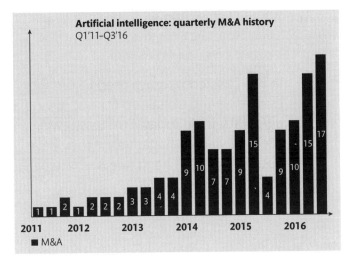

Artificial intelligence, quarterly mergers & acquisitions history 2011–2016

We can expect to see a lot of growth over the coming years as AI breaks into the mainstream. Dave Schubmehl, research director at IDC, predicts that the revenues of companies building AI software (excluding the likes of GAFA) will grow to exceed $10 billion by 2020.

Why we need to pay more attention to AI

By the sheer weight of investment being poured into AI by major tech companies and business disruptors, AI is bound to be in the news regularly. Combing through the hype and plethora of projects, the challenge will be in figuring out how AI can help each company realise its strategic objectives. In today's world, new data is being created daily. Given its volume, complexity and general availability, companies will have to upgrade their capabilities to organise their business and serve their clients better. The temptation to throw AI at all complex and repetitive tasks will draw in many executive teams. The challenge is to link the automation with what customers expect and need. In the past, companies used to be evaluated and penalised for not having a *digital* strategy. Today, businesses will soon be viewed negatively if they have not developed a *bona fide* AI strategy.

> In the past, companies used to be evaluated and penalised for not having a *digital* strategy. Today, businesses will soon be viewed negatively if they have not developed a *bona fide* AI strategy.

As we get better at using artificial intelligence, its value-added nature will improve. This is explained by Scott Brinker in his article '5 Disruptions to Marketing, Part 5: Artificial Intelligence',[8] as he cites the way analyst/rockstar R. Ray Wang lays out the different outcomes that AI can provide. AI's purpose is to be able to do better, faster and cheaper what human beings do. As we will see in the upcoming chapter on big data analytics, the outputs move from the obvious to the more sophisticated.[9]

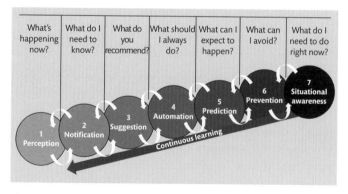

The spectrum of outcomes for artificial intelligence
Source: 2010–2016 Constellation Research, Inc.

Will AI replace all jobs?

After watching a film like *I, Robot*, filmgoers inevitably ask questions. 'Will the computers take over?' 'Will we really see a rising army of robots stand up in unison and fight in en bloc against their inventors?' 'Will all those powers we have given them be used against us?'

> **Press pause, get upskilled, work hard and take responsibility for what will come.**

Robots and computers may not be autonomously attacking the human race any time soon, but the impact of AI will be seen in the furthest stretches of the world, causing some devastation to the global workforce. We have not yet got the widescreen view of the issue, but Will Smith is unlikely to be saving your job in the immediate future by coming to a screen near you. Press pause, get upskilled, work hard and take responsibility for what will come.

> **Some believe AI will affect only factory workers, but that is artificially inaccurate.**

We know machines and technology have affected jobs before, during the industrial revolution. But many of us have not lived through it. In 2016, Foxconn in China reported it had replaced 60,000 assembly line jobs with robots.[10] They call them Foxbots. Some believe AI will affect only factory workers, but that is artificially inaccurate. I have clients in the legal tech space. Many law partners are concerned about how much work machines will end up doing. This transparent, repetitive and efficient way of working will have a huge downward impact on the number of billable hours they can charge. Lawyers are worried, and they have reason to be. As they are often the last ones to give up their positions of power, it is time to take note. The professional working landscape is going to be hit on seismic levels.

AI enables computers to use algorithms to process information quickly, identify patterns and speed up actions. In time, automatic solutions will emerge that are more sophisticated and accurate than manual work. According to Gartner analysis, '85% of customer interactions are projected to be managed without a human by 2020.'[11] Meanwhile, Forrester predicts that by 2025, '16% of all US jobs will replaced by AI.'[12] It is hard to build a wall to protect your country against that.

When one looks at the economics involved, the argument for business to embrace AI is compelling. And it is enticing to look at AI as a way to reduce salaries, overhead, office space, training and staffing costs rather than simply as a value-added extra. Machines do not take holidays or sick days and do not get grumpy or irritated with their clients (or bosses). They simply deliver what is needed.

> We think the scale and magnitude of the changes to the global workforce caused by AI will be one of the big issues of our day, and only has hope of being addressed by wide initiatives operating on many levels.

Sadly, the benefits are not there for everyone, especially those facing forced career changes. This has caused a key debate. Should tech companies whose products cause the loss of jobs hold any responsibility to help equip and find alternative solutions for members of the workforce? If we look at the unsheltered homelessness issues in San Francisco[13] and the numbers of people who were forced out of their tents,[14] it looks unlikely that Silicon Valley will develop such a conscience quickly. Yet, given the large divide between the world's richest and poorest, it was encouraging to see a number of philanthropists and companies who looked to attempt to address homelessness. We think the scale and magnitude of the changes to the global workforce caused by AI will be one of the big issues of our day, and only has hope of being addressed by wide initiatives operating on many levels. Many of us still have time to ensure we are appropriately skilled in areas less likely to be negatively affected by AI.

Every function in a company could, theoretically, benefit from artificial intelligence. Repetitive tasks, such as reporting, invoice processing, sorting through and understanding complex data can all use AI. Areas in business that are currently gaining traction in the use of AI beyond the factory floor are eCommerce, customer service, retail and marketing.

North Face – personalised without my permanent data

Some people happily give away their information, faithfully believing that companies will yet use that information to provide a valuable and customised proposition. However, brands have abused and disappointed customers repeatedly. As people become more reluctant to give away their data, businesses will find it increasingly difficult to provide a personalised service.

Clothing company North Face has provided a light yet smart solution on its eCommerce site.[15] The customer provides a number of inputs based on the projected usage for the item being sought and the site provides an array of best-suited choices based on its catalogue. Depending on the line of enquiry, the site might ask you where you are headed, for what purpose, in which month, your sex and what might be your favourite colour. The nature of the interrogation does not require you to give yourself over to the site, as the data is not retained. In the North Face application, you remain anonymous. Powered by IBM's Watson, the site reviews and understands your unscripted answers. The idea is to provide a perfectly tailored answer to suit your need. If it detects a level of impatience, it will even short-cut the questionnaire.

Under Armour – single customer view

In a fiercely competitive apparel marketplace, Under Armour has continued to stand out with the strategic use of technology. Under Armour created a Connected Fitness division whose purpose is to anticipate and compete as if its biggest competitive threat is Apple or Facebook as opposed to Nike and Adidas. Under Armour's CEO, Kevin Plank, outlined how the company plans to use technology, data and strategic partnerships to drive its future growth. At CES 2017, Plank asked the following question:

> 'The challenge that I give our product teams each season isn't what are we going to do with our current competition, it's what are we going to do if Apple and Samsung decide they want to start making apparel or footwear and if they did then what would it look like and more importantly what would it do?'[16]

Plank has a broad and open approach to partnering and collaborating. In partnership with IBM and HTC, Under Armour launched UA HealthBox,[17] a connected fitness system that provides a single view of a customer's health. The HealthBox system includes a band, scale and heart rate monitor, wireless headphones and connected trainers. These all link to the consumer's hub, UA Record, in an effort to engage with its customer base and help to create better informed, context-rich insights, content and advice. The data and insights are masterminded using artificial intelligence, through IBM Watson. Moreover, Plank has opened up access to this database to other brands. As reported in an article by BCG, 'the company has ... launched an adjacent business that offers other brands access to its fitness community as a way to increase the visibility of their brands and create affinity among consumers concerned about fitness.'[18]

In Plank's strategic vision and his extensive pivot into a technology-infused healthcare and fitness company, there are several important factors. First, Plank has combined the right technologies to support his vision. This includes leveraging the internet of things (connected objects), the smartphone (hub and apps), big data analytics (biometrics) and artificial intelligence (Watson). Second, he has sought the talent and key partnerships in order to pull together this shift. Third, he is operating and developing in communion with consumer input, having accumulated the world's largest online health and fitness community. And, by considering his potential competitors as the disruptive Google, Apple, Facebook, Amazon (GAFA). Under Armour has itself become a pioneer and disruptor. And, in true disruptive manner, Plank has inscribed the walls of the offices with the following maxims:

> 'Expedite the inevitable. Perfection is the enemy of innovation. Respect everyone, fear no one.'[19]

KLM – augmented customer service

Often, people argue and point out that if customer service were left to AI it would be a far inferior experience. Sadly, however, it is often the humans who both make the mistakes and do not follow through resolving the problems. Many would prefer to work with machines as they are able to quickly dissect data, pull out the relevant information and analyse, filter and make sense of it.

It is important to match the technical abilities of one's AI to the task at hand. Moreover, the mix of human and machine is often where AI is best leveraged. KLM, the Dutch airline, is well noted for its experimentation and social media prowess and has been making strides in the use of AI to augment its customer service.

Whereas many businesses are looking to AI to dehumanise their customer service by introducing 'clever' chatbots, KLM has been using an AI system in conjunction with its staff of 235 social media service agents. 'Programming is too limiting and doesn't scale,' said Mikhail Naumov, president of Digital Genius. AI systems such as Saffron (a division of Intel) and Digital Genius look at the historical text-based data, chat logs, emails and social media interactions between customer and agent. They then convert them into a mathematical representation of language, called word vectors. These word vectors are used to create a mathematical deep learning model that can integrate back into the contact centre.

KLM has a strategy in its customer service to be consistently where the customer is. They are strongly active in Facebook and Twitter. The company has over 100,000 weekly mentions in social media and the agents engage in 15,000 conversations. But, in late 2016, they went a step further. KLM opened up a messenger functionality in their app that allows for one-to-one messaging. In the first three months of use, they had four million messages going through this, equalling three messages per passenger, taking the customer journey from booking confirmation through to boarding pass.[20]

The Digital Genius system at KLM works on a historical database of 60,000 logs and on the agent's ongoing actions with the proposed answers.[21] It uses deep learning to constantly learn and refine its suggested messages. In essence, AI is predicting the best answer, leaving validation to the agent, to make sure that the answer is optimally on message.

Do not be late to the party

Despite magazine coverage and the hype and attention that AI receives, not all businesses believe they need it. But these will be in the minority. A business focused on selling reconditioned antique sailing boats to an existing client base may survive without it. But, when there is a lot of data and a need for ongoing and constant improvement, AI is essential.

You could argue that, if your business has an ambition for strong growth, you are left exposed without an AI strategy. Although AI will put people out of jobs and companies out of business, it still provides the opportunity for incredible growth across multiple business departments. We might well feel we are a long way from seeing robots walking round the office, yet we are already experiencing how AI augments the performance of the humans we sit alongside.

> More often than not senior leaders are the gateways for innovation.

One of the challenges businesses face when embracing AI is simply where to start; more often than not, senior leaders are the gateways for innovation. Three common risks confront businesses. First, many leaders feel overwhelmed with all the options available to them and end up being AI procrastinators. Second, with all the improvements AI can bring throughout an organisation, there is a danger that people may attempt to bite off more than is needed. Last, there is also the risk that businesses focus obsessively on trying to be the best in one or two areas, rather than allowing AI to impact on their business in multiple areas.

The benefits to business are clear and the march for AI will continue regardless. One of the biggest effects of the advancement will be on cost reduction. We have historically seen machines reduce staff overheads within factories, but now multiple business sectors are being disrupted. Business owners and shareholders will want to see these changes cause an increase to profit and a growth to their organisations.

Getting started in your business

Within your business, there are many ways that you could incorporate AI. Initially, you could look at what the competition is doing. But, as AI is opaque, it is hard to know who, what and how AI is being used by other businesses in your niche. Competitors are not likely to reveal this information.

So you can look instead at what you are doing. Where is your business working with lots of data? How are you repetitively interacting with customers and what benefit would be brought by an ease in crunching numbers? As you explore the different areas in which AI could be incorporated into your business, reflect on the Pareto 80/20 rule.[22] What small changes could your business focus on that would create the biggest impact? These could range from reducing costs and overheads to increasing customer satisfaction or improving your recruitment processes. Here are some areas to consider.

▋ **Marketing.** 73 per cent of all B2B leads need nurturing and a great way to do this is through content. Using AI could enable your business to pursue the leads and focus on personalising content to each lead. Through examining Twitter activity, website pages viewed, emails opened and questions asked on forums, this could enable your business to send a specific and tailored piece of content to stimulate an engagement.

▋ **General management.** What repetitive decisions are you making that you could avoid? Decision making creates bottlenecks but often managers cannot trust others to make the right decisions for them. AI could gather together the data, understand the important considerations and provide you with a suggested answer.

▋ **Customer service.** The majority of your customers have got similar questions. We have seen it with automated phone systems where you self-direct the message you receive and the people you talk to. The next stage is to personalise your written text activity as a result.

▌ **Commercial and sales.** What activity does someone need to demonstrate to raise their hand and show that they are interested in your product or service? Fill out a form? Register for a webinar? Hand you their business card? You could ask AI to raise people's hands for them, by analysing their activity on your website and social channels, investigating what search terms they are looking for.

▌ **R&D.** Often great development ideas come as a result of trial and error. AI could speed up this process for you by gathering the data, drawing conclusions on the information to provide you with a clear route forward.

▌ **Manufacturing.** Robots have not only improved productivity, efficiency and profits but they have also made a lot of manufacturing environments safer. What else could be created here?

▌ **Finance and accounting.** Get AI and your finance software to instruct your sales team to focus on selling specific items because the margins on these are showing in real time to be producing a greater level of profit once all the numbers have been crunched.

▌ **IT.** Many companies have become familiar with Zapier, where Zapier provides a bridge between different pieces of software. It has become a good entry point tool to explore what is possible with data integration. Take it one step further and explore how AI could enable custom built, personalised and constantly improving dashboards to provide the business data view each person needs.

▌ **Operations.** Do you want AI to streamline activity and reduce inefficiencies? This could range from organising deliveries and ordering stock to managing energy consumption. For many companies there are repeated tasks that happen each day. What could happen on autopilot?

▌ **HR.** Would you like to cut down on your recruitment times and reduce time spent screening candidates? Get AI to spot the necessary keywords, qualification levels, writing styles and experience needed for specific jobs.

❙ Creative. What happens when AI is able to do the creative work? Would AI be acting like humans, meaning real humans are no longer needed to do the work? What creative elements could you strip down and have done repeatedly?

> Get AI to spot the necessary keywords, qualification levels, writing styles and experience needed for specific jobs.

Entrepreneurs and business managers will approach AI from different perspectives. Managers will be focused on the efficiencies, cost savings and improvements generated through AI. Entrepreneurs will lean in to focus on the ground-breaking opportunities that the business can move into.

With all the ways AI can impact business, it is important to remind ourselves that startups and established businesses often need each other. Big data is sometimes at the heart of this collaboration and, though it is important, its close alignment with AI is more significant.

Partnerships and talent

The challenge with startups working in AI is that, quite often, AI *is* their product. They do not have a lot of data to work with but, instead, they work with their client's data. Could your business develop a partnership with a startup working in AI and give them access to your data? Perhaps you could trade data for talent and develop a mutually beneficial relationship. A search for 'AI startups in [Your Industry Niche]' will help focus attention on possible partners. Alternatively, if you are the startup, go and identify those companies looking for you.

If you want to go alone, get in good talent, be sure to identify both strategic and technical expertise. It is important to consider how AI overlaps with the other forces in this book. You cannot treat them in isolation from other disruptive forces. When you are focusing on customers, as well as AI, you will be considering security, big data, cloud, the internet and the smartphone. Without that wider strategic viewpoint, it is possible there will be gaps in your understanding.

'Last year, the cost of a top, world-class deep learning expert was about the same as a top NFL quarterback prospect. The cost of that talent is pretty remarkable.'[23] Finding people who have the combined understanding is a challenge. Businesses, consultants and potential employees who have the necessary and appropriate skills come at a premium. This is often what causes businesses who are exploring AI not to move at the speed that is needed.

What comes at a higher price is moving too slowly in the implementation of AI. Being a laggard can jeopardise your business. Many of us are familiar with, and have read the headlines about, large companies that ignored major moves of innovation, only to be put out of business by disruptors.

> Improve your awareness of artificial intelligence. Download and use the Flipboard app and set up a board on #Artificial Intelligence.

Of all the forces, AI carries the greatest threat to people's livelihoods, jobs and the successes of companies. As the technology improves, leading to enhanced customer interactions and service, businesses will need to respond. Do not put this off, thinking it is a few years yet before you need to think about it. Do not wait for a physical robot to open your office door before you take notice. Get started now. Ask how you will use AI to bring disruption to and through your business.

A slice of PIE

Personal

1. Improve your awareness of artificial intelligence. Download and use the Flipboard app and set up a board on #ArtificialIntelligence.[25]

2. Consider buying an AI home assistant like Amazon's Alexa or Google's Home to become familiar with voice commands. If you have got children or you are simply a big child yourself, you are going to love asking silly questions.

3. Try out the Robot Risk calculator courtesy of the BBC[26] to see if your job or area of expertise is going to be at risk with the tsunami of AI. Consider how you can ramp up your skills in AI.

Internal

1. Make sure you focus on the results, not the technology, when you are looking to sell AI internally. Lead others in discussions to find out which company activities could be done faster and what activities you want to start. Wherever you are in the process and whatever the business, plot a course to include AI in your future plans.

2. According to your strategic prerogatives, check out how your data is being collated and analysed. Seek AI-based solutions that could help to parse through the data and solve the business issues.

3. Enhance decision making. Where decisions need to be taken on a regular basis with rules that are essentially predetermined, AI could be a natural way to enhance and accelerate the process. For example, this can be in forecasting and financial modelling.

External

1. Keep the customers needs central and consider what automatic actions they would find valuable. What AI solutions would help them?

2. How can AI help manage the volume of data around customers so you can glean information, gather insights and improve customer interactions.

3. Explore what grants may be available for AI-related projects. With lots of investment into this space, there will be plenty of opportunities to apply for funding. Go and seek these out.

Big data analytics

What do they do with all our data anyway?

> Big Data is like teenage sex: everyone talks about it,
> nobody really knows how to do it, everyone thinks
> everyone else is doing it, so everyone claims they are
> doing it.[1]

Dan Ariely[2]

What is it?

The word 'data' has two connected meanings. The first and
most broadly used definition is that data is a collection of
facts and stats. It is, literally, the plural for *datum* in Latin,
but we tend to consider data as a *singular* collection. This
becomes somewhat ironic when we talk about *big* data.

The second definition of data is: 'The quantities, characters,
or symbols on which operations are performed by a
computer, which may be stored and transmitted in the form
of electrical signals and recorded on magnetic, optical, or
mechanical recording media.'[3]

So, to begin with, big data is a mash-up of both of these
definitions, brought on by the digitalisation of our world into
code.

Volume, velocity and variety

'Big' data as opposed to 'regular' data is characterised as having three features, the 3Vs:

1. **Volume.** The sheer amount of data.

2. **Velocity.** The speed with which it is being delivered in real time.

3. **Variety.** The number of different sources.

The amount of data already in existence is mind numbing. And much more is on the way. According to MongoDB,[4] 'Facebook ingests 500 terabytes of new data every day; [and] a Boeing 737 generates 240 terabytes of flight data during a single flight across the US.' The number of web pages on the internet continues to climb. It is estimated that there are over 1.1 billion websites in the world,[5] across all languages. With 4.8 billion pages recorded,[6] the average website is estimated to have 4 pages. It should be noted that, according to Netcraft,[7] the web is littered with inactive websites that have not been updated within the last month. In fact, 75 per cent of websites are deemed to be inactive, outlining that as well as the vast swathes of new content being created the graveyard of old content still makes it's presence known. There is a lot of noise one must contend with.

The explosion of data is directly related to the arrival of the digital age, as portrayed in the figure below.[8]

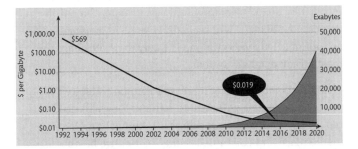

Global data storage cost trends versus data creation explosion

As reported by TechCrunch[9] in 2010, Eric Schmidt, currently executive chairman of Alphabet Inc., famously said that, 'Every two days now we create as much information as we did from the dawn of civilization up until 2003.' Whilst some might refute those exact numbers (e.g. Robert J. Moore[10]), the point remains valid that the volume of new data being created is phenomenally more than in the past.

As content has been democratised, the internet has become a hotbed for data creation. The velocity of this is overwhelming. As well as people creating data, digital devices are also constantly creating it. Twenty years ago, data may have been seen as a steady flowing stream. Now we are experiencing an ocean wide tidal wave that keeps growing taller each day.

Twenty years ago, data may have been seen as a steady flowing stream. Now we are experiencing an ocean wide tidal wave that keeps growing taller each day.

The trickiest component of big data is the variety of sources. With the rapid increase of devices and the imminent arrival of the internet of things, the activity and communication is coming from an unlimited number of sources. On top of that, the data collection is in different formats. This includes text, visual, audio and video and is often geo-located and systematically refreshed. As we reported in the IoT Force 5 chapter, depending on the source, it is estimated that there will be up to 20–34 billion physical items linked to the internet by 2020.[11] Not only will variety come from different devices, but also we will see a divergence in language, code and format. This variety alone is likely to create chaos for most legacy database systems.

With this combination of increased volume, velocity and variety, companies will need to rethink; they will need to repurpose their way of working with innovation, the marketplace and communication. Their entire business processes may well need to change.

> With this combination of increased volume, velocity and variety, companies will need to rethink; they will need to repurpose their way of working with innovation, the marketplace and communication. Their entire business processes may well need to change.

As several studies have portrayed, a good algorithm with poor or little data underperforms a poor algorithm with lots of data. Algorithms and analysis often are rendered less effective because of the lack of good or plentiful data. Algorithms, meanwhile, suffer from being too complicated, not robust or stable enough or improperly maintained. The key will be in being able to compile and scale up the data and then ask the right questions. It will also be important to create algorithms that are simpler.

> A good algorithm with poor or little data underperforms a poor algorithm with lots of data.

Most companies are still grappling with 'small' data or data that was available to them in the analogue world. Businesses have a higher tolerance level for intuition in decision making than might have been expected when discussed alongside correct data. For example, the HIPPO (highest paid person's opinion) principle remains a strong influence in executive teams, as does that of the charismatic leader. Yet, accurate data brings clarity to strategic decisions and good data wins arguments. Otherwise, it can be garbage in, garbage out. It takes a clear and unbiased mind to analyse data optimally.

Big data does not and cannot live in isolation from other technologies; it is, in large part, a function of the combination of new computing power, the web, the smartphone and IoT. In order to manage it, the cloud and artificial intelligence are also essential. What makes big data so powerful is not the data itself, but what you plan to do with it. In the past, product marketing managers would collect data on customers via mail-ins and those postcards would get stashed under the desk, unsorted and collecting dust, until the next marketing manager stepped in and cleared the office of the 'clutter'. One will not solve big data just by hiring a team of data scientists. If the organisation's mindset is not switched on and unified behind a clear, solid and shared purpose, it will be incredibly difficult for it to get its head around the data in a constructive and competitive manner. Marketing, business development, R&D and customer service will need to share the responsibility of collecting, storing, collating, analysing and querying the data in an intelligent manner.

In the management and transformation of big data into valuable business assets, the goal is to move from analysis to prediction and, ultimately, to prescription, as the following figure (adapted from *Analytics Magazine*[12]) represents. AI will be a crucial step in all of this.

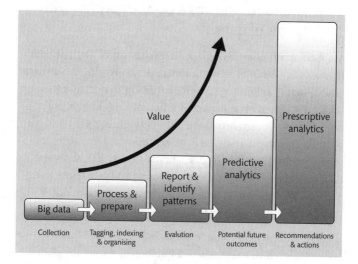

Value chain of data transformation (concept developed by Michael Porter)

Data journalism

We see big data at work in so many different arenas. We are probably familiar with how badly media companies have been rocked by the digital era. One area that has shown a lot of promise for value-added reporting is data journalism, aided by the ever growing amount of open data. Every year for the last three years, I have emceed the Data Journalism Awards[13] created by the Global Editors Network.[14] Data journalism is about the use of data to inform and create newsworthy stories and, just as the new path for journalists may include debunking fake news, in many ways, data and code may be the source of new news. In particular, once the data is identified or revealed, journalists can use their investigative talents to create news. They can look for new correlations, use data to uncover abuse of power or a failure to uphold public interest and create novel stories. Similarly, for businesses and marketing teams, one could imagine how datasets could be used for better storytelling both internally and externally.

> One area that has shown a lot of promise for value-added reporting is data journalism, aided by the ever growing amount of open data.

Why do you need to worry?

One of the biggest risks that businesses face is not having a clear strategy in the first place. Some organisations were poor at small data and are going to continue to be bad with big data. Through the consultative work we both carry out, we have regular conversations with companies where we hear the same internal complaints about the same ongoing challenges.

'We are working off too many systems.'

'Our teams don't collaborate well.'

'The records aren't updated quickly enough.'

'We are not collecting the correct data ... let alone doing anything big with it.'

These are not new issues, but now that a big data strategy is essential for most serious businesses, it needs urgent attention. It is not something that can be wistfully referred to, in the same manner we may apologise for drunk Uncle Harry who makes outlandish statements. Data needs fixing. Businesses need the right software solutions, skilled people and the necessary resources to gather and analyse data. Delays cause consequences. In the best case scenario this may be a loss of market share. In other scenarios we may see some businesses no longer able to compete, causing their extinction.

As well as being slow on the uptake, businesses also risk jumping into big data over-enthusiastically. Unless there is careful thought and consideration, it is easy to see a knee-jerk reaction into launching company big data projects, hiring expensive data scientists, spinning data wheels and spending large sums of money. Often, these do not result in tangible outcomes as they are too vast and overly complicated. We have seen this in the UK, repeatedly with the NHS's handling of people's data.[15] Big data projects need the appropriate expertise, understanding of the organisation and knowledge of what data is crucial. Small iterative circles of learning are more likely to generate more important results than the headline-grabbing large projects.

Here are some examples of big data projects and how they have worked.

Big data – AI and visualisation

It would be hard not to consider Google and Alphabet Inc. more broadly, as a prime model for managing big data. They are, without doubt, at the epicentre of *huge* data. One of the most fascinating zones, with major importance for business, is the treatment of images. Images and video account for a large percentage of the explosion in data we've all seen. Google has been pioneering the use of artificial intelligence to organise crowd-sourced datasets. Google Photos, using the open-source TensorFlow[16] framework, detects the contents of the uploaded images and is able to categorise and tag them into thousands of categories. By the same token, Google is amongst the leaders in using visualisation graphics and tools to present large datasets. Open-source tools include Embedding Projector and Geodetic Velocities Visualisation. It even has a data verbalisation tool that 'automatically generates verbal insights about your spreadsheet data'.[17]

> One of the most fascinating zones, with major importance for business, is the treatment of images.

Healthcare data

The cost and efficiency of healthcare is of strategic importance for any government. With the digitisation of medical records and imaging (including MRI and X-rays), there is a need to analyse the data to improve healthcare, whilst making it more affordable and accessible. As we discuss in Force 12 Genomics, the ever cheaper availability of multi-omic data is on the cusp of exploding into the mainstream. *Analytics Magazine* reported,[18] 'The complexity of healthcare makes it a perfect domain to explore the potential for prescriptive analytics and imaging ... The next step is to use this image analytics to provide real-time insight to healthcare providers during diagnosis and treatment ... The increasing role of algorithmic diagnosis and treatment creates the perfect opportunity to integrate images with prescriptive analytics.'

One of the current challenges is the unstructured nature of the healthcare data, as is seen with the notes that doctors often scribble with unintelligible handwriting. As reported by Bernard Marr, Apixio,[19] a California-based cognitive computing firm founded in 2009 is tackling the thorny challenge of collecting and structuring the data as 'a staggering 80 per cent of medical and clinical information about patients is formed of unstructured data'.[20] Apixio is applying machine learning based on NLP capabilities to better understand the data and rendering models that can be aggregated or drilled down to the patient level. Medical care providers, pharmaceutical manufacturers and insurance companies alike will be keen clients of Apixio.

Shifting the organisation to have big data practices

Organisations face significant challenges when they have not got a good handle on their data. If they were able to take a closer and more detailed look at their data sets, drawing out conclusions often would prevent them from making some of the same basic mistakes. Subsequently, this learning does not filter through into the R&D, sales, marketing, human resources and operational departments. We see a huge waste of resources, as improvements are not made, inefficiency continues and opportunities are missed. The starting point needs to be understanding the value of the data and taking the necessary steps to gather it.

What do you do with the data?

It is one thing to access the data, but it is helpful only if you know what to do with it. Often, we make this more complicated than we need to. For instance, a simple form field on a business' website stating: 'Where did you hear about us?'

is not hard data to collect. It may enable an organisation to assess which marketing channels are achieving the best results. If this data is tracked through to the point of sale, with information about the financial value, margins and cost of marketing in this channel, you have enough data to calculate a basic ROI report on your marketing channels.

Now, admittedly, you are reliant on a form being filled out, and that raises a lot of extra questions. Did they input this accurately or was the response given just because it was the quickest box to tick? What about all those who are not willing to answer the question? This is where software needs to be sophisticated to track this data automatically. In the process, you are able to gain a customer-centric view of the client. But, to arrive at a macro position, often it requires you to start with a small picture and then gradually extend this out for a bigger picture and analysis.

Lean startup – build, measure, learn

Once you are building the approach to gather the data, you need to measure and analyse it, and look at the data to uncover the insights. This build-measure-learn cycle gives you the ability to improve your sources of data, the regularity of collection and the implementation that comes as a result of having it. Going a step further, a dose of well-crafted artificial intelligence can learn to automatically parse through and adjust incoming data.

Many companies claim to be customer-centric: 'We put our customers first.' In a KPMG 2016 survey with 400 executives, fully one-third of all those surveyed indicated that their top three priorities were: 'sustaining customer loyalty, improving customer service and experience and building customer trust'.[21]

But the reality is, if you have not got a big data strategy, and don't fully understand what is important both to your customers and what they want who your customers are and what is important to them, you are sadly a long way away from meeting their needs and being customer-centric. Organisations need to understand who their customers are and the data that surrounds them. It is not enough to have a CRM database and shoot regular emails. There is much more data available outside the transaction, including incoming communications and earning permission. It is important to get a single customer view, and then have the ability to drill down into the areas of communication, interaction, engagement and finance. Big data analytics are optimised when the entire organisation is truly mobilised around the customer.

Alternatively, the other extreme may exist where companies jump on the big data bandwagon. They hire a big data scientist, roll out a programme and use the data to think about the processes and how to streamline costs. But they stop there and inevitably lose sight of the customer journey.

Once you have the data, it is important to understand what changes need to be implemented first and how you have arrived at this decision. You are likely to discover areas of overspending, customer dissatisfaction and wasted sales opportunities. Sometimes, brands just seem to prefer to remain in ignorant bliss. Despite having the data, and knowing the areas that need to be fixed, they are left with the challenge of doing the hard work. This, of course, is carrying out the implementation. But, before you start, the senior team needs to decide what takes priority and which departments need to be involved.

Because of the way an organisation is set up and compensation schemes are arranged, business units may gather, but tend not to share their data internally. The data is divided into silos. This is easily evident in the example of many marketing, sales and finance departments. In marketing, it is often common to have a number of elements and inputs: advertising, digital, social media, content creation, PR, email and events. The task is rendered more complex with third-party suppliers, such as agencies, unless they are treated as part of the team. But how well do the different departments interact and do they have a centralised view of the customer?

For instance, a customer wants to interact with the business and emails help@companyname.com. They receive a reply with a link to the support page to . . . 'raise a support ticket'. After submitting a ticket, later that day, the customer is irritated with the slow response and complains via Twitter. The company does not have a single view of the customer and Twitter is manned by another department. Not being in a position to see the original issue, they tweet back the link to the support page to . . . 'raise a support ticket'. Nothing like delivering customer satisfaction.

Alternatively, a special discounted offer email may have been unnecessary, if the team member had been able to filter out prospects that were speaking to sales advisors five minutes earlier.

What should you do about it?

Have a clear game plan

Having a clear strategy and game plan ensures you kick things off with the right approach. Here are some thoughts you can apply when it comes to starting a big data project.

What data and for what purpose?

Start with an inventory of all the data within the organisation. Bear in mind there is valuable external data, such as Google browsing behaviour. When it comes to data, what are you trying to achieve? What are you hoping the data will tell you? What data is valuable to know and why is this the case? For instance, how could the data increase sales, improve R&D or make operations more efficient? Where would you see improvements to customer service, customer retention and the external perception of the company by its stakeholders?

> Where would you see improvements to customer service, customer retention and the external perception of the company by its stakeholders?

How do you get this data?

Gathering data is a complicated process and always involves software. Many people start looking at software programmes focused on one area of data. Yet that software may specialise in web-based data, but not provide or host the data your business needs. Instead, having established the data you want, research the tools and software that cover all the needs. Or utilise software that has integrations with other data sets if there is no off-the-shelf solution. Involve everyone in the strategic goal and align objectives to ensure two outcomes. First, that everyone gets access from different departments and, second, that everyone is united in the solutions that can come from it.

What database/software/CRM structure do you need to gather all this data?

There is a strong likelihood that, unless your firm is already gathering this data or has robust software in place that you may need to look at alternative software solutions. Software often inadvertently causes businesses to function in silos.

Legacy systems exist and have tended to focus on one area of a business. To get an integrated view of a customer, work with a dashboard that brings multiple sources of data into one viewpoint. Alternatively, you will be spending lots of time working with Excel to develop reports.

Software companies, in wanting to sell their software, sometimes will showcase studies within your sector. This can teach you a lot and becomes a game of joining the dots as you take examples from other companies, piece them together and identify the best data to collect and software solution for your own organisation.

How frequently should you be getting the data?

If one of the core reasons for gathering data is to learn from it, we would recommend an Eric Reis-inspired Lean Startup[22] approach to data. This is typified often by the example of *build, measure* and *learn*. *Building* is the data you are looking to collect and the sources you are looking to collect them from. *Measurement* assesses the data and the information you have collected from it. *Learning* enables you to apply it to decision making for your business. For some organisations, the build, measure, learn loop can happen on a monthly basis but, for others, especially in startup environments, with the ongoing and close analysis of data, it can be studied multiple times each day.

Making the decisions

As has been discussed above, one of the focal points for big data is to make good decisions and improve the results within the business. For non-complex datasets, it is possible that you are equipped to extract and analyse the data. With more complicated requirements, you will need an honest assessment of the skillset and talent you have available.

Consultants and software solutions

Depending on your skills audit, you may need a wider team: internal team members, external consultants and relevant software solutions. The danger with many costly software installations is that, despite paying high licences team members do not understand how to use the software. They end up using 5–10 per cent of the functionality, at a basic level. It sounds ridiculous but I have known companies spend over a £1 million a year on licence fees on great marketing software to find their staff use only basic MailChimp (i.e. at a small fraction of the cost) email functionality. It's like owning a Lamborghini Veneno, and only watching how fast the windscreen wipers can go. During the implementation stage, there needs to be either ongoing training and support for your team or continued relationships with external agencies who know how to maximise the benefits of the software.

In complex big data projects, there are likely to be some disappointments. Sometimes, there can be confusion around the roles and responsibilities between client and consultant. Who is responsible for what data, how is the handoff managed? How are the measured results stacked up against the brief and remuneration?

Software sellers can be like Dell Boy from Only Fools and Horses. They may not reverse odometers, but, they are 'the epitome of used car salesmen'. Those 'amazing features' simply do not exist. My rapidly predictive AI analyser still doesn't give me a head, back and neck massage.

Additionally, the software may have been sold with an over-inflated list of functionality. It may turn out that the software does not provide these solutions or, instead, requires bespoke customisations not previously anticipated. Without wishing to sound derogatory, software sellers can be like Dell Boy from *Only Fools and Horses*. They may not reverse odometers, but some would joke, they are 'the epitome of used car salesmen'. 'These features are mind-blowing.' Sadly, my rapidly predictive AI Analyser still does not give me a head, back and neck massage. My rapidly predictive AI analyser still does not give me a head, back and neck massage.

A slice of PIE

Despite the potential challenges you may face, the opportunities significantly outweigh these and a company without a focus on big data is going to be hugely challenged. It is a long-term consideration and commitment from a business. It is one that is almost guaranteed to provide material benefits if managed well. Yes, it will unearth inefficiencies and open up opportunities. Yes, it will enable greater customer service and increase revenue. And yes, it is big for your business. So what are you waiting for?

Personal

1. On a personal level, be aware of the areas where you are not in control of your data. Check your settings to see who can access your information or get your updates via the various social media sites, starting with Facebook. To get you started, have you got a process to ensure you never miss the birthdays and anniversaries of those important to you?

2. In your Flipboard account, start tracking stories around #Big Data for further examples and ideas.

3. Consider ways to create a central hub of important family, friends, customers and influencers from LinkedIn, Google, Facebook, Instagram and Twitter. We would recommend

▶

for personal use you take a look at Nimble.[23] We also highly recommend learning to tag your contacts for better groupings and connection (e.g. schools, hobbies, interests, languages . . .).

Internal

1. Examine how your organisation could improve the collection and management of data.

2. Consider carefully opening up visibility of and access to your data to foster great collaboration with others.

3. Evaluate the software solutions currently being used to manage your data. Make getting a single view of your customer a key focus. Check to see how effectively data can be hoovered in, structured and queried.

External

1. Consider how you could provide your customers with better service and solutions through a greater understanding of the data you have.

2. Check to see if there are organisations with whom you could partner with to provide further datasets and improve increased understanding of relevant data.

3. Make sure you take responsibility for the data that you are collecting and that you are protecting the privacy of your customers and employees.

8

Blockchain and cryptocurrencies

If I had bought a few thousand Bitcoin earlier, I would now be a zillionaire

> **The blockchain allows our smart devices to speak to each other better and faster.**
>
> *Melanie Swan*[1]

What is it?

Blockchains and cryptocurrencies are inter-related but very different.

Cryptocurrencies are digital currencies, operating independently of any central bank and, through digital encryption, the transfers of these currencies are self-regulated. The most famous and leading cryptocurrency is Bitcoin, though Ethereum* and Ripple** have both grown in popularity. Though Bitcoin had received all the initial attention, it is certainly not the only cryptocurrency in town. Ethereum has seen an incredible rise in value. In fact, there are over 700 cryptocurrencies in existence. Coingecko.com and the coincap app provide up to date pricing information on the different cryptocurrencies.

---

*https://www.ethereum.org/
https://en.wikipedia.org/wiki/Ethereum

**https://ripple.com/

The technology powering Bitcoin and other cryptocurrencies is called blockchain, which is, essentially, a distributed database or a shared digital ledger. These blockchains can be either public or private. A public blockchain runs on open-source software that anyone can read, use or change. The private one has restricted and controlled access, much like an intranet as opposed to the internet. We believe the underlying blockchain technology is a game-changer; a major disruption for business. The beauty of the blockchain is that it ensures transparency, security and integrity for transactions, all at a fraction of the cost charged by traditional financial institutions. In a world where trust is at a premium and privacy a genuine and global concern, the blockchain technology provides a potential solution to both issues.

> In a world where trust is at a premium and privacy a genuine and global concern, the blockchain technology provides a potential solution to both issues.

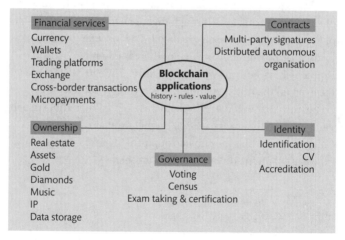

Blockchain applications, combining history, rules and value

As many of the new technologies we are covering in this book roll out, namely the IoT, peer-to-peer marketplaces, automation and AI, we see enormous opportunities for block-chain applications.

Decrypting cryptocurrency

In 2009, Bitcoin was founded and quickly moved from theory to reality. Having always put speculative money aside for buying web domains, I contemplated buying 1,500 Bitcoins in 2011 (approximately worth £1,000 at the time). When I heard a friend discuss the option of 'mining' them, I was really interested.

However, the lure of the golden ticket was always shrouded with 'issues'. Silk Road, a marketplace for illegal goods including drugs, guns and counterfeit items, were often closely aligned with Bitcoin. It looked likely the connection would cause Bitcoin to be quashed. I left it alone and moved on.

You could say that was a mistake. To say that the value of a Bitcoin rose significantly would now be worth £3,202,644. Those 1,500 Bitcoins would now be worth £1,986,203. Approximately. If many people did make their fortunes, it seems like I was not the only one not making an investment. Lily Allen shared that she was offered hundreds of thousands of Bitcoins to perform a concert on the virtual world website, Second Life, and turned it down, replying to the organiser: 'As if.'

As if, indeed.

She was not to know that 300,000 bitcoins would later be worth £640,528,813. Here's to the crazy ones!

So, how did it all start?

Satoshi Nakamoto[2] founded Bitcoin. Nakamoto is a pseudonym, so we do not know whether the founder is a he, a she or even a they. After posting a paper on 'The Cryptography Mailing List' at metzdowd.com, where he described his vision for Bitcoin in October 2008, he released the first Bitcoin software that launched the network in January 2009 but then stepped away publicly from the project in mid-2010. No one has publicly, knowingly met Nakamoto and his identity remains a fascinating mystery.

Here is what you need to know

Before we dive into how to get Bitcoins and what this can mean for your business, it is important to explain how Bitcoin, as a digital currency, differs from the traditional ways that banks and governments work with money. We all use money often, but perhaps do not spend the time to think where it comes from.

Take the Bank of England in the UK. It is owned by the Government and creates money by printing new bank notes or coins. The cost of manufacturing a £20 note is about £0.05 and the Government, by creating the note, has made a profit of £19.95.

'From the time the Bank of England was formed in 1694, it took over 300 years for the banks to create the first trillion pounds. It took only 8 years for the banks to create the second.'[3] (See also: positivemoney.org.)[4] Many of these banks create money through the process of creating loans and mortgages. The significance of institutions and governments creating money is that it gives them a windfall of most of the amounts they create and, although they provide governance, they maintain control and wield their power on the economy.

With all this money being created, despite the overheads they face, the banks are making astounding levels of profit. What ordinary people could buy with this money diminishes due to the value of money decreasing, as a result of inflation. House prices, meanwhile, continue to rise.

In 2008, along came the credit crunch and, of course, the recession. Our trust for governments had decreased, our confidence in financial institutions was at an all-time low and anxiety around centrally owned economic systems was widespread.

It was in this climate of the collapse of Lehman Brothers in September 2008 that Nakamoto presented his paper[5] on 'The Cryptography Mailing',[6] before launching Bitcoin three months later. Critics may argue that Bitcoins are no different from the banks, in that Nakamoto set up a structure where money could simply be created and he also would be set to make large windfall profits. There are a number of key differences about Bitcoin that make it a real threat to existing financial institutions and a potentially major disruptor.

It is cheaper with Bitcoin

Bitcoin differs in a number of ways from how ordinary currencies work. Because transactions are recorded on a blockchain, through peer-to-peer verification, there is no need for large costly institutions to verify these transactions.

As Nakamoto wrote in an email to Mike Hearn, one of the Bitcoin core developers: 'The existing Visa credit card network processes about 15 million Internet purchases per day worldwide. Bitcoin can already scale much larger than that with existing hardware for a fraction of the cost. It never really hits a scale ceiling.'[7] Where financial companies and institutions charge 2–4 per cent to process transactions, this decentralised approach has huge financial savings, when the current percentage for processing Bitcoin transactions is around 0.1 per cent.

The main reason for the lower transaction costs is that the infrastructure is distributed and the manual labour is done by 'miners' who, for a tiny fee, paid in the form of cryptocurrencies, will verify each transaction and validate the provenance and delivery of the currency. Just like in a ledger, for each transaction, there is an 'in' and a corresponding 'out'. And, on top of not requiring an institutional stamp of approval, the parties on either end of the transaction will be anonymised.

There is a cap at 21 million on the number of Bitcoins that can ever be in existence. This built-in limitation means the currency is protected from inflation or hyperinflation. Of course, the intrinsic value of the Bitcoin can go up and down for *other* reasons.

Bitcoin has been a volatile currency in its first few years. It is still largely a poorly understood concept and its effectiveness at the scale of a worldwide currency is far from proven. The value has also been impacted by websites storing Bitcoins, often on behalf of other people, being hacked and having their Bitcoins stolen. The highest profile of these was Mt. Gox, which was hacked in 2014, when $700 million worth of Bitcoins were stolen. In August 2016, a further $700 million worth of Bitcoins were stolen from Bitfinex. Another reason for this volatility has rested with its close association to those individuals and sites who benefit from the anonymous nature of the site. Silk Road, an underground marketplace trading in illegal items, was a prime example.

Of course, the issue with anonymity creates a headache for law enforcement agencies that wish to stop the sale of illegal drugs. It is easier to transport electronic digits than large suitcases stuffed full of cash. But there is a secondary issue of tax that is also a huge issue. Suddenly, this decentralised currency, which can stay off the radar of government transactions, is able to transfer funds without detection. This, potentially, has a wide economic impact.

As Michael Carrier[8] writes: 'The largest economy in the world is not the U.S. or China, it is the Internet, and the Internet has for the first time, just invented its own money. This change is potentially more significant than the invention of the Internet itself.'

On the positive side, this provides those who need to move their funds out of unstable economic environments the means to do so. But, for many, there is a greater reliance on those who are earning money in Bitcoin to declare this to the authorities. And I imagine that many don't!

And then there was blockchain

> If cryptocurrencies have captured a good deal of PR and are shaking up the financial world, it is highly likely that the most disruptive element of the cryptocurrency force is the underlying blockchain technology.

If cryptocurrencies have captured a good deal of PR and are shaking up the financial world, it is highly likely that the most disruptive element of the cryptocurrency force is the underlying blockchain technology. In *Forbes*, Laura Shin wrote:

> *'Blockchain technology is likely to disrupt financial services first by making existing processes more efficient, secure, transparent and inexpensive, and then later by creating new products that we can't even dream of.'*[9]

Blockchain, in essence, operates as a proof-of-existence. Tamper-proof until today, the blockchain's fundamental benefit in a digital world is as yet totally untapped. What are the features of blockchain that these entrepreneurs are seeking to leverage?

Why do you need to worry?

Looking first at cryptocurrency, which is already in circulation, the first port of call are financial services. Cryptocurrency is, by definition, 'fintech' or financial technology, meaning that it represents an alternative to traditional banking and payment systems providing a new, more accessible, flexible and scaleable approach to meet the customer's financial services needs. Any monetary transaction can, theoretically, be converted into an exchange of cryptocurrency. Whether Bitcoin comes out as the core leader is less important than the resounding proof of the innovative opportunities that the internet is providing.

> 'There's not any one particular use case that the big financial institutions are all interested in. The way they look at it is, where are the opportunities to reduce costs without creating incremental risk, whether that's compliance risk or otherwise? Then, where are the opportunities to generate revenue?'
> Barry Silbert, founder of SecondMarket.[10]

There is a strong chance that cryptocurrencies will materially disrupt the foundations of currency. They might also challenge how financial exchanges can or should be conducted; for example, in terms of pricing, tracking and accountability. As Brian Forde, director of digital currency at MIT Media Lab, said, the open protocol of blockchain: 'actually disrupts the disruptor'.[11]

Here are a few examples of startups that show promise.

Bitland[12] is an NGO, based in Ghana, looking to help revitalise 'dead capital' in the form of unregistered land and home ownership. In Africa, some 90 per cent of rural land is undocumented and has no associated official title of ownership. As a result, for many, it is impossible to use one's home as collateral for a loan. It is complex to buy and sell property, and fraud and corruption is rife in any land transaction. Bitland, which runs on the OpenLedger[13] blockchain, enables individuals to digitally codify their land title, using a combination of GPS coordinates, satellite photos and written descriptions. The blockchain 'miners' will verify the information as a transparent and unfalsifiable record. If Bitland can succeed in its mission, it will enable individuals to use their 'dead capital' and convert it into a useable and more liquid source of funding.

Another example is in the music industry. The context here is that all the power is centralised in the hands of record labels and distributors, including music streaming services such as Spotify, Tidal, Google Play Music or Apple Music. The vast majority of artists receive just a sliver of the royalties, scant data on their music and zero control over how or where their work is circulated. Award-winning recording artist Imogen Heap has been working on a project, under the banner of Mycelia[14], that is considering blockchain technology to resolve at least part of the problem. The concept would be to have artists upload their own music into the blockchain, distribute it in a multivariate manner and price it differently as they see fit. Royalties would be paid diligently to the proper parties and verified information would be recorded about the music in a decentralised database.

The music industry has been in massive upheaval for the past 20 years, ever since the arrival of peer-to-peer file sharing. After being aggressively opposed to Napster and other similar sites, the music industry would do well to adjust its attitude towards innovation. As Heap says, 'If you are open and share your data, more work comes to you. It's a way of being. Closed data, protective databases and being possessive over the flow of data, is actually what is biting record labels in the bum.'[15]

Would any of these areas be a potential opportunity or threat to your business model? It is still early days. We will see a lot more being built on blockchain in the coming years.

Amongst financial institutions, it is interesting to see that, rather than invest in lawsuits to combat cryptocurrencies, there has been a concerted effort to onboard the underlying technology. With the savings that are made, and the lack of centralised accountability, there is a strong case to be made. Meanwhile, there is a peer-to-peer model that could challenge sectors such as finance, insurance and legal service suppliers significantly. On the positive side, due to the digital nature of the currency, it is likely that there will be new ways to explore and analyse the data of transactions.

What should you do about it?

The first port of call is to make sure that, if your customers are interested in using Bitcoins to pay, then your business should explore being able to give that option. Second, and far more profoundly, you might consider how the underlying blockchain technology can provide you with new ways of doing business. The first area of particular focus should be on all forms of transactions, financial or otherwise. In any event, if you have a laboratory for working on new tech, blockchain could be one of the raw materials. Where are the opportunities?

> If you have a laboratory for working on new tech, blockchain could be one of the raw materials.

Blockchain technology opens up new ways to tackle old problems. It could be appropriate in your sector, if:

▌ There are many middle people, who are taking a chunk of the margin.

▌ Multi-party contracts are involved and the timing and coordination is of concern.

▌ The industry is fraught with a lack of transparency.

▌ Ownership needs to be tracked.

▌ Underlying trustworthiness is an issue amongst the parties involved in the transaction.

▌ Fraud is prevalent.

▌ There is a stranglehold on distribution by just a few players.

▌ Institutions are required to validate, oversee and control the flow of papers and transactions.

Blockchain and Bitcoin are likely to be names that become a part of the wider public's future understanding and vocabulary. With the levels of venture capital funding being invested into this space, and hugely influential investors, from Peter Thiel to Mark Andreessen speaking so publicly about its impact, this gives entrepreneurs and businesses like yours an opportunity to get ahead of the curve. How are you going to take advantage of that?

> Break down your business flow into transactions and see if any part of these need authentication that could be attributed to the blockchain.

A slice of PIE

Personal

1. Go to a conference on Bitcoin via CoinDesk.com.[16] Read about the latest news on Bitcoin via reddit.com/r/Bitcoin[17] and consider meeting with some blockchain entrepreneurs through meetup.com.[18] Visit Futureproof.ly to find the best sites to explore.

2. Investigate what companies allow you to make a transaction with a Bitcoin. Check out the price chart of Bitcoin on CoinDesk;[19] open up a Bitcoin wallet and buy some Bitcoin, securing it wisely. Keep track of what your Bitcoin and other cryptocurrencies are currently worth, using cryptocompare. com[20] and, if need be, take some money out of a Bitcoin ATM. You may need to take a little drive to find one! Find a Bitcoin ATM via Coinatmradar.com.[21]

3. Compare Bitcoin to other cryptocurrencies. If you are looking to experiment with other cryptocurrencies, you may see that some of these have greater fluctuations. There are some 700 currencies from which to choose. Our recommendation is to start with another that has a market valuation of more than £10 million and buy from an additional cryptocurrency. Take advantage of the Coincap

▶

app. There's a huge amount of speculation and increase in values in cryptocurrencies as has been seen in the rise throughout 2017. But be aware of the risks of market bubbles.

Internal

1. Think what areas of your business are reliant on third parties for verifications. Break down your business flow into transactions and see if any part of these need authentication that could be attributed to the blockchain. Are there many intermediaries that could be sliced out of the chain? Review what parts of the business flow require regular contractual agreements.

2. Bring an external speaker or consultant into your organisation to explore-how Cryptocurrencies could be applied into your business.

3. Could you buy your staff members a nominal amount of Bitcoin as a gift, which is released to them at retirement age? It may not rise in value at the same rate, but it allows others to share in the excitement of an increasing asset (and also provides a good reason to stay in touch).

External

1. Find out if any of your clients would like to pay in Bitcoin, or if any of your staff would like to be paid in Bitcoin. Be sure to think through the tax ramifications.

2. Are there people inside your organisation who may be interested to think through how an appropriate blockchain solution could work for your business? Alternatively, are there consultants you can work with?

3. Start building out a blockchain solution or work alongside someone who is already implementing a similar solution.

3D printing

Can you print me a time machine?

The maker movement is about people who want to gain
more control of the human design world that they
interact with every day. Instead of accepting off-the-shelf
solutions from institutions and corporations, makers
would like to make, modify, and repair their own tools,
clothing, food, toys, furniture, and other physical objects.[1]

Mark Frauenfelder[2]

What is it?

With Fabien, a geeky friend, I spent a few hours trying to
design a little plastic megaphone that would slide on top of
my iPhone so that the speaker volume would be mechanically
amplified. Once we came up with the design on CAD
software, we input the instructions into the small 3D printer,
which had cost over $1,000. The printer took about 30
minutes to produce the item, using about $5 worth of plastic
beads. Once we had extracted the opaque white object, which
was close to 3 cm^3 in size, we removed the iPhone from its
case and realised that it was not very ergonomic. Moreover,
the phone sat awkwardly on the desk. We went back to the
drawing board. Three iterations later, we came up with a
solid prototype. The sound coming out was perceptibly

louder and the sounds from us were ones of jubilation. We had printed that megaphone. Fabien and I high-fived one another. We were members of the 3D printing alumni.

Many are familiar with laserjet and inkjet printers. These printers create graphics and words on paper or card and have been in people's offices and homes for decades. 3D printing is a fast-evolving technology that prints physical items in three dimensions. Initially, to some, this may not sound overtly disruptive, it is just printing after all, but do not be mistaken. 3D printing is significant.

> Initially, to some, this may not sound overtly disruptive, it is just printing after all, but do not be mistaken. 3D printing is significant.

3D printing certainly has the power to influence and help manufacturing move from a traditional approach using expensive moulds and casts to a process that builds through a layer-by-layer additive process. It is a bit like building something brick by brick with lego. As a result of using a 3D printer to create a product, one ends up saving an excessive amount of time and money on communication, on the expensive building of moulds and casts and on unnecessary shipping costs. If you had access to a printer that could print an object – any object – what would you print?

There is, additionally, vastly improved computing power and increasing miniaturisation that is boosting the potential of 3D printing. Nonetheless, 3D printing is not limited to the printing of small objects. There are many projects that can be imagined where 3D printing provides the best solution for creating large-scale objects. Winsun, a Chinese company, has taken it beyond the imagination stage. Using 3D printing, it is allegedly building houses and apartment buildings with a cost of $5,000 per house. The single houses measure

33 × 132 × 20 feet, take 24 hours to construct and, by building components of the houses off site, they have reduced waste by 70 per cent and labour by 50–80 per cent per building, when compared to bricks and mortar construction.

> Through the way people use 3D printing, we will also see efforts in sustainable development, a focus on the maker movement and a desire and opportunity for personalisation.

The impact that 3D printing currently is having, and will grow into further, is far wider than simply manufacturing. Some would go as far as to call it the third industrial revolution. Through the way people use 3D printing, we will also see efforts in sustainable development, a focus on the maker movement and a desire and opportunity for personalisation. Moreover, it is not hard to imagine how 3D printing may completely revolutionise the canons of distribution logistics, where one could have print-on-site as opposed to manufacture-and-deliver. These fundamental trends are at the heart of 3D printing and, along with the cost savings, the maturing of the industry and the rate of adoption, one can say with confidence that this 3D printing idea is not a passing fad.

In fact, it has been around for some time.

Duncan Stewart, director of technology, media and telecommunications research at Deloitte Canada, explains, '3D printing, where machines take computer files and make objects out of metal or plastic, building them up one layer at a time, has been around since the 1980s.'

3D printing has not fully broken out and matched the promises of recent years, especially the media-embraced hype during 2012–2014. Despite being around for 30 or so years in more or less primitive forms, the machines were cumbersome, materials limited, production slow and the cost immense.

However, all this is changing with 3D printing quietly gathering speed, momentum and investment and this is opening it up to all levels. As well as self-funding or asking friends and family for investment, people are raising money through selling advance orders of 3D printers for home use through Kickstarter or Indiegogo. In fact, four of the top 50 all-time funded campaigns on Kickstarter have been for 3D printers, with over 10 3D printing campaigns raising over $1 million. Alternatively, there are specialist investors working specifically in 3D printing at seed funding level (iMakr.vc, Asimov Ventures, Disney Accelerator) through to venture funding (Lux Capital, Balderton Capital, Autodesk Spark). This helps the sector achieve growth.

In this climate it is important to see what has changed over the last few years of development. Whilst still principally used in business, as the economics of 3D printing improve and new printable materials are introduced, there will be many more opportunities for 3D printers to be used in the home.

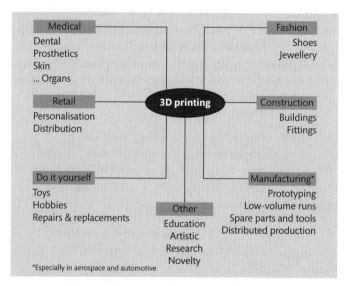

Applications for 3D printing

Why do you need to worry?

You may not be planning to build a new house any time soon, but how will 3D printing affect you and your business?

3D printing presents far more opportunities than causes for concern; but, for a number of people, again, the realities of lost jobs *is* a tangible concern. As 3D printing methods improve and the number of materials increases, with gains in cost savings and time saved, we are going to see companies investing more in this space, resulting in lost jobs. Instead of having a manufacturing line with eight members of staff working, you can print the parts to the product and have robotic arms assemble the products efficiently. It is more economical and the finances will drive change. Instead of paying salaries, the cost of this approach to manufacturing is maintenance, materials and electricity. Foxconn, known as the world's largest manufacturer, has a customer list that includes Apple, Microsoft, Google, Sony and Amazon and has over 1.3 million staff members. Its CEO, Terry Gou, once described 3D printing as 'just a gimmick'. But following the company's news in 2016 that it was going to reduce its staff count by 60,000 and replace them with Foxbots to help in it's manufacturing, it also outlined that it will be using 3D printing as part of its research and development work.

As well as manufacturing, we are also likely to see a loss of jobs in other spaces: fashion, retail, food, architecture and construction, to name a few. In short, anywhere you can identify products and objects will be affected.

Moral implications

Before we explore how businesses can harness and take advantage of this advancement in technology, it is important to look at some of the concerns to be considered. 3D printing raises a series of moral questions. When you are able to print all manner of objects, what does this mean for the creation of products that you would expect to be licensed or regulated?

> When you are able to print all manner of objects, what does this mean for the creation of products that you would expect to be licensed or regulated?

In 2013, the *Mail on Sunday* newspaper, in the UK, highlighted the dangers of 3D printing and firearms. Two journalists downloaded blueprints from the internet, created by Cody Wilson, who was a US law student at the time and is now the author of *Come And Take It*, detailing how to create a plastic gun, from 16 parts.[3] It was created in 36 hours and cost the newspaper £1,700 to buy the printer and materials. The gun was made of plastic, except for ammunition and a small firing pin, and could be broken down into smaller objects for transportation. This resulted in the gun not setting off metal detectors or showing up in body and bag scanning devices. The journalists tested this by passing through security to get on a Eurostar train from Kings Cross to Paris. Once inside, it took them 30 seconds to assemble the lethal weapon.

In 2013, 100,000 of these blueprints had been downloaded within two days of them being published before the US State Department took down the files. But, in 2015, accessibility increased again even further. It became possible to create a plastic gun for £25, if you already had the printer to do this.

In 2016, the issue of transport security and plastic guns had still not been resolved. The Transport Security Administration discovered a plastic firearm in a carry-on bag bound for a plane. They had discovered this one, but the more concerning reality is how many guns could go unnoticed in the future and what devastating news may lie ahead for us as a result. Could we witness a future hostage or terrorist activity 30,000 feet?

Is there a need to be concerned? How should this be regulated? How do we protect ourselves from these dangers? An important point to highlight is that we should always allow morality to be in conversation with technology.

> We should always allow morality to be in conversation with technology.

3D printing in health

Aside from the dangers of weaponry, one of the areas where 3D printing is already beginning to take off is in medicine. Whilst we are far from being able to print body parts, there are many pertinent applications where a small device or part may be necessary for a specific and one-of-a-kind size. Whether for dentistry or hearing aids, 3D printing has already become a norm. As Duncan Stewart writes, 'Hearing aid shells and dental copings are almost exclusively made with 3D printers today,[4] as are most braces for teeth,[5] some orthotics for shoes,[6] and even some titanium hips.'[7] As the use of different materials becomes more viable, more opportunities will arise.

Additionally, there are in excess of an estimated 10 million amputees globally, with approximately 185,000 amputees each year in the USA. 90 per cent of these amputees suffer from hindered mobility. A prosthetic limb is a recognised solution to this. However, as William Root points out, through his Exo project, many prosthetic limbs look robotic. This can further affect the self-esteem of someone who has lost their limb and, due to the cost, many are prevented from being able to access them. Through 3D printing, William Root[8] has designed his prosthetic limb called Exo, resulting in the only cost being the materials.

In Spain, surgeons of Salamanca University inserted a
3D-printed artificial rib cage, made out of titanium, into a
54-year-old cancer patient. Dental labs can accurately and
rapidly produce crowns, bridges, stone models and a range of
orthopaedic appliances, as is shown with Javelin Tech.[9] Ed
Smith, a paediatric neurosurgeon at Boston Children's
Hospital, has been using 3D-printed models of brains to
practise on before operations, helping to reduce the length of
his surgeries by 12 per cent.[10]

Chicago-based Colombian designer, Carlos Arturo Torres[11]
created the Funtastic Hand using a 3D printer for certain
parts of a modular prosthetic arm for children. The concept
was to allow the child to programme and own his/her
prosthetic extension rather than inherit an adult-made
mechanical tool. The first particularity of this project was
that Torres reached out to LEGO and, in a truly collaborative
spirit, the Danish company was happy to work on creating a
prototype whereby LEGO pieces were to be used as part of
the arm. As a result, the child is able to affix the LEGO plastic
bricks in any way he/she wants. The child's arm became
whatever toy or concept his or her imagination could create.
If there was an element of entertainment, the functionality
remained central to the process.

The second particularity of this project was the impact on the
other children in the child's class at school. By donating their
own LEGO pieces, they felt that the child's arm suddenly
became an object of joy rather than a reason to tease their
classmate.

The third was that the prosthetic could evolve with the
child's age, size and enjoyment of toys. The cost of the arm is
projected at $5,000, with a $1,000 recurring fee for the
adapted 3D-printed sockets.

The examples of the Funtastic Hand and the Iko Creative
Prosthetic System, shows how 3D printing can be leveraged

when applied with the right mindset mix: collaboration, empathy and purpose.

What should you do about it?

Businesses should not ignore 3D printing. There will be many who do, only to find that others in their sector are making 50–70 per cent cost savings and it has destroyed their own business model. There is an early mover advantage where the lessons and cultural preparation is crucial. Yet, this is also a sector where the technology has had trouble finding a successful business model. Many of the high-flying 3D startups have folded and several of the largest publicly traded 3D printing companies (e.g. Stratasys SSYS, 3D Systems Corp DDD or Arcam AB) are down heavily from their hyped highs due to disappointing sales.

There are some blockers that prevent people's appetite for 3D printing and these are partly mindset issues. First, businesses at the early stage of 3D printing will not have ownership over all of the printers and the printing processes they may like. Where a manufacturing company is familiar with a line of production, to suddenly have a third party print components for them negates their need to have studied manufacturing. A number of managers will have legacy infrastructure *and* bruised egos and will need to get over it. It will require a desire to work collaboratively with those who have the right hardware. For some, this could be a cultural challenge to build out their processes and accept that they need to relinquish some levels of control.

3D printing challenges the notion that a department based out of one factory or location is the norm.

Second, 3D printing challenges the notion that a department based out of one factory or location is the norm. As 3D printing is more mobile by nature, when compared to a manufacturing plant, it allows for quicker prototyping and more opportunities for each idea to be explored. This notion naturally will challenge the *status quo* of many organisations, and raise issues of who has ownership and control over their work. As a result of the proximity to 3D printers and organisations working more collaboratively, we are likely to see people wanting to work together and crowdsource the intelligence. What would be some of the obstacles to your business exploring 3D printing?

The luxury of personalisation

To some degree, the advent and sophistication of 3D printers could lead to some interesting opportunities for luxury goods companies. Luxury is about hyper customisation, personalisation and exclusive production. One example of such is the one-of-a-kind production of exquisite 3D-printed guitars by Steampunk. The Steampunk guitar, based on the iconic Telecaster, has a 3D-printed body whose moving parts are printed as a single component. According to its creator, Olaf Diegel, the Steampunk body is printed 'using selective laser sintering (SLS) by 3D Systems … on an sPro 230 SLS machine out of Duraform (nylon) material'.[12] Each guitar is custom ordered and costs the customer $4,000.

The time taken to produce the final object, including the artistic coat of painting, is three months. In the case of the Steampunk guitar, the use of 3D printing is to render a personalised and customised guitar. Not one guitar resembles another because the identity of a guitar lies in its body. The remainder of the guitar, the fretboard, tuning heads and pickup, is made using standard equipment. The key is to use the 3D printer where it provides a solid differential value without compromising the quality of the object. How could this personalised approach be incorporated into your business?

Commercial opportunities

There are many exciting applications for 3D printing from a business standpoint. In exploring physical objects, there are, potentially, endless ways that 3D printers could be useful. From a business perspective, below are some of the key ways 3D printing can already be used. What are the key benefits of the 3D printer versus alternative methods of manufacture? If your business requires, or has, any of the following characteristics, that could make 3D printing a legitimate area of exploration:

▊ Production in small runs.

▊ Personalisation to products, e.g. adding a name.

▊ Customisation and adapting to the specific situation or person.

▊ Experimentation with iterative improvements.

▊ To accompany regular change, e.g. a child that is growing.

▊ Transportation to the final destination is complicated.

▊ Decentralisation of the production.

Examples where businesses should or could be using 3D printing:

▊ Rapid prototyping.

▊ Quick design iteration, e.g. A/B testing of physical products.

▊ Low volume production.

▊ Mass customisation.

▊ Virtual inventory, e.g. distributed delivery.

▊ Production of less common spare parts.

▊ Prosthetics (especially for children who continue to grow and need new size updates).

If you use manufacturing suppliers or deliver work internally, check to see whether 3D printing is being used. In the past, to create moulds and then fabricate temporary mockups would take 5–10 days. It is cheaper to use 3D printing, as this allows you a rapid approach to iterations and improvements.

Every manufacturing unit needs to look at and explore exhaustively where and how their spare parts are being provided. There is an industry that is growing up and around 3D printing. Some of the sectors that are likely to embrace 3D printing the quickest would range from product designers and manufacturers, fashion designers and manufacturers, to those within the auto industry, construction, architecture, packaging or health.

Where 3D printing is both the future of manufacturing and, as some would argue, the third industrial revolution, how will you respond personally? How will your organisation take advantage of this disruptive technology? Excitement over 3D printing is becoming contagious. Creativity has been raised to a new level. Embracing this disruption might take your business into areas you had not considered and, you may find as you push out into this new dimension, they are just around the corner.

A slice of PIE

Personal

1. Add a specific feed on #3D printing in your Flipboard or Feedly account.

2. Download some design files from 3D community sites such as thingiverse.com,[13] youmagine.com[14] or treasure. is[15] and locate a 3D printer to print these off.

3. Are there any problems you have solved with product ideas? Consider whether someone could help bring your idea to life using 3D printing.

Internal

1. Check to see if or when you need to have a small quantity of prototypes built. Or are any of your products personalised? Use Tinkercad.com[16] or solidworks.com[17] to create your own designs.

2. Use 3D printing marketplaces like 3dhubs.com[18] or shapeways.com[19] to find access to a 3D printing service.

3. Consider printing off marketing merchandise for trade shows.

External

1. Check out how you could work with your suppliers to help them implement 3D printing and cut down on the time involved building out prototypes.

2. Could your organisation consider buying a 3D printer? As an operating model, it might be beneficial (at least for a period of time when the printer is not fully occupied) to become a 3D hub so as to be more embedded in the 3D printing community.

3. Are there partners or clients that you could introduce to 3D printing? Perhaps you could go along to a 3D printing conference together to deepen the relationship and learn more at the same time.

Energy storage
When will my phone last me a week?

> **Whenever we witness art in a building, we are aware of an energy contained by it.[1]**
>
> *Arthur Erickson[2]*

What is it?

One of the biggest challenges of alternative energy sources is the intermittent nature of the generation and the disequilibrium between when it is created and when it may be needed. For example, typically, solar panels collect energy during the daytime, but aside from air conditioning during the day, it is in the evening that the energy is needed. Thus, there is a critical need to store that energy for the vital moment. At its core, energy storage is about the ability to capture, retain and distribute energy in the most efficient and effective manner. In today's context, energy storage is becoming an evermore critical issue and, fortunately, technological advancements have been accelerating.

> One of the biggest challenges of alternative energy sources is the intermittent nature of the generation

and the inadequacy between when it is created and when it may be needed.

Our world is producing around 35 billion tonnes of CO_2 per year and climate change is accepted as a reality. As a result, there is a strong undercurrent and focus on renewable energy and how it is stored efficiently. As reported by Carbon Brief:[3] 'Averaged over the last decade, emissions from fossil fuels and industry account for 91% of human-caused CO_2 emissions, with 9% coming from land use change.' As Mike Scott says, '[energy storage] is going to be one of the most important features of the 21st century's energy landscape.'[4] With better energy storage, new exploration opportunities will open up, energy transformation will be more efficient and mobility will be enhanced.

There are five main technologies in energy storage (with chief benefit in brackets):

1. **Thermal:** hydrogen (with high storage capacity) and liquid air energy storage or LAES (long duration, large scale).

2. **Compressed air:** energy storage or CAES (with the use of underground caverns to store the compressed air).

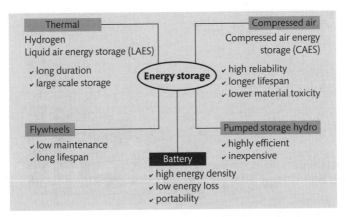

The five principal methods of energy storage with their chief benefits

3. **Pumped storage hydroelectricity:** or PSH: (highly efficient and inexpensive)

4. **Flywheels:** (low maintenance and long lifespan).

5. **Battery:** including lithium ion (solid state – high energy density, low energy loss), redox-flow (long life span, ease of recharge), lead acid (cost effective), nickel cadmium (low selling price, easy storage).

Whilst the mainstream focus has long been on developing renewable energy, there is now an increased focus on energy storage. Energy storage technologies range from very mature to highly speculative. It is a subject that has attracted the interest of companies and governments around the world. The investment in the sector is growing, even if interest from venture capitalists isn't quite as large as it has been. According to data from GTM Research and ESA's U.S. Energy Storage Monitor, 'Corporate investment in energy storage reached an all-time high in terms of quarterly investments in Q3 2016 ... bringing the annual total to $812 million.'[5]

The size of the market for energy storage is about to explode, with residential and non-residential usage helping to accelerate

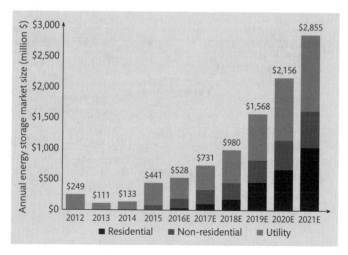

US annual energy storage market size, 2012–2021E (million $)[6]

the growth. The following figure shows the projected growth according to the bullish U.S. Energy Storage Monitor.

Advancements in energy storage are bound to follow, including improved efficiencies and lower costs. There are promising new battery technologies that are looking to break below $100 per kWh, with Elon Musk's enterprising ventures leading the way. In *No Ordinary Disruption: The Four Global Forces Breaking All the Trends*,[7] the authors from the McKinsey think tank anticipate that the price of lithium-ion battery packs could drop by one-third in the next ten years. There will be significant disruptions in industries directly affected, such as transportation and energy (oil and gas, power generation). Cities will also be impacted.

There are some amazing new technologies being established. These include ways to conduct energy, for example graphene. This creates many prospective technologies including cryogenic or liquid air energy storage and synthetic diamonds.[8] As has been a recurring theme in this book, no technology really lives in isolation. Energy is connected to the IoT, with objects ranging from wearable tech, homes, highways and factories all connected. We will see a massive increase of sensors using low-power wide-area network (LPWAN) technologies. Moreover, IoT will be instrumental in rendering energy grids smarter, thanks to the distribution and recuperation of new data points.

One of the areas of improvement to watch will be the standardisation of the way that energy storage technologies are measured when it comes to looking at the environmental impact and efficiencies.

Why do you need to worry?

Energy consumption remains a strategic issue for the world. As much as there is worry and debate about climate change, the finite nature of energy resources is also a long-term threat to world order. In 2015, industry was responsible, according to the IEA,[9] for 29 per cent of the total world consumption of fossil fuels. Therefore, the manufacturing sector has many reasons to be attentive to energy consumption and storage. Finding ways to produce renewable sources of energy has long been a preoccupation of the Western world. Politics will continue to play an important role in leading the charge, with China staking a claim by announcing, in January 2017, the investment of $360 billion in renewable energies between then and 2020.[10] With a supply of renewable energy comes the inevitable challenge of effective, efficient and environmentally conscious storage.

How can energy storage play a role for your organisation in the future?

Imagine this . . .

On my way to a meeting yesterday in our company's shareable electric multi-pax vehicle (SEMP-V), I was on a video conference with four other people also on the move at the same time in four different countries. That was a first for me. It is so convenient not to have to keep one's eyes on the road and to be able to work at the same time. Plus, the SEMP-V is exceptionally noise-proof. Our SEMP-V has a new glare-proof screen, which makes the video quality so much better on sunny days. When I arrived at Covent Garden, I was able to print out the 3D prototype just in time. It is so handy having all that equipment, like the 3D printer and coffee machine, in the work zone of the SEMP-V.

I plugged in to the ground terminal (that uses compressed air energy storage) and then went to join the team for our 'AI-storm'. We have been pioneering in the use of AI as part of our brainstorming sessions with clients. We all wear these pre-charged vests and headgear that harvest and store external energy, all the while synchronising our heartbeats and mindwaves. We like to think of it as hyper-IoP, the interchange of people. The battery-charged vests and headgear now can last for a full day of use. They are so comfortable, you do not even need to take them off for lunch. What is more, when there was a big thunderstorm outside, it was nice to know that not only were we protected, but that the energy from the storm was being applied into our energy packs.

When I got back into the SEMP-V at the end of the day to head home, I was happy to lie down in my bed and have an electronic massage. Some days, I think I would just rather live in the SEMP-V, it is so convenient and self-reliant. That said, as soon as I can upgrade to the latest SEMP-D (the shareable electric multi-pax drone), I'll be a taker.

If the above scenario is futuristic, the reality is closer than one might think. What are the implications for business?

The different groups affected by energy storage

Changes in the storage of energy have an impact on us all, but we have identified three groups who will experience the change in differing ways. The first group are directly involved in producing and storing energy, the second create products that need access to energy and the final group are businesses and households whose working and living environments are impacted by energy storage.

For those involved in producing energy, over the last few decades we have noted a strong prioritisation on the need for renewable energy. We have seen the dangers and limitations of fossil fuels, with international conflicts and wars focused on access to these resources. There have also been environmental disasters like the Deepwater Horizon oil spill, in 2010, which have highlighted the damaging impact and dangers of fossil fuel production. Put plainly, fossil fuels do not get a good press.

The challenge we have faced with renewable energy is the inefficient manner in which the energy created through renewables has been stored. This is now changing and, with the coming improvements in energy storage, there will be a much greater opportunity and an increased call for renewable energy as a serious alternative to fossil fuels. It will also help shift the balances of power. Energy storage will become a matter of strategic importance for countries wanting to improve their autonomy. The same will be true of plants that wish to run using renewable energies.

> Energy storage will become a matter of strategic importance for countries wanting to improve their autonomy.

Highview power storage

With the development of new ways to store energy, companies will be able to rethink the way they operate to pursue more efficient operations. One company that is innovating in this space is Highview Power Storage.[11] Using liquid air as the storage medium, Highview designs bespoke liquid air energy storage (LAES) plants that can efficiently deliver large volumes to service the energy storage market.

Whereas hydro-electric plants are constrained by needing to be located where there are large volumes of water, Highview's technology does not have the same geographic constraint. It is able to deliver low-cost LAES plants essentially anywhere. Using the cryogenic technology, where low-temperature or cryogenic liquids are used as energy storage, Highview plans to open the largest cryogenic energy storage plant in the world.[12] This will be a GigaPlant providing 200 MegaWatt (MW)/1.2 GigaWatt/hour (GWh), in Manchester, England. 'Cryogenic energy storage helps renewable energy sources to sidestep the problem of environmental factors by allowing intermittent (and sometimes unreliable) energy to be stored.'[13] Technologies such as cryogenic energy storage could radically change the way manufacturing plants are designed.

Energy on the move with wearable technology

But, as well as bigger plants, changes in energy storage are needed in small places, too. Technology increasingly is being embedded in our clothes. As such, a key to development will be the ability to store energy in small and efficient cells. Researchers from King Abdullah University of Science and Technology[14] have created micro-batteries that are ever thinner and more efficient. Measuring only a few micrometres, these new micro supercapacitors will bring key new opportunities to wearables.

One standout example is the Superflex Aura powered body suit,[15] an undergarment designed for the older age group. Based on technology originally designed to help US soldiers to carry heavy loads, the suit features hexagonal pods around key muscles, storing batteries, motors and control boards. These lightweight suits are being specifically designed to enhance the mobility of the elderly. Aura's tentative consumer release date is mid-2018.

Tesla – more than a car company

Elon Musk has, almost single-handedly, been leading the narrative and initiatives in energy storage. The Tesla electric car is a beacon in its space. But Tesla is going well beyond the manufacture of a disruptive vehicles. It has moved into energy itself. Tesla broke ground on its Gigafactory 1, a 4.9 million square-foot facility producing lithium-ion batteries, in June 2014 in Nevada and began cell production in 2017. The Gigafactory has planned annual battery production capacity of

35 GigaWatt-hours (GWh), where one GWh is the equivalent of generating or consuming one billion watts for one hour. As such, Musk claims that the output of 'Gigafactory will be bigger than the sum-total of all lithium-ion batteries in the world.'[16] By 2018, the Gigafactory 'will double the world's production capacity for lithium-ion batteries and employ 6,500 full-time ... workers.'[17] As a representative modern facility, Gigafactory will produce all its own energy as well.

> If Tesla is one of several 'new age' enterprises looking to push space travel, energy storage is clearly an important component of such ventures.

Great exploration

If Tesla is one of several 'new age' enterprises looking to push space travel, energy storage is clearly an important component of such ventures. SpaceX (Musk), Blue Origin (Bezos) and Virgin Galactic (Branson) are three of the most heralded private initiatives. The benefits of improved energy storage will be important for space travel and also impact satellites. Down on earth, exploration and 'adventure' travel will also be revolutionised. For example, the Enza New Zealand catamaran (of Sir Peter Blake fame) has been retooled to be autonomous with a zero carbon footprint. Called Energy Observer, the refitted 31-metre boat uses a combination of energy storage technologies, most original of which is the use of seawater. The technique consists of stripping the hydrogen out of the water and stocking it under high pressure (350 bars) in the hull.

If space and ocean exploration seems a far cry from regular business preoccupations, the take-away for business is the opportunity to render all electricals more portable, including the insertion of entertainment centres in a boat or car, for example.

The changing face of product design

Changes in energy storage bring changes in product design. We have seen this in everyday items. The mobile phone, once known to look more like a brick, has, over the years, been replaced with more streamlined designs, due to, amongst other things, a reduction in battery size. We are still waiting however, for the battery that will last a week.

> Changes in energy storage bring changes in product design.

As we have seen changes in the production of energy, we're left asking an important question. What if everyday items previously powered by fossil fuels or plugged into electricity sockets can be powered through batteries or other forms of energy storage? How will this affect design and functionality? What do manufacturers need to consider?

The electric car is an obvious signpost of what is to come, where a large rechargeable battery replaces the need for petrol or diesel. The capacity of these batteries has increased, the time taken to recharge them has decreased and, as a result, the distances able to be travelled have grown significantly. This has brought a change in the designs of cars, as there is no longer a need for a large fuel tank.

In 2015, IKEA brought to the home a series of lamps and tables that enable easy phone charging, by placing phones on an inbuilt charging hotspot. Starbucks did a similar thing in its coffee shops, making it easy for customers to access wireless charging without cables. As phones, tablets, laptops and now, increasingly, IoT devices have shown, we are, increasingly, wanting and needing to charge our items on the go. On arriving at someone's house, along with the offer of a cup of tea, the ability for a relaxed and convenient device charge may become the expected. It is likely we will see all smartphone manufacturers build into the phones the capability for wireless charging. Further iterations will enable proximity wireless charging, where devices can be charged without even having to be placed on a mat or device, but simply by being in proximity to a charging hub.

Will some products need to be clustered? Could we see appliances we had commonly seen at home appearing in vehicles as they function as energy hubs? After all, if there is a reason why we would want access to an appliance or electronic device whilst we are in our new vehicles, how are we designing these products with that in mind?

Whether it be solar panelled rucksacks, wearable clothing or electric-based vehicle hubs, there is a growing and increasing demand for access to charged technology as and when we need it.

If much has been focused on the Tesla electric car, the opportunity for energy storage at the residential level is also important, especially for areas that do not have easy and consistent access to energy. The Tesla Powerwall[18] is a rechargeable lithium-ion battery designed to store energy at a residential level for load shifting, backup power and self-consumption of solar power generation. Tesla has a focus on providing a threefold solution: generating energy through solar panels on the whole roof of a building, storing energy in Powerwalls and then using it in electric cars.

Often, effective communication and storytelling from forward thinking companies enable a broader adoption of technology. These brands help shape an idea, grab the attention of the market and make it accessible and tangible to others. Tesla has succeeded in doing this with its cars, but this is just a small part of the impact it will have. Where previous solar panels were costly, and often considered unattractive bolt-ons, Tesla's move into this market has paved a way for a greater level of adoption. You don't have people showing off their combi boiler. But they'll be proud of their Solar Powerwall combination.

The impact on your business and work

Where the workforce has developed to become flexible, mobile and remote, this move will increase further. Transportation will become work hubs and, with the advancement of self-driven cars, the experience we will all have will be remarkably different. As soon as solar panels, good energy storage, improved batteries and ease of charging become the norm, we will see a different relationship with, hunger and desire for portable devices. The growth of IoT devices is increasing this demand for portable charging.

> As soon as solar panels, good energy storage, improved batteries and ease of charging become the norm, we will see a different relationship, hunger and desire for portable devices.

So, when it comes to you, your family and your business, what would be some of the important questions for you to consider? Before making investments in technology or solutions that may quickly become outdated is it worthwhile to reflect on some key points?

For those directly involved in the production and storage of energy, there are important and near-term strategic actions you can take:

▌ Evaluate the impact on your business model.

▌ Search for new talent in energy storage.

▌ Identify potential non-traditional competitors.

▌ Brainstorm for durable competitive advantages.

▌ Check on safety and legal responsibilities.

For businesses whose products and services are directly associated with energy and energy storage, there are other important questions to be asked over the near-to-medium term:

▌ How will products that require energy (e.g. printers, refrigerators, electric razors, toys with batteries) be adapted?

▌ How will the usage of products that require energy change with enhanced mobility?

▌ What are the implications in terms of legislation and administration?

▌ What new products and services will be possible and/or required with enhanced and cheaper energy storage capabilities?

For businesses in general, even if energy storage is not a central part of your enterprise, here are the types of questions you need to be asking yourself over the longer term:

▌ How will work flow and the office space be impacted?

▌ How can energy costs be reduced using energy storage?

▌ How will commuting and transportation be changed?

▌ How can overheads be reduced and productivity increased?

▌ Do you want to make a choice to go solar?

A slice of PIE

Personal

1. Would you consider getting a Tesla Powerwall or integrated solar panels for your home?

2. What would stop you from getting an electric car? Even if you are not looking to buy a car currently, why don't you book a test drive to understand more about this option for when you are?

3. What energy storage solutions could you combine with IoT within your home?

Internal

1. Evaluate what additional routes to energy storage your firm could embrace in order to be environmentally responsible.

2. Reflect on how transportation and productivity will be impacted, and how you can be at the forefront of these implementations.

3. Are there any changes to your business model or working space that you may experience as a result of the changes in energy storage? This may include products not needing to be plugged into the mains and the greater level of portability and mobility this will bring.

External

1. Ensure that your external messaging is aligned with the internal reality when it comes to your organisation's energy consumption and environmental responsibilities.

2. Have your organisation cater for your customers' device charging needs when they are in your premises.

3. What changes to your products or services will become expected as we see a dramatic increase in energy storage? Are there new products? Will people grow an expectation that equipment and devices would no longer be using mains power?

Self/assisted driving

Are the days of mum being taxi driver numbered?

> The self-driving car is coming. And right now, our best supply of organs come from car accidents ... Once we have self-driving cars, we can actually reduce the number of accidents, but the next problem then would be organ replacement.[1]

Bre Pettis[2]

What is it?

Back in 2002, when the film *Minority Report* came out, I thought it would be amazing to have a car like that; but it felt like 2054 was a long time to have to wait for a driverless car. However, I grew up in the 1980s and I am of the *Knight Rider* generation and, having spent years longing for a 'KITT', my childhood had taught me to be patient when it came to predictions of the future.

The depiction of the car and travel in *Minority Report* showed no traffic and that clean green travel can be the norm. There was the ability to summon your car, be driven to wherever you wanted and, of course, use the journey time however you pleased. The dream is still there.

Forget 2054. When it comes to driverless cars, we are now well ahead of the game.

So, what is a self-driving car?

> '*A robotic vehicle that is designed to travel between destinations without a human operator. To qualify as fully autonomous, a vehicle must be able to navigate without human intervention to a predetermined destination over roads that have not been adapted for its use.*'[3]

If that seems too out of reach, remember, this all started with assisted driving, a car using functions that have been augmented by a computer, but still require a human driver. Or, to put it in other words, power-steering and automatic parking – something most new cars come with nowadays.

There has been significant growth and development in both assisted driving and the march to autonomous vehicles, with Google, Apple, BMW, Uber, Audi, Volvo and Tesla leading the charge.

Here's what you need to know

As presented by McKinsey in an article written by Anne VanderMey, 'The 12 disruptive tech trends you need to know':[4] 'Autonomous cars are coming, and fast. By 2025, the "driverless revolution" could already be "well underway".' Elon Musk, CEO of Tesla Motors and ever the optimist, believes that the technology for fully autonomous cars will be ready by 2020.

Tesla is, arguably, leading the way with the miles of testing it has managed through its widely adopted assisted-driving vehicles. In 2017, Tesla announced the Model 3 and it could be the turning point of the industry. Priced at £30,000, it makes electric cars available to a much wider audience than before. It is now comparable to the price of traditional family cars (albeit with hefty government subsidies for the time being). The car receives software updates so, rather than buying a new model every year, you can wait for the next software release.

But what about safety?

On 7 May 2016, Joshua Brown's Tesla's autopilot mode failed to distinguish an 18-wheel truck and trailer crossing the highway and, sadly, he died as his Tesla crashed into it. These are problems that Tesla believes its September 2016 software upgrade has addressed but clearly and sadly, any improvements could never bring Joshua back to his family and friends.

It is impossible to think of driverless cars or assisted driving without stopping to think about the safety implications. After all, would you want your loved ones to drive in a car where they do not have their hands on the steering wheel?

> It is impossible to think of driverless cars or assisted driving without stopping to think about the safety implications.

Tesla pointed out in its response, at the time, that this was the first known 'Autopilot' death in 130 million miles driven by customers; but, amongst all drivers in USA, every 100 million miles in 2015 there were 1.12 fatalities. When this is compared to 1921, the first year these statistics were gathered, the ratio was 24.09 fatalities for every 100 million miles.[5]

In its response, Tesla wrote: 'Every time that Autopilot is engaged, the car reminds the driver to "Always keep your hands on the wheel. Be prepared to take over at any time."'[6] But, as the technology continues to improve, it is easy for drivers to be lulled into putting their confidence in the car's computers. There are likely to be more than a half million Teslas on the road by 2019 and, with the extensive data they gather, this will help them make their cars safer and enable them to get to the point of being driverless more quickly.

To further demonstrate its preparation plans, one of the Tesla Model 3 sedan features is for seats to be folded down to act as a cabin bed. Why is that? I do not imagine Tesla is going after the VW Campervan market at this stage. Tesla is building its 'hardware' to prepare for the software improvements that will follow: a car that drives at 70 mph, so you can catch 40 winks.

▌ How would these developments impact your life each day and what questions emerge as a result?

▌ Is it appropriate to use a self-drive car to drive home if someone is too drunk to drive?

▌ If your boss gives you access to the car for work, are you expected to work in it on the way home?

▌ Will others track your journeys online to see where you really are? Who owns the data?

▌ If someone were to steal your car, would it drive itself straight to the police station?

▌ How much power do we give to cars and is that power in safe hands?

The next step in hacking

This brings us on to the issues of car hacking. In September 2016, researchers from China were able to hack the Tesla Model S and remotely control the braking system, front door locking, sunroof, chair, boot, indicators and side view mirrors of the vehicle. Craig Smith, who is author of *The Car Hackers Handbook*, stated that, although this was not the first incident of car hacking, he believed it was the first incident that targeted a Tesla.[7] The implications of this are concerning. A car being unlocked remotely by someone else making theft easy or the risk of dangerous accidents being caused by sudden braking is worrying. Tesla created a software upgrade to fix this problem within 10 days, but we can expect many further stories like this to emerge from multiple car manufacturers.

There is a wider issue that also needs thinking through, and this is not one of safety or security, but one that has more of a philosophical leaning.

The moral question

How should the vehicle be programmed to react in the situation of an *unavoidable* accident? Should the focus be to save as many lives as possible, even if that means that the driver and their passengers may die, or should it be to protect those inside the car at all costs? Jean-Francois Bonnefon (PhD) at the Toulouse School of Economics, carried out a study where he asked several hundred people through Amazon's Mechanical Turk to answer questions so he could understand their thoughts. Those asked were given scenarios where one or more pedestrian could be saved if they swerved into a barrier, killing the car's driver or passengers. They had to make a choice as to which they believed was right. They discovered that most people want the cars to sacrifice the drivers and passengers to save pedestrians, but that was only the case so long as those being questioned weren't *in* the car.

The Massachusetts Institute of Technology (MIT) created the Moral Machine, to ask passengers to answer questions that also raised the notion of how we value different types of people. Would your answer be different if it were known that the person ahead of you was a criminal? Or if they were elderly, obese or dying of an incurable disease?

Why don't you take the test yourself? It is interesting to see what questions it raises. To take the test and then compare your results against other participants, go to http://moralmachine.mit.edu.[8]

The governments' response

How have different governments responded to the issues around driverless cars? In the UK, in mainland Europe, Asia and in the USA, there has been a great level of support for these developments. The major advantage that governments cite are the life-saving benefits, the reductions in accidents and the associated financial benefits. The consulting firm, McKinsey & Company, mapped out some of the changes it believed driverless cars would bring. The biggest prediction applied to the USA is that self-driving cars would reduce car accidents by 90 per cent. The argument is that most of these are caused by human error. If that data played out, there would be annual savings to the US economy that would be in the region of $190 billion. Michele Bertoncello and Dominik Wee demonstrate this in their report, 'Ten ways autonomous driving could redefine the automotive world'.[9]

In the USA, the NHTSA and the US Department of Transportation outlined the following 15 core areas that manufacturers should assess in the development of this technology. They produced a report entitled 'Federal Automated Vehicles Policy', published in September 2016. The areas covered are: data recording and sharing, privacy, system safety, vehicle cybersecurity, human–machine interface, crashworthiness, consumer education and training, registration and certification, post-crash behaviour, federal, state and local laws, ethical considerations, operational design domain, object and event detection and response, fall back (minimal risk condition) and validation methods.

Self-driving, like all the other forces explored in this book, is not a standalone technology. It involves big data, AI and, of course the need to ask mindset questions. The US Government's response to the issues around self-driving cars recognises this.

In September 2016, Germany looked to create the first Driverless Car Highway Code. Alexander Dobrindt, Germany's Transport Minister, put forward a bill to provide the first legal framework for autonomous vehicles. The focus was on three areas: that a car chooses property damage over personal injuries, that humans are treated equally, regardless of age or race, and that, if a human were to take their hands off the steering wheel to check their phones, that the car's manufacturer would be liable in the result of a crash.

Regardless of the value of human beings treated, if there is a choice between which two people are killed and which stay alive, there is still a choice to be made. No doubt car manufacturers would want to prioritise those within a car to show that their car was the safest. But how is this worked through, when the law is not clear? And how are firms held accountable when the technology is sophisticated? Additionally, where many of these companies are in competition with each other, how is crucial data shared between direct competitors? Tesla opened up its patents in 2014 to speed up innovation towards driverless cars, which is a great start. Some may argue this also increases the likelihood of others supporting and developing solutions that tie into Tesla's infrastructure, ensuring a stronger commercial outcome for Tesla. Car manufacturers including Tesla, however, have been slow in sharing the data from the miles that have been driven.

Why do you need to worry?

For companies in the automotive space, the implications are clear. The competition is coming from multiple directions, including many non-traditional players. The regular rules of engagement are being upended. And for the person who makes their living driving a car, the impact will be significant.

In short, if your cousin is looking to become a London cabbie, now is the time to recommend a different career path.

Outside of the auto sector, there are many industries and niches that will be affected by the growth and development of driverless cars. And, for a number of people, this impact will be significant in jobs that would be lost.

Taxis and ride-sharing The drivers of taxis and ride-sharing vehicles would be affected, as driverless cars would be more economical and safer to use.

Car parks As ride-sharing and autonomous driving services take off, the number of individual cars needing parking will decrease.

Auto-repair companies Driverless cars would take themselves off to be fixed, so auto repair companies may suffer as a result.

Petrol stations These will need to reinvent themselves, if not pivot entirely.

Freight transportation With the development of driverless lorries, we would see larger areas of transportation affected.

Couriers Courier journeys through the likes of DropIt Shopping* and Deliveroo would be changed for driverless alternatives.

Chauffeurs No longer would there be name boards held at up at airports but, instead, driverless cars would do pick-ups.

Auto manufacturers Ride-sharing apps that bring vehicles to people on demand reduce the need for them to own a vehicle. Additionally, some traditional car manufacturers would be laggards in their own innovation towards self-driving vehicles and this could have a devastating impact on their businesses.

---

*https://www.dropit.shop/

Trains and subways Potentially, travelling by the underground and subway could be seen as highly outdated, versus point-to-point service. Time is lost travelling to and from the station and up and down escalators. This is time that could be saved by grabbing an on-demand ride with a colleague.

Driving and parking fines As people would not have the need to own their own cars, there would be reduced driving infractions and parking fines. Moreover, speed limits and traffic lights will always be respected.

Oil The oil industry would be significantly impacted by the growth in electric cars.

Emergency services People may access driverless cars to get to hospital when they previously would have called an ambulance. Additionally, you could possibly see a time when police cars and fire engines would no longer need drivers.

Military Increased use of self-drive vehicles will reduce the headcount of those who are employed as drivers, resulting in fewer casualties in war-torn areas. More front-line fighters, fewer supply personnel.

Aeroplanes People would be more willing to drive longer distances and, as a result, driverless cars may become more appealing for some in comparison to the inconveniences of air travel. With people able to relax or work in the comfort of their own cars, it would trump some of the hassle of air travel. This would be the same for trains.

Insurance On the assumption that there will be fewer accidents then, subsequently, there will be a large drop in the insurance policies taken out for both auto and life insurance. You will still have to have insurance, but the cost would reduce dramatically, perhaps up to 75–80 per cent of current costs.

Retail Due to the increased speed and convenience of deliveries from online purchases, there may be further impact on retail as fewer people make the journey to the shops. Alternatively, a shopping trip becomes more social and less hassle, as there is no driving or parking involved. For commuters, it will be easy to order from a healthy food shop on the way home and pick it up from the store your car would pass by. Perhaps we would see drive-by supermarkets?

Hotels Where drivers are able to sleep in a vehicle, and cars are built with this in mind, more people will consider sleeping in vehicles instead of a hotel. Additionally, as car ownership decreases, garages will be converted into short-stay accommodation. This would result in the likes of Airbnb gaining further market share from hotels.

Service jobs that pay high hourly rates (e.g. consultants, lawyers) As executives look to maximise the value of their time, consultancy companies may provide vehicles that enable work to take place during journeys. As the car drives back to the base from the executive's destination location, the consultant is busy researching and writing up the work.

Small offices/meeting rooms Vehicles could be created to host meetings or act as small offices. Instead of coming to a central location, the vehicle would pick up individuals from their homes or an easy access location. It could drive to a suitably inspirational working location. The roof opens up, the sides come down and it is an office by the beach. Variations of this could be used by training companies and team away-days, reducing the costs for businesses.

Radio, music and podcasts Audio media that has long had a stronghold on commuters, may become less popular as people have greater freedom to embrace other forms of entertainment and learning in self-driving cars (e.g. video).

Matching services Whether it be combining ride-sharing and dating apps or ride-sharing and consultancy apps, people would be able to share journeys and be connected with the relevant matched party.

Places of beauty With great locations situated near good public transportation links, new areas are opened up to those who can now be driven there. More trips to beaches, places of natural beauty and a chance to embrace the great outdoors.

Try it on – test it out Some retailers will combine the retail experience with a ride home. Fashion, jewellery, make-up, electrical goods; commit to a minimum monthly spend and receive a ride home whilst trying items on. Beats having to find time to go to a store to touch products.

On demand Whether it be massage vehicles, make-up and hair journeys, personal coaching sessions, different service providers may offer their services as a combined journey and service solution.

Travelling with friends People could have more time with friends as vehicles pick up multiple people from nearby city centre locations and drive them back to their individual homes.

Multi-tasking As the car becomes more of a homely experience, many companies will create add-on experiences: food on demand, entertainment on demand, relaxation or language tutorials based on what cameras in the car can see. Where people are cash-rich and time-poor, many services that can comfortably and realistically be achieved in a vehicle will be considered.

What should you do about it?

Imagine a city with fewer cars parked, then consider what that redesigned space could look like. How many cars are just parked, hour after hour doing nothing? They just take up space. As the driverless car comes, our cities may feel more futuristic, but they will also become more beautiful.

> As the driverless car comes, our cities may feel more futuristic, but they will also become more beautiful.

The driverless car is further away than assisted-driving technologies. For the companies involved directly in the automotive space, this is a technology that addresses both convenience and safety needs. For many complementary industries, such as delivery and transportation, there will be significant impacts. Meanwhile, there will, undoubtedly, be interesting opportunities for co-branding and the co-development of new services as the technology becomes more democratically available.

Two big questions that will arise for people will be: 'Do I need to own a car or is it better having access to transportation?', alongside 'How much is my time worth to me?' For many people in the developed world, having a car is considered standard, but the economics of this is changing. With the convenience of ride-sharing apps and the reduction of cost, how does this compare to the depreciating value of owning a car that also requires payments for insurance, tax, roadworthiness and maintenance costs?

Additionally, when you own and drive a car, you do not have the same freedom to make use of this time as you would if you were being driven. Some solutions outlined above may take a few years to emerge. But we can be confident that vehicles that give time back to the driver will become available. With the support of multiple governments, countries racing to be the leading pioneers of driverless technology and some of the biggest companies and most talented entrepreneurs focused on this solution, there is the energy to make driverless cars happen. The question is not,

'Will it make sense for you to take advantage of this technology?' but, perhaps, '*When* will it make sense for you to take advantage of this technology?'

Safety and cost remain two big stumbling blocks for many. Safety is the big issue that many will wrestle with. No doubt this will improve significantly over time but, at the same time, it is already statistically safer than driving in a normal car. When the technology is seen to be as trams and planes, will we choose to accept statistics and recognise a mode of transportation that for my children will be the norm in years to come? Statistics are one thing, but it becomes hard to let go and leave your family in the trust of a computer, when culturally we are so familiar with the need to be in control behind a steering wheel. This will be the initial reaction that many people will give but, as more self-driving options appear on the road and it becomes the norm, gradually there will be an adjustment to it. Assisted driving cars will no doubt be a stepping stone to broader acceptance of self-driving.

Cost will be the other factor. With Tesla pricing its Model 3 at just £30,000, it is likely we will see ever wider adoption of these cars. For many professional middle-class people, that price is affordable, especially when one questions the value of someone's time. Even if it is more than what people typically would be prepared to pay for a car, if it gives back one and a half hours a day, as a regular commuter, to be able to work during this time, it would pay for the difference in cost. What would you do with your time if you no longer had to drive?

Whether it is additional overtime for your company, increased profits if you run your own business or micro-consultancy sessions during the journey, the gained time is certainly valuable. Would the additional price tag be worth it? If you are a working professional, living in a major city and, typically, drive to work on a commute that is longer than 30 minutes, I am sure it would be. You may want to consider making a decision in the coming months whether you will be an early adopter when they are released to the public. If it is likely, perhaps build a team of people around you who are also committed to maximising their time, embracing new product or service ideas and taking advantage of the changes with driverless technology. Create a timeline and a roadmap for implementation and get inspiration and ideas from those in your group.

As for me, having waited for my 2054, 2020 feels only moments around the corner. The next stage is that the car learns to talk to me. Actually, that feels too easy. I want it to sing. *Bohemian Rhapsody*: 'Is this the real life? Is this just fantasy?'

A slice of PIE

Personal

1. Research self-driving cars and subscribe to #driverless cars on your Flipboard or Feedly app.

2. Assess what your time is worth and start tracking what you would do if you had your travelling time available to you.

3. Take a test drive of a car that either has assisted driving or is a self-drive car. Make a decision as to whether you would be looking to buy one. If so, what are the circumstances that would enable that to happen?

Internal

1. Evaluate whether the growth of driverless cars has any effect on your business or your startup's business model. What advantages could you make the most of? What disruptions do you need to prepare for?

2. If your organisation has fleet vehicles, weigh up in advance the financial impact of switching over to driverless cars. You could do a benchmark by leasing a suitable vehicle

▶

with a work space for a member of your staff and, by employing a driver, test the productivity levels and the additional value of the work completed.

3. What are some of the ways that staff could make the most of time spent in the vehicles? Consider whether time spent in a driverless car is considered work time or personal time.

External

1. What new product lines or services could your business prepare for on the basis of the changes that driverless cars would bring?

2. Reflect on how driverless cars would improve the quality of people's lives.

3. What do you think are the wider societal and moral issues of driverless cars? Take part in MIT's Moral Machine.[10]

12

Genomics
What won't we be able to cure?

DNA is like a computer program but far, far more advanced than any software ever created.

Bill Gates, The Road Ahead

Google's cofounder Sergey Brin had his genes decoded by genetic testing company 23andMe.[1] The results gave him reasons to be concerned. 'The exact implications of this are not entirely clear,' he wrote on his blog. 'Nonetheless it is clear that I have a markedly higher chance of developing Parkinson's in my lifetime than the average person.'[2]

In relation, no doubt partly influenced by these results, but also as a result of his mother having Parkinson's since 1999, Brin has donated over $100 million[3] to help discover a cure for the disease. He wrote: 'This leaves me in a rather unique position. I know early in my life something I am substantially predisposed to. I now have the opportunity to adjust my life to reduce those odds.' He cites that, 'there is evidence that exercise may be protective against Parkinson's.'

Fast forward a few years and we can see that DNA testing is significantly on the rise. People are left with the simple question of whether they would like to have access to their genetic code to understand their ancestry, take pre-emptive action against illness and see improvements to their health and fitness. How will humans respond to this information and in what ways will this affect businesses?

Admittedly, if you were met with concerning news, you may not have $100 million kicking around to put towards research for cures, but would you feel empowered to make changes and adjustments where you can? And, even if you did not directly know what to do with the information and what changes you could make, many testing companies provide a context for support or give recommendations for DNA consultants and genetic counsellors to help.

Once, genomic testing was accessible only to the elite and rich but, now, getting a partial genomic reading costs as little as £150. The changes in genomics in the last few years makes this topic a disruptive, important and sensitive one to grapple with.

What is it?

According to the *Oxford English Dictionary*,[4] 'Genomics is the branch of molecular biology concerned with the structure, function, evolution, and mapping of genomes.' Unless you are a biologist, it is hard to get your head around the relationship between genetics, genomics, chromosomes and DNA. If you are a biologist, you may want to skip the definitions and fast forward to the impact genomics will have on people and business. For the rest of us: hang in there.

Chances are, this whole topic has been, at best, the subject of an article you read diagonally or watched a documentary about.

All human cells have two sets of chromosomes, which carry DNA. One set is inherited from the father and the other from the mother. Cells can be found in the blood or you can take a swab from inside the cheek. There are companies like Illumina that provide a whole genome sequencing test or, like 23andMe and Karmagenes, that provide a partial test.*

*http://karmagenes.co/

Here is a rudimentary explanation of genetics and genomics:

▌ **Genetics:** is the study of the gene. A gene is considered the
functional genetic material in our DNA that is capable of
programming. 'A "gene" refers to a specific sequence of
DNA on a single chromosome that encodes a particular
product,'[5] such as a hormone or enzyme.

▌ **Genomics:** a genome is an organism's complete set of DNA,
including all of its genes. Genomics is the study of the full
genome, including *all* genetic material, whether it is
considered *functional* or not. Roughly 2 per cent of our
genome is allocated to the genes that 'code', with the
function of programming or encoding a particular *product*.
The remainder is filled with other DNA sequences, some of
which modify the way the genes are expressed.

If many are aware that progress on decoding the genome has
been made, most are unsuspecting about the massive wave of
new genetic information that is about to flood the world.

> If many are aware that progress on
> decoding the genome has been made,
> most are unsuspecting about the massive
> wave of new genetic information that is
> about to flood the world.

Decoding the human gene

In 1990, the publicly funded $3 billion research project to
decode the human genome was kicked off. Aided by the
private initiative, Celera Genomics, that used a different
approach at considerably less cost ($300 million), this
combination of teams successfully announced on 14 April
2003 they had cracked the code. Today, the leader in genetic
decoding is Illumina. It provides services to a number of
companies that directly connect with consumers, including
the already mentioned Google-backed 23andMe. In addition

to the Illumina-backed initiative, Helix,[6] there are dozens of companies that are listed on Wikipedia[7] offering consumer DNA-testing. The cost has continued to come down, at a rate far exceeding Moore's famed law, which relates to computing power. Illumina came out with an $850,000 machine that can sequence over 20 whole genomes per day, as it aims to bring the per-genome cost down to just $100.

At a cost of around $1,000 per person for a full reading and £150 for an FDA-approved, if partial, reading, the market for decoding the human being's gene could quickly move north of $20 billion per year.

What is the impact on people?

The process for getting a test done is easy. It involves spitting into a sample tube, sending it in the post to a laboratory and then receiving a report two weeks later. What can these results tell us?

Bearing in mind, within a report there will be a healthy dose of ranges and probabilities, the first thing you will be able to see is the breakdown of your ancestry. It is often quite surprising to people when they discover that they are not 100 per cent one nationality, but their DNA shows they are from multiple countries and regions. People rarely stop to think about that reality.

A recent engagement campaign called 'The DNA Journey' was carried out by travel company Momondo.[8] In it they filmed 67 global citizens, who took the DNA test and then were shown the results. The results were interesting, even if, due to the dramatic entertainment value, one takes the complete accuracy with a pinch of salt. There were certainly poignant moments. In one segment, there was the anticipation of two people discovering they were, in fact, cousins, having never met before. Could there be some relatives of yours working in the same niche or, if you work for a large enough organisation, even working for the same company?

Some of the participants initially showed a prejudicial attitude towards other nationalities not their 'own'. The results estimated someone's ethnicity based on their DNA and caused some to own and acknowledge that some regions and countries they had in their ancestry were those they had been negative about moments before. As viewers, it further acted as a reminder for us all to live like we are in a global village, and celebrate the fact we have more in common than we realise. This message would serve as an alternative to the nationalist and racist undertones we still hear in the media and sadly at times in Politics. Perhaps it would be an interesting exercise for senior national leaders to carry out their own DNA tests to help break down global barriers between countries. Additionally, how could these be used within your organisation to bring a greater sense of collaboration, collaboration, to enable people to work better together. We may, after all, be more alike than we have realised.

Second, as well as understanding your ancestry further, the test results can help reveal if you are at risk of passing on an inherited condition to your children. For instance, if you are soon to be a parent and have a cystic fibrosis gene, would you want this gene to be treated through a process called 'gene editing' in order to minimise the likelihood of passing it on? As gene editing becomes more advanced, the thought of this may seem, initially, incredibly positive. However, some may hold a different view and would want people to consider those who have cystic fibrosis. Over time, how would society view this condition or, indeed, people with other conditions who were not in a position to receive gene editing. Would they become ostracised? How would it affect relationships if one party has a genetic disorder that cannot be treated? Could we see a change in marriage vows: 'For better or worse, for richer or poorer, for good genes or bad genes'?

Third, by understanding any genetic risks you have, you can make informed changes about your health or at least manage the areas you cannot change. As a result, you may have clarity as to how you would respond to specific drugs or treatments, and receive a bespoke line of treatment that takes into consideration your DNA. There will be a benefit in understanding more about your health and how to approach your nutrition and fitness. There are a growing number of companies, like DNAFit,[9] that have emerged to help people apply solutions to their DNA reports and results. The results help explore whether they are naturally inclined to power sports or endurance sports and how quickly their body will recover between sessions. Nutritionally, it can reveal one's reaction to salt, saturated fat and carbohydrates. It will also show risks to being gluten and lactose intolerant, how well one's metabolism reacts to caffeine and alcohol intake and what vitamins and antioxidants are needed. It is easy to imagine companies needing to consider different catering and wellbeing options.

Keeping it in the family

If you are sold on the benefits and are wanting to jump online and purchase your testing kit, it is worthwhile considering some of the potential impacts of having your genes decoded. Some firms even insist you have genetic counselling in advance of receiving some information.

As identified, you may learn about your ancestry and may discover significant information that reveals that you are not related to someone you have always considered family. This is most commonly the case in areas of paternity, causing painful questions to arise and a deep level of turmoil. Additionally, you may discover relatives that were never made known to you. Or, if you were adopted, you may find yourself in a position to find your biological parents. Are you ready to navigate all the emotions that come with these issues?

Furthermore, because genetic information is hereditary and affects more people than you alone, you may find that your family do not want to know either the ancestry or the health information you discover. This may put you in a difficult situation of not knowing what to communicate and where it is safe to share the information. Additionally, if you discover you have a genetic defect, you may be able to adjust your living patterns. But, if the condition is not curable, as is currently the case with Parkinson's or Alzheimer's, it can be difficult to come to terms with the possibility that you may develop this disease many years from now. Will you receive the support you would be looking for? There is a strong argument that it is better to take pre-emptive action; this sense of uncertainty may cause emotional challenges to some.

Imagine this . . .

My watch's haptic resolutely tapped my wrist. It was time to drink more fluid. I got up and stretched, before refilling my water bottle. Since I had had surgery on my knee, I was doing my best to keep up with my physical therapy routines. But, the motivation to do more had come from the re-reading of my genetic and epigenetic results. Living in England, where the climate is decidedly dismal, I had a 10 x higher risk of thrombosis, which meant that I had a 10 out of 1,000 chance of having some kind of embolism versus the standard 1 out of 1,000. Since I had been identified as someone who is prone to muscle tears through dehydration, I now carried around a water bottle with me everywhere I went. My watch's sensors were able not just to detect my inactivity, but also to monitor and indicate my electrolyte levels.

To my surprise, my genetic ancestry readings had been the big win for me. And it was all the more useful to be able share with my wife and kids. To begin with, we all enjoyed the fact that I had a trace of African roots. But, when I went about writing the story of my grandfather, that knowledge helped me come to terms

▶

with some odd familial differences. More importantly, it set me on a path to find out more about my great grandmother's history.

More saliently, and certainly more concretely, we then got the genetic readings for all the family. It turned out that my youngest had a coding indicative of dyslexia. As a result, we found a therapist and bought a raft of new toys and interactive 'books' that were designed for dyslexic children in their pre-reading years. The field of medicine has evolved so much thanks to the stimulus of genetic readings. Moreover, there are now many complementary goods and services tendering to these new genetic readings. They say that, thanks to the phonological intervention we have undertaken for our youngest, she should not suffer as much as I did in slogging through books that were veritably a torture for my own dyslexic brain.

Meanwhile, I thought it a citizen's duty to accept that my genetic reading become anonymised and entered into the world databank. But, to begin with, I was much more reluctant to share the data with the GOADER, Genomic Office of Anonymised Data for Efficient Returns. The initial premise was that each person would get paid £5,000 for handing over their genetic data and, in return, companies would be able to consult the data for better marketing purposes. It was not entirely clear how much the major corporates paid to GOADER, but it was reported on *GenoLeaks* that the minimum corporate subscription was £10 million per annum. At the start, insurance companies were the only interested parties. But, now, even marketing companies such as L'Oréal and Unilever have become interested to see if they can adapt and customise better their on-demand supply of household and beauty products. I am chuffed to get the annual subscription payment of £1,500. I'm thinking of upgrading to the gold level next year, where my data can be shared with banks and the police. I wonder if the £10,000 signing bonus is worth it?

The changes and impact of genomics is creeping up on us and it is not only personal. It is business.

What is the impact on companies?

As the number of people wanting to take genetic tests increases, businesses will find themselves both with a responsibility and an opportunity. On a macro level is there concern we could end up living in a world as depicted by the film *Gattaca*? It tells the story that, through genomics, some people are 'created' and classified as 'valids' and others are conceived and, therefore, more prone to natural disease and classified as 'invalids'. In the film, genetic discrimination is illegal but, in reality, due to genetic profiling, 'valids' qualify for professional employment whilst 'invalids' are relegated to menial jobs. Is there a risk that testing companies cannot be trusted with our data or even that, due to the value of this information, a black market for trading it could emerge? How much would it be worth to companies, during recruitment processes, to find out key information about potential staff members' health and behavioural traits?

Would staff want their employers to know their genetic disposition and would they trust them with the data? How could we ensure that companies do not abuse this data? And, even if some do not want to provide their data, some companies may run company-wide schemes and, if someone was not to consent, would they be treated fairly? It is likely that the firms we work for will not be the custodians of this genetic data. It will be more common that, in most cases, people will gather their own data, much as they would gather their own credit report and, through the APIs available from services like 23andMe, the individual would have the option to share their personal data with others.

Alternatively, once the data is read, anonymised and made available via open source, how will companies layer information on top of that? Centralised companies that deliver this service will offer up an API that other solutions can access. This API will act as a central route to market for many solutions, as third-party companies offer ways to interpret, make use of the data and build services on top of this information. Additionally, some may choose to store and share their data through blockchain technology.

There are some areas where there would be more contention. As hinted, could it ever become the case that genetic tests become a part of a recruitment process? Perhaps, it is feasible to see sports clubs extending the range of the pre-signing medical to include genetic tests. In fact, DNAfit started working with two premiership football clubs in the UK in 2014.[10] Marios Kambouris, the Yale University geneticist, previously worked with a Premiership club in 2011 to see how injury-prone different players may be.[11]

Where there is strong competition, high financial rewards and incentives, it is not unusual to see sportspeople and other high-performing individuals subject themselves to requirements many other 'workers' would not be prepared to. It is equally quite likely that we will see gene editing, if people consider changes could make them or their offspring better sportspeople. Could this raise issues, much in the same way as performance-enhancing drugs do?

Are we likely to see a time where providing our genetic code is a compulsory requirement for job applications in the short term? It seems the common wisdom would say no. In all but the outlier examples, I think the legal issues would prevent this from taking place for some time. It is easy to imagine a lawsuit against discrimination for an unsuccessful job applicant from someone who had performed well but was turned down in the final stages. They would argue it was not down to their eligibility as a candidate but that their DNA test showed a high probability of developing Alzheimer's. That would be enough for HR departments to steer clear of for some time. The potential impact of this discrimination will be enough for legal and HR departments to steer clear of requesting such tests. Will that hesitancy last forever?

As with the individual benefits that businesses will experience, there are additional words of caution. Some companies may be able to save money on business insurance premiums if they were able to provide genetic reports to their insurers. One must take care not to breach the trust staff have put in the company. If companies are slow to respond to the needs of their employees, will there be claims brought against them? And, if data is provided to a company, how is this data stored in a way that takes responsibility for the privacy of the individual? Who will do the oversight? Will there be a global standard?

What could your business do with such data? On a micro level, when an employee comes to HR outlining a disposition to be depressed due to a lack of sunlight, and their genetic report demonstrates this, you would be able to base them closer to the window to ensure a greater level of care. Companies could also offer DNA tests to team members to help them manage their health, nutrition and foster greater working patterns and diversity. The Momondo senior management team agreed to have their DNA tested, resulting in a greater awareness that they did not have a balanced ethnicity in their senior management team. As Momondo CEO Hugo Burge said in a BBC report, 'Anything that makes you question your decisions and perspectives is good. We're all prone to pre-judging people … and if you come to terms with the fact that you're not the person you thought you were, it definitely changes your perspective about prejudice when meeting other people.'[12]

> If you come to terms with the fact that you are not the person you thought you were, it definitely changes your perspective about prejudice when meeting other people.

For some business sectors, the future will open up lots of opportunities. If you are within health, nutritional, well-being, training, development, educational, learning, personal branding, marketing, counselling, ancestry, private investigation security, legal, police, pharmaceutical, insurance, human resources, travel, real-estate, family planning arenas, the applications are there to be imagined.

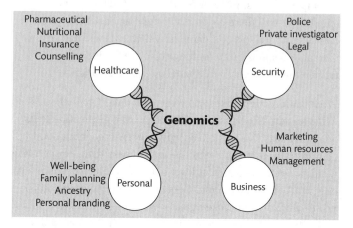

Potential opportunities with genomics

As the study of genetics gets more lab time and spills into the wider domain, we are bound to see new analyses and applications. For example, in the marketing sphere, well beyond the healthcare space, one can imagine the discovery of genetic predispositions to certain products, pitches and channels. Researchers at King's College London, in a study published in the journal *PLoS One*, concluded that, 'Our results support an active model of the environment, where young people choose their online engagements in line with their genetic propensities.'[13] The research, which studied online media use in 8,500 teenage twins in the UK, suggests that we inherit a certain predisposition to media consumption. In terms of opt-in marketing, such readings could be gold for brands and customers alike. How would it affect your business, if you could segment out your marketing message to those who have a predisposition for video?

> The study of genetics remains embryonic in terms of its exploitation in businesses outside the medical and genetics sphere.

Meanwhile, a whole other related area of study is epigenetics. As defined in the *Oxford English Dictionary*,[14] epigenetics is 'the study of changes in organisms caused by modification of gene expression rather than alteration of the genetic code itself'. As such, epigenetics includes environmental components that, as with evolution, have an impact on our bodies and our deviations, whether they are neurological, more widely biological or psychological. The study of genetics remains embryonic in terms of its exploitation in businesses outside the medical and genetics sphere. However, the analysis and interpretation of epigenetics brings with it the hope for greater robust business applications.

> The analysis and interpretation of epigenetics brings with it the hope for greater robust business applications.

With a better understanding of our past and the potential for our future, the opportunity to operate both differently and better in the present is now a potential reality for many of us. Although businesses' relationship with genomics is in its infancy, we can expect to see significant changes in this area in the coming years. Will it take hold? The next few years will be fascinating to watch.

> With a better understanding of our past and the potential for our future, the opportunity to operate both differently and better in the present is now a potential reality for many of us.

> How would you ensure you take responsibility to show respect, appropriate support and the provision of care if you knew someone's genetic information?

A slice of PIE

Personal

1. Consider how you could benefit if you had information about your genes. What would you take responsibility for?

2. Read up on genetic edits and take a position on the ethics.

3. Consider taking a genetic test with the likes of 23andMe[15] or AncestryDNA.[16] AncestryDNA or look to receive a Personal Development programme through a test with Karmagenes.*

Internal

1. Evaluate what advantages your company would have if staff shared genetic information with you.

2. How would you ensure you take responsibility to show respect, appropriate support and the provision of care if you knew someone's genetic information? What might be the insurance consequences?

3. Are there any company initiatives you could support people with to explore genetics further? Could it help with collaboration and diversity training?

External

1. How could genetic data enable you to communicate more meaningfully with your customers?

2. What is important to consider in the protection of DNA data? How should others also take responsibility?

3. What is your ethical position on the use of DNA data? Is it right for marketeers to use such data?

---

*Bookmark-Karmagenes.com

Conclusion – futureproofing for disruption

There is no time like now to get started. Which disruptive force is most strategic to you and your organisation? The good news is that, on one level, getting started can be as easy as subscribing to *WIRED* or some new podcasts. Check out our website, futureproof.ly, where there will be blog posts, guest articles and interviews to give you further inspiration. We want to hear of your stories and how you have been able to implement these solutions. As we said right at the beginning of the book, we want to be your companions as you look to Futureproof your business.

> Tie the initiatives directly to your strategy in order of priority.

As you go down the path of assessing and selecting technologies, people and partners to help drive your business forward, we want to remind you of several key points we have addressed throughout this book.

- Tie the initiatives directly to your strategy in order of priority.
- Carry out an honest assessment of yourself and your organisation against the three key mindsets: meaningfulness, responsibility and collaboration.
- Evaluate which technologies will work with each other and how they will integrate best in your organisation.
- Check to see what skills or capabilities you might be missing.

▌ Make sure the customer is always at the heart of your goals.

▌ Get your hands stuck in as you explore and use the technology.

▌ Do not give up when you face mistakes but, with tenacity, keep learning, improving and growing.

Get your hands stuck in as you explore and use the technology.

As we consider what it takes to be truly ready for disruption, we believe there is a certain alchemy that comes when you know *why* you are doing it, that you strongly believe in the cause, and you are ready to get your hands dirty in participation. We call this the Head-Heart-Hands approach.

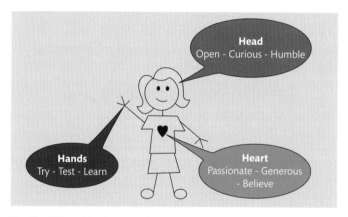

The Head-Heart-Hands approach to help futureproof your business

Head

As a business leader, it is crucially important to make sure the strategic goals are clearly defined and that the disruptive forces are appropriately targeted to solve the company's core challenges. Putting the right *head* first, means removing the arrogant I-know-it-all attitude. It means being curious, embracing constant learning, reading hungrily, assessing the quality of your network, being open to diverse opinions and having the humility to listen attentively whilst welcoming criticisms. We all know how important it is to have a good head in business.

Heart

> You need to know that somehow your organisation contributes to society and makes the world a better place.

To the extent that every employee who engages is contributing to your competitive edge, it is important that you and your team have a level of energy and engagement that outstrips your competition. Being big hearted enables you to be passionate and wholeheartedly committed to your business, fulfilling the call to make a difference. You need to know that somehow your organisation contributes to society and makes the world a better place. That requires heart and courage and a strength to keep going through the pain. The attitude we like to embrace is one of giving before receiving. You are building something far bigger than you.

> Digital transformation and the onboarding of these new technologies cannot be delegated.

Hands

Digital transformation and the onboarding of these new technologies cannot be delegated. You need to stand up and be counted. Whether you are a business leader, entrepreneur or an employee in the company, everyone needs to get their hands dirty and try things out. Even in the early stages of development, it is useful to understand what these technologies can do now, and what is to come. Within your organisation, it is imperative that you understand the improvements to be implemented for your team and your customers, so that all areas of your organisation grows and flourishes.

If you are, indeed, nervous in any areas, don't worry. Many people when they allow their thoughts to catch up with them are nervous. But this is not a time to be glass half empty. This is a time to dream of what is to come. We are absolutely convinced that the future with all the threats and fears, is exciting and fulfilling. But it won't be handed to us on a platter. We believe a new style of leadership is needed to passionately embrace and fearlessly grow through the challenges that lie ahead. Leaders who are able to embrace new technologies. Leaders who understand how the sociological, ecological and geopolitical trends are changing the expectations of workers and customers. Leaders who have the courage to listen and live lives of humility, integrity and passion. Do you want to be a great leader?

> Above all, it is about having the courage to lead by example, in front of the pack living lives of humility, integrity and passion.

How do you feel when you evaluate the opportunities that lie within these disruptive forces. Are your thoughts positive or negative? Many, including ourselves, will, at times, straddle both. We encourage you to embrace these forces with a measure of scepticism, a healthy dose of experimentation and a strong community of allies to cheer you on. At times you may need the tough love, to give you more courage as you make space to grab hold of the future. Do not wait for the world to disrupt you and push you out of a job. Get ready for the change, anticipate what is coming and swivel to make sure you grow through it. We repeat; don't let you or your organisation be crushed or left behind by the disruption. Yes, AI and robotics will put some out of a job, but that does not need to be the defining story. There will always be people who point to impending doom. You are formed from something deeper. The greater challenge and adventure will be to recognise these transforming trends and learn to work with AI and robots. That is the future.

We are incredibly excited to see how these new technologies, in partnership with big-hearted people, will help create a better world. We hope that this book has brought you insight, inspiration and encouragement as you grapple with the issues. We hope you make both a meaningful difference *and* a handsome profit.

> Get ready for the change, anticipate and swivel to make sure you benefit and grow from it, without getting crushed by the disruption.

And, in it all, we hope that you will put your head, heart and hands into creating something beautifully disruptive. As new technology constantly emerges and new challenges arise, through it all, we long for you to create something that's deeply meaningful. For others. For yourself. My friends, it's time to create an legacy. After all, that's what's truly Futureproof.

Notes

Introduction

1 Christensen, C. (2013) *Innovator's Dilemma: When New Technologies Cause Great Firms to Fail*, (reprint edn), Harvard Business Review Press.

2 https://www.wired.com/insights/2014/04/digital-darwinism-disruptive-technology-changing-business-good/

3 http://www.businessballs.com/maslow.htm

4 https://www.forbes.com/sites/johnkotter/2013/04/03/how-to-lead-through-business-disruption/#60dfc3bf2644

5 An Intrapreneur is an individual working in a larger organisation who operates as an entrepreneur.

6 https://techcrunch.com/event-type/disrupt/

7 After closing down, it has acquired and has traded hands twice and was merged with Rhapsody.

8 https://en.wikipedia.org/wiki/Sean_Parker

9 http://sethgodin.typepad.com/the_dip/

10 http://theleanstartup.com/

11 http://cdoclub.com/

12 http://www.forbes.com/sites/falgunidesai/2016/06/13/the-many-faces-of-the-chief-digital-officer/

13 http://myndset.com/2012/05/raising-your-digital-iq-why-its-important-for-all-the-c-suite/

14 The T-shaped manager profile was first explored in the *HBR* article by Morten T. Hansen and Bolko von Oetinger, March 2001. https://hbr.org/2001/03/introducing-t-shaped-managers-knowledge-managements-next-generation.

It was then re-used by people, including Ross Dawson, to describe conceptually the T-shaped expertise profile. http://rossdawson.com/blog/building-future-success-t-shaped-pi-shaped-and-comb-shaped-skills/ Dineli Mather (Deakin University, Australia) is credited with the pi-shaped expertise profile. http://www.deakin.edu.au/about-deakin/people/dineli-mather

15 https://www.producthunt.com/ – Product Hunt was acquired in Nov 2016 by AngelList.

16 http://ted.com

17 https://www.bloomberg.com/technology

18 Masterclass.com

19 Udemy.com

20 https://basecamp.com/

21 http://infed.org/mobi/peter-senge-and-the-learning-organization/

22 https://www.marketingcloud.com/blog/35-digital-marketing-quotes-to-memorize-and-tweet/ Marc Benioff, CEO of Salesforce, from his speech at Dreamforce 2014.

23 http://www.briansolis.com/2012/03/10-tenets-to-survive-digital-darwinism/

24 https://www.siliconrepublic.com/companies/digital-disruption-changed-8-industries-forever

25 *HBR* article, 'What is Disruptive Innovation?' https://hbr.org/2015/12/what-is-disruptive-innovation

26 https://www.prophet.com/thinking/2016/04/the-six-stages-of-digital-transformation/

27 https://thebusinessleader.co.uk/2014/11/10/its-good-but-its-not-a-digital-transformation/

28 https://www.slideshare.net/Pure360/smart-insights-bdmf2014

29 http://cloudblog.ericsson.com/the-seven-stages-of-digital-transformation

30 https://techcrunch.com/2015/04/18/you-dont-need-a-digital-strategy-you-need-a-digitally-transformed-company/

31 http://www.statista.com/statistics/193710/concert-revenue-of-live-nation-entertainment-since-2008/ and Deloitte estimates for 2015.

Mindset 1 Meaningfulness

1 https://www.theguardian.com/technology/2017/jan/11/robots-jobs-employees-artificial-intelligence

2 https://www.wired.com/2017/02/self-driving-cars-wont-just-watch-world-theyll-watch/

3 http://www.cnbc.com/2016/05/02/bitcoin-inventor-satoshi-nakamoto-finally-revealed.html

4 Millennials is a term to describe the generation between 1980 and 2000, who all came of age with the internet in existence.

5 https://www.inc.com/nicolas-cole/why-millennials-would-rather-make-less-money-working-a-job-they-love.html

6 http://www.gallup.com/businessjournal/188033/worldwide-employee-engagement-crisis.aspx

7 http://www.newoaksconsulting.com/assets/docs/Impact_of_Employee_Engagement_on_Performance.pdf

8 http://ww2.kqed.org/stateofhealth/wp-content/uploads/sites/27/2015/04/Are-Entrepreneurs-Touched-with-Fire.pdf

9 https://www.harpercollins.com/9780066620992/good-to-great

10 Collins, J. (2001) *Good to Great*, Chapter 3, Random House Business.

11 http://www.bbc.co.uk/news/magazine-18723950

12 https://www.enneagraminstitute.com/

13 http://www.strengthsfinder.com/home.aspx

14 http://www.gallup.com/businessjournal/186044/
employees-strengths-outperform-don.aspx

15 http://spencerjohnson.com/

16 http://www.gallup.com/businessjournal/182321/
employees-lot-managers.aspx

17 Maxwell, J.C. (2007) *The 21 Irrefutable Laws of
Leadership* (2nd rev. edn), Thomas Nelson.

18 http://www.herdwisdom.com/seven-fundamentals-
infographics.php#.U59YUo1dU00

19 https://www.accenture.com/us-en/
insight-un-global-compact-sustainability-mining-metals

20 http://www.sustainability-reports.com/81-of-sp-500-
companies-published-sustainability-reports-in-2015/

21 Greenwashing is the practice of pretending to be more
environmentally friendly than one is in reality. It's more
of a marketing ploy than a substantive action.

22 http://www.blackrockimpact.com/

23 http://www.sourcemap.com/

24 L'Oreal teamed up in 2015 with Organova, which 3D
prints synthetic skin. http://www.bbc.com/news/
technology-32795169

25 L'Oreal's stock price traded in a range of 50–100 euros
from 1999 to mid-2012.

26 https://www.greatplacetowork.com/

27 http://www.theacsi.org/

28 https://www.glassdoor.co.uk

29 https://www.ted.com/talks/ricardo_semler_how_to_run_
a_company_with_almost_no_rules

30 https://en.wikipedia.org/wiki/Maslow's_hierarchy_of_needs

31 http://www.kstoolkit.org/Samoan+Circle

Mindset 2 Responsibility

1 In the original text of *The Fountainhead*, there is a dialogue between the protagonist Howard Roark and the Dean. Dean: 'My dear fellow, who will let you?' Roark: 'That's not the point. The point is, who will stop me?' – Chapter 1, p. 17

2 http://gs.statcounter.com/press/mobile-and-tablet-Internet-usage-exceeds-desktop-for-first-time-worldwide

3 http://www.ooyala.com/videomind/blog/video-make-nearly-80-Internet-traffic-2020

4 http://www.robinsharma.com/

5 Ronson, J. (2015) *So You've Been Publicly Shamed*, Picador.

6 http://www.darkreading.com/endpoint/91--of-cyberattacks-start-with-a-phishing-email/d/d-id/1327704

7 http://audible.com

8 https://iag.me/socialmedia/how-to-do-a-facebook-personal-profile-security-audit/

Mindset 3 Collaboration

1 Lash, J.P. (1980) *Helen and Teacher: The Story of Helen Keller and Anne Sullivan Macy*, p. 489, Delacorte Press/Seymour Lawrence.

2 *OuiShare Magazine* – http://magazine.ouishare.net/2014/04/lisa-gansky-and-the-value-capture-in-the-collaborative-economy/

3 http://crowdcompanies.com

4 https://www.flickr.com/photos/jeremiah_owyang/15928658251/sizes/k/

5 http://www.betrustman.com/

6 http://www.fastcoexist.com/3046119/defining-the-sharing-economy-what-is-collaborative-consumption-and-what-isnt

7 'How the Sharing Economy Can Create Value from Waste,' by Lisa Gansky, *Huffington Post*, http://www. huffingtonpost.com/lisa-gansky/sharing-economy-value-waste_b_8522490.html, 10 November, 2015

8 'Show me the money,' a phrase used by characters in the 1996 film, *Jerry Maguire*.

9 https://www.renttherunway.com/

10 http://chic-by-choice.com/

11 https://rentez-vous.com/

12 http://www.bagborroworsteal.com/

13 http://www.chicagotribune.com/lifestyles/travel/ct-chicago-airbnb-money-helps-me-travel-1127-20161107-story.html

14 https://medium.com/@GregMuender/how-renting-my-place-on-airbnb-is-funding-my-startup-4de9ad014ce4#.785ol63mr

15 'Transforming the bank for the digital era,' *WIRED* UK edition, 15 October, p. 107

16 http://www.bbc.co.uk/news/technology-21043693

17 http://www.leetchi.com/

18 https://www.mangopay.com/

19 'Payments need to collaborate,' *WIRED* UK edition, 15 October, p. 104

20 Scott Monty, CEO and co-managing partner of Brain+Trust Partners.

21 *World Café* animation is a style of workshop that is great for sharing ideas and, with right context, is ideal for surfacing collective intelligence.

22 https://us.drive-now.com/

23 http://onefinestay.com/

24 http://slack.com

25 http://trello.com

26 www.ouishare.net

27 http://ouisharefest.com/

Force 1　The web

1　Berners-Lee, T. (2000) *Weaving the Web: The Original Design and Ultimate Destiny of the World Wide Web*, HarperBusiness.

2　https://www.statista.com/statistics/278414/number-of-worldwide-social-network-users/

3　https://www.statista.com/statistics/264810/number-of-monthly-active-facebook-users-worldwide/

4　http://www.pewInternet.org/2015/08/19/the-demographics-of-social-media-users/

5　http://www.metafilter.com/user/15556

6　http://www.emarketer.com/public_media/docs/eMarketer_eTailWest2016_Worldwide_ECommerce_Report.pdf = 9.9% in 2017e

7　https://www.coursera.org/

8　https://www.khanacademy.org/

9　http://www.open.edu/itunes/

10　https://www.lynda.com/

11　http://calnewport.com/books/deep-work/

12　https://basecamp.com/

13　https://uk.drive-now.com/

14　https://www.car2go.com/

15　For Mercedes https://mieten.mercedes-benz.de/ and Daimler https://www.daimler-financialservices.com/mercedes-benz-rent/

16　https://www.audiondemand.com/

17　https://flinc.org/

18　https://www.tamyca.de/ – Opel is based in Rüsselsheim am Main, Germany.

19　https://media.ford.com/content/fordmedia-mobile/fna/us/en/news/2015/06/23/ford-smart-mobility-shifts-from-research-to-implementation.html

20　https://www.zopa.com/public-loan-book

21 https://www.fundingcircle.com/uk/statistics/

22 https://www.ratesetter.com/aboutus/statistics

23 £6,502,783,000 http://p2pfa.info/data

24 https://www.duolingo.com/

25 https://www.talmix.com/

26 Clarity.fm

27 https://www.upwork.com/

28 http://kickstarter.com

29 http://indiegogo.com

30 buzzsumo.com

Force 2 The smartphone

1 http://www.newyorker.com/culture/susan-orlean/hello-its-me

2 https://www.gartner.com/newsroom/id/3339019. According to IDC https://www.idc.com/getdoc.jsp?containerId=US42065716, the total number of phones (feature + smart) purchased in 2016 was 1.93 billion. Gartner predicts smartphone sales will reach 1.9 billion in 2020.

3 http://insight.globalwebindex.net/device

4 http://gs.statcounter.com/press/mobile-and-tablet-Internet-usage-exceeds-desktop-for-first-time-worldwide

5 http://www.pewInternet.org/2015/10/29/technology-device-ownership-2015

6 According to Nielsen, the number of apps has been stalled at around 27 since 2012. http://www.nielsen.com/us/en/insights/news/2016/wanna-get-away--travel-app-usage-increases-among-americans-who-w.html

7 https://www.comscore.com/Insights/Blog/Q3-2016-Digital-Commerce-Hits-84-Billion-as-MCommerce-Accounts-for-20-of-Sales-for-1st-Time

8 http://wayoflifeapp.com/

9 http://Lynda.com

10 https://testmysite.thinkwithgoogle.com/

11 https://www.snapchat.com/geofilters

Force 3 The cloud

1 https://www.salesforce.com/ca/cloud-computing/

2 https://www.srgresearch.com/
articles/2016-review-shows-148-billion-cloud-market-growing-25-annually

3 UCaaS = Unified Communications as a Service (UCaaS) is a delivery model in which a variety of communication and collaboration applications and services are outsourced to a third-party provider and delivered over an IP network, usually the public internet.

4 Also known as FOMO = Fear Of Missing Out.

5 *The Croods* (2013), produced by Dreamworks. http://m.imdb.com/title/tt0481499/quotes?qt=qt1902297

6 https://medium.com/@glengilmore/6-digital-transformation-takeaways-from-a-global-leader-huawei-d62a329abbaa#.8ykuf015h

7 https://www.hubspot.com/

8 https://www.xero.com/

9 http://Salesforce.com

10 https://zapier.com/

11 nozbe.com

12 rememberthemilk.com

13 https://evernote.com/

14 https://www.typeform.com/

15 https://gsuite.google.com/

16 http://gotomeeting.com

17 https://basecamp.com/features/clientside

18 https://ifttt.com/

Force 4 Security

1 http://ittoday.info/AIMS/DSM/82-01-02.pdf Earliest available reference to the quote in 1982, that refers back to an image with the quote http://awarenessmaterials. homestead.com/Toothbrush.html

2 https://en.wikipedia.org/wiki/Malware

3 https://www.juniperresearch.com/researchstore/strategy-competition/cybercrime-security/financial-corporate-threats-mitigation

4 http://www.takethislollipop.com/

5 https://www.ted.com/talks/alessandro_acquisti_why_privacy_matters

6 http://www.danah.org/

7 http://www.datasociety.net/

8 https://episode1.donottrack-doc.com/en/

9 http://gawker.com/you-can-safely-read-the-entire-sony-leak-right-here-1698253271

10 In a 2011 G Data Software survey with nearly 16,000 users in 11 countries, 48 percent of respondents believed that a computer could not get infected simply by visiting a website.

11 http://anthonyrhoward.com/

12 https://www.propublica.org/

13 https://1password.com/

14 https://lastpass.com/

15 https://twofactorauth.org/

16 https://ico.org.uk/for-organisations/improve-your-practices/training-videos/

17 http://www.iso9001.com/

Force 5 Internet of things (IoT)

1 http://www.huffingtonpost.co.uk/geoff-mulgan/its-life-jim-but-not-as-we-knew-it_b_2550912.html

2 https://en.wikipedia.org/wiki/Geoff_Mulgan

3 As Jim Hunter Chief Scientist & Technology Evangelist at Greenwave Systems indicates, @theiotguru

4 http://www.juniperresearch.com/press/press-releases/iot-connected-devices-to-triple-to-38-bn-by-2020

5 SIGFOX uses ultra-narrow band transmissions. LoRa uses a chirp spread spectrum approach, distributing information across the transmission band. LTE-M is low data rate via cellular modems.

6 LPWANs explained: http://info.link-labs.com/lpwan

7 https://www.aylanetworks.com/

8 http://www.eurotech.com/en/

9 https://filament.com/

10 http://marketrealist.com/2015/10/projected-impact-of-the-Internet-of-things-on-the-economy-in-2025/

11 http://www.preventice.com/products/bodyguardian/

12 http://ambyint.com/

13 http://www.wellaware.us/

14 https://med.stanford.edu/news/all-news/2017/01/wearable-sensors-can-tell-when-you-are-getting-sick.html

15 http://www.pitpatpet.com/

16 http://www.actuarialpost.co.uk/article/pet-insurance-market-worth-potential-%C2%A32--5bn--856.htm

17 https://www.theguardian.com/world/2017/feb/17/german-parents-told-to-destroy-my-friend-cayla-doll-spy-on-children

18 http://www.telegraph.co.uk/technology/2016/12/20/hackers-could-take-control-plane-using-in-flight-entertainment/

19 https://shodan.io/

20 https://www.shodan.io/search?query=refrigerator

21 https://nest.com/

22 https://workswith.nest.com/products

23 https://www.smartthings.com/uk/

24 https://www.amazon.com/Amazon-Echo-Bluetooth-Speaker-with-WiFi-Alexa/dp/B00X4WHP5E

25 https://nest.com/

26 https://www.apple.com/uk/ios/home/

27 http://Namely.com

28 https://www.amazon.com/b2b/info/amazon-business

29 https://www.amazon.com/dash

Force 6 Artificial intelligence (AI)

1 Kristoff, J. and Kaufman, A. (2015) *Illuminae: The Illuminae Files, Book 1*, Rock the Boat.

2 https://www.nvidia.com/object/deep-learning.html

3 http://linkilaw.com

4 https://www.theguardian.com/technology/2016/dec/22/bridgewater-associates-ai-artificial-intelligence-management

5 https://www.ibm.com/think/marketing/artificial-intelligence-is-nothing-without-artificial-empathy/

6 https://www.cbinsights.com/blog/top-acquirers-ai-startups-ma-timeline/

7 https://www.cbinsights.com/blog/top-acquirers-ai-startups-ma-timeline/

8 http://chiefmartec.com/2016/12/5-disruptions-marketing-part-5-artificial-intelligence/

9 http://blog.softwareinsider.org/2016/09/18/mondays-musings-understand-spectrum-seven-artificial-intelligence-outcomes/

10 http://www.bbc.co.uk/news/technology-36376966

11 https://www.gartner.com/imagesrv/summits/docs/na/customer-360/C360_2011_brochure_FINAL.pdf

12 https://www.forrester.com/Robots+AI+Will+Replace+7+O
    f+US+Jobs+By+2025/-/E-PRE9246

13 http://www.bbc.co.uk/news/world-us-canada-37629559

14 https://www.nytimes.com/2016/12/17/opinion/sunday/
    the-tent-cities-of-san-francisco.html?_r=0

15 https://www.thenorthface.com/xps

16 http://www.thedrum.com/news/2017/01/07/
    under-armour-puts-biometric-single-customer-view-the-
    heart-digitisation-against

17 http://www.underarmour.co.uk/en-gb/healthbox.html

18 https://www.bcgperspectives.com/content/articles/
    growth-innovation-in-2016/ by Michael Ringel, Andrew
    Taylor, and Hadi Zablit, Jan 2017

19 http://www.inc.com/magazine/201602/tom-foster/kevin-
    plank-under-armour-spending-1-billion-to-beat-nike.html

20 https://www.salesforce.com/video/309487/ At about 1'10

21 From KLM Press release http://news.klm.com/klm-runs-
    pilot-with-artificial-intelligence-provided-by-digitalgenius
    and my podcast with head of Digital Genius

22 https://en.wikipedia.org/wiki/Pareto_principle

23 Peter Lee, Vice President, Microsoft.

24 https://snips.ai/content/
    intro-to-ai/?ref=producthunt#ai-metrics

25 To create a board in Flipboard (www.flipboard.com), first
    search for 'artificial intelligence' and then pick at least
    one or two proposed hashtag topics to follow.

26 http://www.bbc.co.uk/news/technology-34066941

Force 7 Big data analytics

1 https://www.facebook.com/dan.ariely/
   posts/904383595868. The structure of this quote has been
   around for decades and applied to many new
   technologies. We advise that it is true about many

companies, but there are more and more companies using big data effectively.

2 https://en.wikipedia.org/wiki/Dan_Ariely

3 https://en.oxforddictionaries.com/definition/data

4 https://www.mongodb.com/big-data-explained

5 http://www.internetlivestats.com/total-number-of-websites/
By 'website' we mean unique hostname (a name which can be resolved, using a name server, into an IP Address).

6 http://www.worldwidewebsize.com/

7 https://www.netcraft.com/active-sites/

8 @KPCB: Y axis on graphic is logarithmic scale. Source: John Hagel, Deloitte May, 2014, http://www.statisticbrain.com/average-cost-of-hard-drive-storage/; the black line predicts exponential growth of data from around 3 zettabytes in 2013 to approx 40 ZB by 2020. An XB = 1 x 10^{18} bytes. Source IDC's Digital Universe Study, December 2012, https://www.emc.com/collateral/analyst-reports/idc-the-digital-universe-in-2020.pdf

9 https://techcrunch.com/2010/08/04/schmidt-data/

10 https://blog.rjmetrics.com/2011/02/07/eric-schmidts-5-exabytes-quote-is-a-load-of-crap/

11 IHS (https://technology.ihs.com/576648/tech-companies-creating-strategic-platforms-to-support-the-internet-of-things-ihs-says) predicts 30 billion IoT connected devices while Gartner's estimate (https://www.gartner.com/newsroom/id/3165317) is 20 billion by 2020. Business Insider's IoT Ecosystem Research Report puts the number at 34 billion (https://www.businessinsider.com/intelligence/bi-intelligence-iot-research-bundle-reports-store)

12 http://analytics-magazine.org/images-a-videos-really-big-data/

13 https://www.datajournalismawards.org/

14 https://www.globaleditorsnetwork.org/

15 https://www.theguardian.com/society/2013/sep/18/
   nhs-records-system-10bn

16 https://www.tensorflow.org/

17 https://research.google.com/bigpicture/

18 http://analytics-magazine.org/images-a-videos-
   really-big-data/

19 http://www.apixio.com/

20 http://www.forbes.com/sites/bernardmarr/2016/08/25/
   the-most-practical-big-data-use-cases-of-
   2016/3/#f1058db56725

21 https://home.kpmg.com/xx/en/home/insights/2016/06/
   becoming-hyper-customer-centric.html

22 http://theleanstartup.com/book

23 https://www.nimble.com/

Force 8 Blockchain and cryptocurrencies

1 Swan, M. (2015) *Blockchain: Blueprint for a New
  Economy*, O'Reilly Media.

2 Satoshi Nakamoto's profile and entries on P2P
  Foundation: http://p2pfoundation.ning.com/profile/
  SatoshiNakamoto

3 http://positivemoney.org/how-money-works/
  how-much-money-have-banks-created/

4 http://positivemoney.org/

5 White paper: 'Bitcoin: A Peer-to-Peer Electronic Cash
  System' https://bitcoin.org/bitcoin.pdf

6 http://satoshi.nakamotoinstitute.org/emails/cryptography/1/

7 https://bitcoinfoundation.org/forum/index.php?/
  topic/54-my-first-message-to-satoshi/

8 Michael Carrier – Bay Area Crypto Entrepreneur,
  @michaelpcarrier

9   http://www.forbes.com/sites/laurashin/2015/09/14/
    bitcoin-blockchain-technology-in-financial-services-how-
    the-disruption-will-play-out/

10 http://www.forbes.com/sites/laurashin/2015/09/14/
    bitcoin-blockchain-technology-in-financial-services-how-
    the-disruption-will-play-out/

11 http://www.wired.co.uk/article/
    wired-money-2015-future-of-finance

12 http://www.bitland.world/

13 http://www.openledger.info/

14 http://myceliaformusic.org/

15 TechCityNews.com, Issue 10, Spring 2016

16 http://www.coindesk.com/events

17 https://www.reddit.com/r/Bitcoin/

18 http://meetup.com

19 http://www.coindesk.com/price/

20 http://cryptocompare.com

21 https://coinatmradar.com/

Force 9 3D printing

1   https://www.forbes.com/sites/danschawbel/2014/08/15/
    mark-frauenfelder-how-the-maker-movement-will-create-
    new-entrepreneurs/#3884fd3261a5

2   http://www.markfrauenfelder.com/

3   Wilson, C. (2016) *Come and Take It: The Gun Printer's
    Guide to Thinking Free*, Gallery Books.

4   http://www.forbes.com/sites/stevebanker/2013/10/15/3d-
    printing-revolutionizes-the-hearing-aid-business/

5   http://investor.aligntech.com/alignar_final_7-8-14/align-
    advantage.html

6   https://www.sols.com/

7 http://shanghaiist.com/2015/09/02/3d-printed_hip_
   implant_approved_for.php

8 https://www.behance.net/williamroot

9 http://www.javelin-tech.com/3d-printer/industry/dental/

10 http://www.wired.co.uk/magazine/archive/2015/10/
   start/3d-printing-neurosurgery

11 http://carlosidea.com/

12 http://www.oddguitars.com/steampunk.html

13 https://www.thingiverse.com

14 https://www.youmagine.com/

15 http://treasure.is/

16 http://Tinkercad.com

17 http://solidworks.com

18 https://www.3dhubs.com/

19 https://www.shapeways.com/

Force 10 Energy storage

1 http://www.arthurerickson.com/about-arthur-erickson/
   speeches/1/

2 http://www.arthurerickson.com/

3 https://www.carbonbrief.org/
   what-global-co2-emissions-2016-mean-climate-change

4 https://www.forbes.com/sites/mikescott/2014/03/21/
   ge-taps-into-the-coolest-energy-storage-technology-
   around/#485bad4b699e

5 https://www.greentechmedia.com/articles/read/
   corporate-investments-in-energy-storage-at-660-million-
   in-q3-2016

6 https://www.greentechmedia.com/research/
   subscription/u.s.-energy-storage-monitor

7 Written by McKinsey directors Richard Dobbs, James
   Manyika and Jonathan Woetzel.

8 http://www.treehugger.com/gadgets/new-battery-made-nuclear-waste-and-diamonds.html

9 https://www.iea.org/publications/freepublications/publication/KeyWorld2016.pdf

10 https://www.theclimategroup.org/news/china-invest-360bn-renewable-energy-2020

11 http://www.highview-power.com/

12 http://www.highview-power.com/conceptual-gigaplant-200mw1-2gwh/

13 http://www.allaboutcircuits.com/news/could-cryogenic-energy-storage-solve-renewable-energys-biggest-problem/

14 http://www.digitaljournal.com/tech-and-science/technology/microscale-energy-storage-devices-advance-wearables/article/480778

15 http://www.thetimes.co.uk/edition/news/grankini-body-suit-empowers-the-elderly-with-motorised-fabric-v30rp8fgl

16 https://www.tesla.com/gigafactory

17 https://www.bloomberg.com/news/articles/2017-01-04/tesla-flips-the-switch-on-the-gigafactory

18 http://www.teslamotors.com/en_GB/powerwall

Force 11 Self/assisted driving

1 http://fortune.com/2014/08/15/if-driverless-cars-save-lives-where-will-we-get-organs/

2 https://en.wikipedia.org/wiki/Bre_Pettis

3 http://whatis.techtarget.com/definition/driverless-car

4 http://fortune.com/2015/07/22/mckinsey-disruptive/

5 https://en.wikipedia.org/wiki/List_of_motor_vehicle_deaths_in_U.S._by_year

6 https://www.tesla.com/en_GB/blog/tragic-loss

7 Smith, C. (2016) *The Car Hacker's Handbook: A Guide for the Penetration Tester.* No Starch Press.

8 http://moralmachine.mit.edu/

9 http://www.mckinsey.com/industries/automotive-and-assembly/our-insights/ten-ways-autonomous-driving-could-redefine-the-automotive-world

10 Go to http://moralmachine.mit.edu

Force 12 Genomics

1 https://www.23andme.com/en-gb/

2 http://too.blogspot.ie/2008/09/lrrk2.html

3 https://www.bloomberg.com/news/articles/2015-02-04/parkinson-s-study-dims-ambitions-for-gene-flaw-carried-by-brin

4 https://en.oxforddictionaries.com/definition/genomics

5 http://www.nchpeg.org/bssr/index.php?option=com_content&view=article&id=95:genetics-vs-genomics

6 https://www.helix.com

7 http://isogg.org/wiki/List_of_personal_genomics_companies

8 https://www.momondo.ie/letsopenourworld/dna

9 https://www.dnafit.com/

10 http://www.independent.co.uk/sport/football/news-and-comment/two-premier-league-teams-commission-genetic-profiles-of-their-players-9196470.html

11 http://www.thesundaytimes.co.uk/sto/news/uk_news/article799536.ece

12 http://www.bbc.co.uk/news/business-38183937

13 https://www.ft.com/content/419733b2-e181-11e6-9645-c9357a75844a

14 https://en.oxforddictionaries.com/definition/epigenetics

15 https://www.23andme.com/

16 https://www.ancestry.com/dna/

Index